INSIGHT GUIDES

SYDNEY

smart guide

Discovery CHANNEL

APA PUBLICATIONS L
Part of the Langenscheidt Publishing Group

Contents

Areas

Sydney 4
Central Business
    District.......................... 6
The Rocks and
    Foreshore.................... 8
The Opera House and
    the Domain.................10
Darling Harbour and
    Chinatown..................12
Kings Cross District........14
Paddington and
    Surry Hills...................16
The Inner-West
    Suburbs......................18
Eastern Suburbs.............20
Eastern Beaches.............22
The North Shore.............24
The Blue Mountains........26

A–Z

Aboriginal Culture 28
Bars 30
Beaches 38
Cafés 42
Children 46
Environment 48
Essentials 50
Fashion..........................56
Festivals 58
Film...............................60
Food and Drink 62
Gay and Lesbian 66
History 68

Below: Sydney's famous Bondi Beach.

2

Left: dusk descends on Sydney Harbour.

Atlas

East Balmain to
     Kings Cross **132**
Potts Point to
     Woollahra **134**
Surry Hills and Inner-West
     Suburbs....................**136**
Paddington and
     Centennial Park **138**
Central Business District
     and the Rocks **139**

*Inside Front Cover:
     City Locator
Inside Back Cover:
     New South Wales*

Hotels **70**
Literature **78**
Museums and
     Galleries **80**
Music and Dance **88**
Nightlife.........................**90**
Pampering **92**
Parks and Gardens **94**
Restaurants **98**
Shopping.....................**110**
Sport............................**118**
Theatre **124**
Transport **126**
Walks and Views **128**

*Street Index: 140
General Index: 141–4*

Below: Aborigines busking on The Rocks.

3

Sydney

The Harbour Bridge and the Opera House may be the city's icons, but the thing that Sydneysiders value most is their lifestyle. Blessed with a temperate climate, countless beaches and that world-famous harbour, locals spend much of their lives outdoors. For that rare overcast day, there are plenty of other options, including fascinating museums and a world-class dining scene.

Destination Fact and Figures

Population: **4.2 million**
Indigenous population: **1 per cent**
Years of human habitation: **more than 50,000 years**
Area: **12,145sq km**
Population born outside Australia: **31 per cent**
Number of languages spoken: **140**
National parks and state conservation areas: **39**
Beaches: **more than 100**
Suburbs: **over 300**
Length of harbour foreshore: **230km**
Length of harbour foreshore open to the public: **135km**
Number of fatal shark attacks since 1937: **1**

Natural Beauties

Many of the best things in Sydney are free: Swimming at surf beaches such as Bondi and tranquil harbour beaches like Nielsen Park, exploring the countless foreshore walks, strolling through the beautiful harbourside Royal Botanic Gardens. Certainly few other cities have so much harbour foreshore, that they are willing to dedicate a large chunk of it to, of all things, a zoo. But then, few cities can match Sydney's suburban sprawl, either. Sydney covers around the same area as London, despite having less than half the population.

The upside of this penchant for low-density living is the many patches of bush and parkland, home to a range of native fauna. Do not expect to find cuddly koalas: apart from native birds such as magpies and kookaburras, the wildlife you are most likely to encounter is the large lizards known as goannas and the nocturnal possums. The city is also ringed by a series of stunning national parks, the highlight of which is the Blue Mountains, a dramatic World Heritage-listed wilderness.

Urban Delights

While the city's setting is stunning, much of its appeal rests on its cosmopolitan lifestyle. Sydney is the nation's powerhouse, a fact reflected in its skyrocketing property prices, and its inhabitants enjoy spending the money they earn. The restaurants are top-class, from world-renowned fine dining temples such as Tetsuya's to cheap and cheerful eateries offering some of the best Asian food around. Artistic ensembles such as the Australian Chamber Orchestra, the indigenous Bangarra Dance Theatre and the Sydney Dance Company, under the leadership of Graeme Murphy, have global followings. And many of Hollywood's biggest names, including Cate Blanchett, Nicole Kidman, Naomi Watts and Russell Crowe, call Sydney home (at least part-time).

Fashion is another field where locals have excelled: not surprising, given the importance Sydneysiders attach to looking good. The renovated terraces of the inner-city and the city's ornate Strand Arcade are where you will

Below: it is hard to think of another city with as much leafy foreshore space as Sydney.

find acclaimed local labels such as Collette Dinnigan, Sass and Bide, and denim kings Ksubi (known here as Tsubi).

Grim Beginnings

The glitz and glamour of today's Emerald City is a long way from the early days of settlement. Before the First Fleet arrived, this land belonged to the Eora tribe. They were largely wiped out by the Europeans and the diseases they brought with them. Their presence is remembered principally by some scattered Aboriginal carvings and by place names such as Woolloomooloo and Bondi.

The motley group of soldiers and convicts who made up the First Fleet huddled in the area today known as The Rocks, for the sandstone cliffs that provided the convict workforce with its building material. For many years the city's most notorious area, The Rocks is now a lively atmospheric mix of cafés, shops and markets, with some of Sydney's most historic surviving buildings. While too much of the city's past was swept away in the building frenzy of the 1960s and 1970s, some outposts survived on Macquarie Street, the city's traditional seat of power, and in the western centre of Parramatta. The sandstone barracks and gaols scattered throughout the inner-city are further, incongruous reminders of the city's grim past.

Highlights

▲ **Sydney Opera House**, Sydney's postcard-perfect building, is also its premier arts venue.
▶ **The Rocks**, Sydney's birthplace is an atmospheric mix of narrow alleys, workers' cottages and pocket-sized pubs.

▲ **Taronga Zoo**. See Australia's oddest animals, from koalas and kangaroos to the platypus.

▶ **Bondi Beach**, this sweeping, surf-fringed arc is Australia's most famous stretch of beach.

▲ **Pubs** play an enormous role in Sydney's social life, from after work drinks to all night sessions.
▶ **Sydney Harbour Bridge**, for 75 years this elegant span has linked the two sides of the harbour.

Central
Business District

Sydney's narrow, twisting streets, based on the random paths created by convicts and soldiers, are a rare reminder of the colony's early days. Today's CBD is dominated by soaring buildings, punctuated by a few surviving Victorian beauties and the green expanse of Hyde Park. New skyscrapers continue to be unfurled, the latest a batch of massive residential towers. Their presence has brought at least one benefit, with an influx of restaurants, bars and clubs livening up the city immensely.

See Atlas Pages 132–133 & 139

Above: the Archibald Fountain in Hyde Park.

Macquarie Street

Sydney's single most historic stretch of road starts at the Opera House and runs past the Royal Botanic Gardens all the way to Hyde Park. The corner where the Cahill Expressway ramp meets the

For the past 30 years, Sydney's skyline has been dominated by the AMP Tower, known to locals as Centrepoint Tower. At 303m, it is the city's highest structure. As late as the 1960s, that honour was held by the AMP building at Circular Quay, now dwarfed by all its neighbours.

Royal Botanic Gardens offers a snapshot of three very different faces of Sydney. On one corner is the solid respectability of the **State Library**; opposite lies a row of elegant 1920s art deco apartment buildings; and on the third corner stands Sydney's latest architectural trophy, Renzo Piano's **Aurora Place**, a celebration of Sydney's emergence as a global city.

Heading south from here you pass the city's most impressive stretch of heritage buildings, including the old **Mint**, **Parliament House**, **Sydney Hospital** (originally known as the Rum Hospital

because its construction was funded by the revenue from the government's rum monopoly) and **Hyde Park Barracks**. The latter, dates back to 1817 and was designed by convict Francis Greenway in 1817 to house male convicts. It now contains a museum. SEE ALSO MUSEUMS AND GALLERIES, P.81–2

Hyde Park and the Shopping District

At the far end of Macquarie Street is **Hyde Park**, the CBD's main green space, which contains the exuberant **Archibald Fountain** and the

Left: the skyscrapers of the Central Business District, with the Queen Victoria Building in the foreground.

art deco **Anzac Memorial**.

Opposite Hyde Park, on the corner of Elizabeth and Market streets, the discreet glamour of Sydney's premier department store, **David Jones**, marks the beginning of the city's principal shopping precinct. Arrayed chiefly along Market and Pitt streets, particularly Pitt street Mall, you will find outlets including a second David Jones store, Myer Department Store, and Centrepoint shopping centre, which lies at the foot of the **AMP Tower.**

Also on Market Street is one of Sydney's most beautiful relics, the **State Theatre**. Acclaimed at its opening in 1929 as the greatest theatre in the British Empire, its ornate interiors, including the second-largest cut-crystal chandelier in the world, have been beautifully preserved.
SEE ALSO FASHION, P.57; PARKS AND GARDENS, P.94; SHOPPING, P.114; THEATRE P.125

Martin Place and George Street

The **Strand Arcade**, a beautiful Victorian arcade leading from Pitt Street Mall to George Street, is the address favoured by some of the country's best designers, with the likes of Alannah Hill, Bettina Liano and Zimmermann all on the second floor.

Emerging on George Street, you are facing the **Queen Victoria Building** or QVB, a Victorian landmark designed to resemble a Byzantine palace, complete with enormous stained glass windows. Four storeys high and covering the entire block between Market and Druitt streets, it is a shoppers' delight. At the Druitt Street end it opens onto the equally grand Victorian **Town Hall**.

From the Town Hall, head back north along George Street to **Martin Place**, the

city's largest pedestrian plaza. Stretching all the way to Macquarie Street, it is lined with corporate headquarters, as well as upmarket bars such as Wine Banq and shops like Paspaley Pearls headquarters.

Martin Place's crowning glory is the **General Post Office** (GPO). This was once Sydney's most imposing building, with sumptuous interiors, a grand colonnade and an ornate clock tower. However, the tower was removed during World War II to prevent Japanese bombers using it as a navigation aid during raids (which never came) and not replaced until the 1960s. After decades of neglect, the GPO was refurbished as part of the Westin Hotel complex.
SEE ALSO BARS, P.30; SHOPPING, P.112–3

Right: the General Post Office.

The Rocks and Foreshore

The colony's harsh early days took place here but, apart from a few grim reminders such as the Argyle Cut, a tunnel hewn out of sandstone by chisel-wielding convicts, The Rocks has managed to leave behind its dark past. Today it is a thriving tourist centre and home to some of Sydney's best restaurants. Wander off the main strip, however, and you will find traces of an earlier time: narrow alleys, tiny workers' cottages, and perfectly-preserved working-men's pubs, the oldest in the country.

George Street

While George Street's western side is dominated by a series of gaudy tourist-oriented duty-free shops, pubs and cafés, the eastern side of the street has some of the area's most interesting buildings. To properly appreciate the clean lines of the **Museum of Contemporary Art**, walk around to the harbour side, where the front door of this art deco landmark is located.

Next door, overshadowed by its neighbour, is **Cadman's Cottage**, Sydney's oldest building and the oldest residential building in all Australia. It dates back to 1816 and is open to visitors. On the other side of the cottage lies **Sydney Visitors' Centre**, staffed by knowledgeable locals. Every weekend, the far end of George Street hosts **The Rocks Market**, where 150 stalls sell a wide range of

souvenir items, including graceful fruit bowls made from Australian hardwoods. SEE ALSO ESSENTIALS, P.55; MUSEUMS AND GALLERIES, P.80, 86; SHOPPING, P.117

The Back Streets

The Rocks was once Sydney's most notorious area, a squalid, crowded maze of narrow streets where prostitutes and razor gangs preyed on passers-by, and where the bubonic plague swept through as late as 1900. To get a glimpse of those days, wander the grid of hidden lanes on the slope between George Street and Cumberland Street. Narrow walkways such as Nurses' Walk, Bakehouse Place, Kendall Lane and Gloucester Walk are a

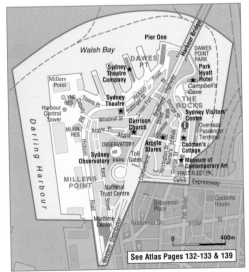

See Atlas Pages 132-133 & 139

From the early 1900s on, the State Government repeatedly announced plans to redevelop The Rocks, most recently in the 1970s. The proposal met with fierce resistance from residents and the construction unions. Led by activist Jack Mundey, the unions placed 'green bans' on the project, a move which not only resulted in the scrapping of the plans, but also launched Sydney's heritage movement.

Left: George Street leads into the heart of The Rocks, with the Harbour Bridge beyond.

Cruise and **Wildfire**, while further along at **Campbell's Cove**, vast, atmospheric 19th-century storehouses contain more eateries. From here, it is just a few steps to the low-lying sandstone flanks of the **Park Hyatt Hotel**, Sydney's best-situated luxury hotel, with its own respected restaurant. The building nudges the edge of **Dawes Point Park**, under the mighty span of the Harbour Bridge, a popular spot for wedding photos.

Continuing around the foreshore you come to the former **Bond Wharves** along Hickson Road. While some of the wharves have recently been redeveloped into multi-million-dollar apartments, wharves 4 and 5 are home to the **Sydney Theatre Company** and the **Wharf Restaurant**, with its 180-degree views.

Opposite the Wharf Theatre, on the other side of Hickson Road, is the recently refurbished **Sydney Theatre**, which has its own restaurant.
SEE ALSO HOTELS P.71–2; RESTAURANTS, PAGE 99–100; THEATRE P.125; TRANSPORT P.126

reminder that this area once looked very different.

Gloucester Walk opens onto **The Cut**, a section of Argyle Street carved out of the towering sandstone by the convict workforce, who used the stone to construct the colony's buildings. The walls of The Cut still bear the marks of the convicts' chisels. Argyle Street is also home to one of the area's best-preserved buildings, the **Argyle Stores**. The four-storey warehouse constructed around a cobbled courtyard is now home to upmarket shops and the Bel Mondo restaurant.

Continuing up Argyle Street, you reach the heights of **Millers Point**. This is the real Rocks, where public housing tenants live in tiny workers' cottages and drink in beautifully-preserved pubs. The Palisade, dating from the early 20th century, is one favourite, as is the Lord Nel-

son Brewery on Kent Street, a sandstone building that has housed a pub since 1831. From here, either continue down Kent Street towards the discreet luxury of the Observatory Hotel, or head back towards the Quay via Argyle Place and Lower Fort Street, past the **Garrison Church** and the Hero of Waterloo, which challenges the Lord Nelson for the title of oldest pub in town. Turn left into Cumberland Street to reach the steps taking you to the **Harbour Bridge** and the Bridgeclimb offices.
SEE ALSO BARS, P.32–3; SHOPPING P.110; WALKS AND VIEWS, P.128

The Foreshore

The superbly scenic stretch of foreshore starting at the Museum of Contemporary Art contains some of Sydney's best restaurants. The **Overseas Passenger Terminal** houses glamorous eateries such as **Quay**,

Below: one of The Rocks' many quirky sights.

The Opera House and the Domain

In Sydney, it is all about the harbour and foreshore, and there is no finer stretch of foreshore than this. From the bustle of Circular Quay, flanked by the famous white sails of the Opera House, along the sinuous green curves of the Royal Botanic Gardens and down to the eateries lining the elegant Finger Wharf, this is Sydney's favourite playground. Away from the waterfront, the Royal Botanic Gardens and the Domain provide leafy breathing spaces in the heart of the city.

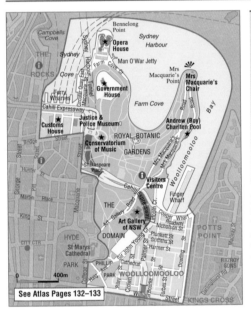

See Atlas Pages 132–133

Several famous Sydneysiders are commemorated in the area around the Royal Botanical Gardens: Bennelong Point is named after an Aborigine 'adopted' by the early settlers, Mrs Macquarie's Chair was apparently a favoured scenic spot of Governor Lachlan Macquarie's wife, while the Andrew 'Boy' Charlton Swimming Pool *(see p.122)*, appropriately, commemorates a 1920s Olympic champion swimmer.

have discovered that East Circular Quay is a great venue for a night out. You can catch an arthouse film at the **Dendy Opera Quays**, enjoy world-class food and views at **Aria** restaurant, or explore a very different drinking environment at **Minus Five**, a bar made entirely of ice.

SEE ALSO BARS, P.33; FILM P.61; RESTAURANTS, P.100

Sydney Opera House

The **Opera House** is so famous that it is hard to imagine Sydney before its sails were unfurled. Danish architect Joern Utzon won the design competition, but the 14-year building process was fraught, both for the architect – who walked out halfway through the project –

East Circular Quay

Set back from the bustle of the ferry wharves on Alfred Street, the gorgeous **Customs House** (1885) became an immediate favourite after its refurbishment in the 1990s.

The redevelopment of neighbouring **East Circular Quay** around the same time was hugely unpopular, although you would never guess it from the crowds that

flock there now. After the first phase of construction removed the existing 1960s office buildings, opening up views through to the Royal Botanic Gardens, locals vociferously opposed any further development, and gave the squat apartment building erected on the site the derisory nickname, 'the Toaster'. Today, however, all is forgiven, as Sydneysiders

Left: Sydney's most recognisable landmark.

...ment House, the former residence of the State Governor; and the **Sydney Conservatorium of Music**, inspired by two Scottish castles. Both are open to visitors.

South of the gardens lies the **Domain**, an extensive public space which at weekends serves as Sydney's Speakers' Corner and in January as the venue for free evening concerts. Within the Domain is the **Art Gallery of New South Wales**, which contains a number of major collections of Australia's art.
SEE ALSO MUSEUMS AND GALLERIES, P.81, 85; MUSIC AND DANCE, P.88; PARKS AND GARDENS, P.95–6; SPORT P.122

Woolloomooloo

Near the art gallery, a flight of stairs runs down to Woolloomooloo, until recently one of the city's more run-down areas. The redevelopment of the **Finger Wharf** into upmarket apartments and a dining complex has created another delightful harbourside hang-out. For a cheaper meal option, the pies at **Harry's Café de Wheels** in a nearby van are an essential Sydney experience.
SEE ALSO CAFÉS, P.42–3

and for the government, which saw construction costs soar $95 million beyond budget. (The shortfall was inventively made up through a series of lotteries.)

Today, the Opera House is one of the world's most recognisable buildings, as well as Sydney's premier cultural space. Beyond catching an opera or play, you can enjoy a meal at the acclaimed **Guillaume at Bennelong Restaurant**, a cocktail at the **Opera Bar**, take in a front-of-house or backstage tour, or just walk around the perimeter and marvel at the close-up view of the tiled sails.
SEE ALSO BARS P.33; MUSIC AND DANCE, P.88; RESTAURANTS P.100; THEATRE, P.125

Royal Botanic Gardens and the Domain

The **Royal Botanic Gardens** mark the site of the colony's first farm, set up in 1788, and cover almost 30 hectares of green space. The magnificent foreshore walk is a highlight: it stretches from the Opera House around **Mrs Macquarie's Chair**, past the scenic **Andrew 'Boy' Charlton Swimming Pool** to the Domain and the Art Gallery of NSW. However, the magnificently landscaped gardens offer plenty of other attractions. Favourites include the Palm Grove, home to over 140 types of palm, as well as a succulent garden, a herbarium, and the Tropical Centre, housed in a striking pyramid-shaped glasshouse. You are also likely to encounter plenty of local fauna on a stroll through the gardens, including white cockatoos, brush-tailed possums, fruit bats and ibises.

On the Macquarie Street side of the gardens, you will find two historic Gothic Revival buildings: **Govern-**

Right: the CBD seen from the Domain.

Darling Harbour and Chinatown

The south-west corner of the inner city has been enlivened in recent years by these two ever-growing districts. Darling Harbour has expanded since its creation in 1988, with the adjacent Cockle Bay and King Street Wharf now vibrant elements of the city's bar and restaurant scenes. The Chinese have had a presence in Sydney since the city's earliest days, and Chinatown remains the best place in town to grab a late-night meal or find cheap and cheerful fashion bargains.

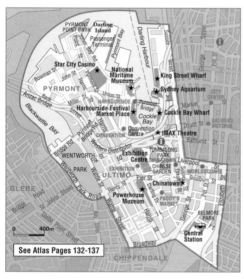

See Atlas Pages 132-137

willows and waterfalls make for a tranquil sanctuary during the week, but becomes crowded on weekends. Two other popular attractions are nearby: the **IMAX cinema** and **Tumbalong Park**, where a busy programme of free festivals attracts families.

Head north along the eastern shore to reach **Sydney Aquarium**, which houses more than 5,000 sea creatures. Walking through transparent tunnels with sharks and massive manta rays gliding over your head is a highlight.

Flanking the aquarium are two of Sydney's favourite places to party: **Cockle Bay** and **King Street Wharf**. Cockle Bay's best restaurants include the colourful, friendly Malaysian eatery **Chinta Ria Temple of Love**, and the more upmarket **Coast**. King Street Wharf is popular with the after-work crowd, who flock to the indoor/outdoor

East Darling Harbour

Developed as one of the State Government's major projects for the 1988 Bicentennial, Darling Harbour wraps around

three sides of a harbour inlet and contains a number of separate precincts. At its southern edge is the walled **Chinese Garden**. Its ponds, weeping

Left: historic vessels moored by the Maritime Museum.

on the North Shore, the city's official Chinatown is in the heart of the city, centred along Dixon and Sussex streets.

It stretches from the corner of Liverpool and Sussex to Haymarket (a produce market still exists in the bottom floor of the massive **Market City** shopping and restaurant complex); Darling Harbour and George Street mark the boundaries to the north and east.

Dixon Street became the official heart of Chinatown in 1980, when Chinese business owners, in cooperation with the local council, introduced the ceremonial archways and lions that have become the area's main monuments. However, for visitors who come to explore the colourful mix of cheap and cheerful food halls, jewellery shops, Asian supermarkets and tiny boutiques, nearby Sussex Street offers more options. The area has a profusion of restaurants, from no-frills favourites such as **BBQ King** on Goulburn Street to grand dining rooms such as the renovated **East Ocean** (entrances on both Dixon and Sussex streets).

The area around the Capitol Theatre on the far side of George Street also houses a number of interesting shops.
SEE ALSO RESTAURANTS, P.101; SHOPPING, P.112

Cargo Bar and chic **Loft**, a vast drinking space decked out in warm colours and compelling textures.
SEE ALSO BARS, P.33; CHILDREN, P.46–7; FILM, P.61; PARKS AND GARDENS, P.94; RESTAURANTS, P.102

West Darling Harbour

From the aquarium, take the pedestrian Pyrmont Bridge to the **National Maritime Museum** on Darling Harbour's western shore. This exhibition space deals with all aspects of Australia's extensive history with the sea. Inside you will find exhibits dealing with Aboriginal seafaring and the maritime exploration of Australia, while outside a number of ships, including the destroyer *Vampire* and the submarine *Onslow*, are anchored for exploration.

Opposite: dusk falls on Darling Harbour, a popular centre for entertainment, shopping and nightlife.

North of the maritime museum lies the raucous **Star City casino**, best avoided. Instead, head south, past the **Harbourside Shopping Centre** (among predictable tourist offerings is the indigenously owned and operated **Gavala Art Gallery**) to the **Powerhouse Museum**. Housed in a converted power station, it contains 380,000 items covering decorative arts and design, transport and social history. The fascinating collections include 20th-century fashion and arts, indigenous dance, music, television and film.
SEE ALSO ABORIGINAL CULTURE, P.29; MUSEUMS AND GALLERIES, P.83, 85; NIGHTLIFE, P.90; SHOPPING, P.111

Chinatown

Although the Chinese community has a long history in Sydney, it has grown exponentially in recent years, and now constitutes the city's most significant overseas-born group. Although many Chinese live

Until the early 1900s, the Chinese community was based around The Rocks. Later, many Chinese market gardeners and traders moved closer to the city's hay and produce markets. When the markets moved to the site now known as Haymarket, the Chinese followed, and today's Chinatown was born.

Kings Cross District

For decades, Kings Cross was a byword for glitz and glamour, and infamous for its crime and sleaze. 'The Cross' still has a raffish, bohemian feel to it, so it is somewhat surprising that today the suburbs on its fringes, such as Elizabeth Bay and Potts Point, are among some of the city's most desirable neighbourhoods. The Cross still maintains its edgy mix of strip shows and upmarket apartments, and visitors come as much for the gambling joints and happening nightlife as for the trendy cafés and green harbour parks. Consequently, that this area is considered by many to be Sydney's throbbing heart.

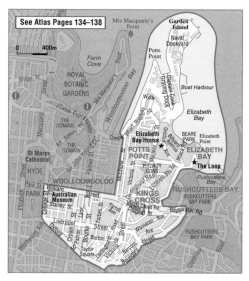

See Atlas Pages 134–138

In the 1970s and 1980s, 'The Cross' became associated with organised crime and drug trafficking, particularly in the person of Abe Saffron, a night-club owner and property developer known as the 'Boss of the Cross'. Saffron died in 2006, but drugs remain a problem; Sydney's first legal injecting room was opened here in 2001.

William Street into Victoria Avenue, where leafy trees, Victorian terraces and upmarket bars, such as Jimmy Liks, give an atmosphere of urban elegance.
SEE ALSO BARS, P.34; RESTAURANTS, P.103

Kings Cross

Kings Cross's most famous landmark, the giant red Coca-Cola sign that looms above William Street, is a suitable welcome to the city's most notorious red-light district. Heading north along the main drag of Darlinghurst Road, it is hard to find much to like in the tawdry mix of strip shows, sex shops and backpacker hostels, culminating in The Bourbon, now a vibrant nightspot but previously, as

the Bourbon and Beefsteak, one of the city's most disreputable venues.

Fortunately, the area's backstreets have a very different feel. East off William Street is happening Bayswater Road, where the wall-to-wall nightspots include two of the city's most chic bars, **Hugo's Lounge** and **Hugo's Bar Pizza**. Angling off Bayswater Road, Kellett Street is lined with tiny terrace houses containing stylish bar-restaurants. Turn west off

Potts Point

Shaped like a giant dandelion, the **El Alamein Fountain** in the Fitzroy Gardens marks where Darlinghurst Road turns into Macleay Street, and Kings Cross turns into the classier Potts Point. But even if the fountain disappeared tomorrow, the boundary would still be unmistakeable, with the strip clubs being replaced by elegant 1920s apartment houses (many with glorious harbour views), buzzing bistros and quality delis.

Left: the backstreets around Macleay and Victoria streets contain fine Art Deco buildings.

open to visitors.
SEE ALSO MUSEUMS AND
GALLERIES, P.80–1;

Darlinghurst and East Sydney

To the south of William Street lie Darlinghurst and East Sydney, where you can find some of Sydney's most thriving nightlife. **Victoria Street** in particular is lined with an impressive array of restaurants and cafés, including the **Victoria Room** and **Fu Manchu**. For a pizza-and-pasta fix, turn west down Liverpool Street, and then via Crown Street into Stanley Street, the inner city's Little Italy.

Running parallel to Liverpool Street is Burton Street, the site of the elegant sandstone edifice that was formerly **Darlinghurst Gaol**. It was built on a conspicuous hill for maximum visibility, and 79 people were hanged in the building, which bizarrely is now an art college (visitors welcome, tel: 9339 8744). From here, Forbes, Darlinghurst and Victoria Roads all open onto the bustling Oxford Street near Taylor Square.
SEE ALSO BARS, P.35;
RESTAURANTS, P.103

Rather than wandering too far down Macleay Street – it runs out of steam as it heads downhill towards Woolloomooloo *(see p.11)* and the naval base at Garden Island – spend some time exploring the small backstreets connecting Macleay Street with Victoria Street. They contain some of Sydney's finest architecture, including art deco buildings such as the former Metro Theatre in Orwell Street (now the base of Kennedy Miller Productions, the makers of *Babe* and *Mad Max*) and **Tusculum** in Manning Street, a glorious 1830s mansion with a two-storey Ionic colonnade.

More splendid architecture can be found by turning east down Elizabeth Bay Road, which culminates in the cul de sac known as **The Loop**, home to some of Sydney's most glamorous apartments. Wander down Ithaca Road to **Beare Park**, perhaps the city's prettiest harbourside park, then walk back along Billyard Avenue and Onslow Avenue to **Elizabeth Bay House**, one of Sydney's grandest mansions. Originally built for Alexander Macleay in 1839, it is now administered by the Historic Houses Trust, and is

Right: the El Alamein Fountain in the Fitzroy Gardens.

Paddington and Surry Hills

It is a rare visitor who does not fall in love with the inner-city suburbs of Paddington and Surry Hills. Foodies love the array of restaurants, particularly along Crown Street. Fashionistas love Paddington's upmarket boutiques and Surry Hills' more cutting-edge labels. The gay community clusters around the lower reaches of Oxford Street, where their favourite clubs are located, and those who appreciate fine architecture all but swoon when confronted with the area's renovated Victorian terraces.

Paddington

There is no Paddington without Oxford Street. The thoroughfare that separates Paddington from Surry Hills is Sydney's best shopping street, and is also home to the suburb's oldest buildings. Situated at the edge of the suburb, near the corner with Greens Road, is the elegant Georgian edifice **Juniper Hall**, built in the early 1820s for Robert Cooper, ex-convict and gin distiller. Opposite stands the **Victoria Barracks**, a convict-built military complex dating back to 1848. At the far end of the barracks, on the corner of Oatley Road, is the **Paddington Town Hall** (1891), now home to the vibrant, arthouse **Chauvel Cinema**.

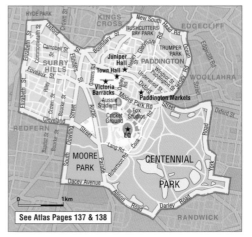

See Atlas Pages 137 & 138

Behind Juniper Hall, narrow streets are still lined with the small terraces that were built to house the artisans working on the barracks. These narrow lanes are as typically Paddington as the wide tree-lined avenues such as Paddington and Windsor streets, where the spacious Georgian homes sell for millions of dollars.

Oxford Street is lined with beautiful boutiques all the way to Woollahra, but smart shoppers know there are treasures hidden in the side streets.

Browse the galleries and boutiques on Glenmore Road until you reach the gourmet haven of **Five Ways**, where you will find cafés, restaurants and **Le Gerbe d'Or**, one of Sydney's best patisseries. Stop for refreshment at the **Royal Hotel** before heading along Heeley and Underwood streets to William Street, where you will discover everything from hand-made shoes to star designer Collette Dinnigan to chocolatier Just William.

SEE ALSO BARS, P.35; FILM, P.61; MUSEUMS AND GALLERIES, P.84; SHOPPING, P.110

Left: look for a bargain at Paddington Markets.

Left: wrought-iron balconies are characteristic of the area.

occupy their traditional turf near Central Station, as does Rupert Murdoch's media empire.

If Surry Hills' abundance of pubs attests to its working-class origins, the trendy bistros and imported beers that have transformed locals' favourites affirm the suburb's gentrification. Not everything has changed, however: Sydney's most famous brothel, A Touch of Class, still occupies its long-term premises in Riley Street.

Surry Hills' trendiest highway is **Crown Street**, which runs between Oxford and Cleveland streets and has a concentration of chic boutiques and smart restaurants at either end. Bourke Street, running parallel, has more restaurants near the Cleveland Street end, although the St Margarets development near Oxford Street is worth checking out, not least for the exquisite Object Gallery.

Up-and-coming is the area closer to Central Station. Following the success of sophisticated restaurants such as **Longrain** and **Lo Studio**, a number of furniture and interiors outlets are opening up around Campbell and Commonwealth streets.

SEE ALSO RESTAURANTS, P.104–5

Centennial and Moore parks

Between Paddington and Surry Hills lie two of Sydney's biggest parks. Built on reclaimed swampland, **Centennial Park** was dedicated 'to the people of New South Wales' in 1888 to mark the centenary of white settlement, and was the venue for the inauguration of Federation in 1901. Its ponds, playing fields and grasslands can be explored by foot, bicycle, inline skates or even on horseback, and in summer the popular Moonlight Cinema takes place here.

Moore Park is rather bare in comparison, and flanked by the **Aussie Stadium** and the **Sydney Cricket Ground**. Also nearby is **EQ**, an entertainment precinct with cinemas, restaurants and playgrounds, next door to **Fox Studios**, where the

Star Wars series and *Matrix* trilogy were filmed.

SEE ALSO FILM, P.60; PARKS AND GARDENS, P.94; SPORT, P.119–120

Surry Hills

Surry Hills covers the area to the west of Oxford Street, from the valley around Central Station to the heights of Crown and Bourke streets, up to Cleveland Street where Redfern begins.

In the 1930s, this was Sydney's most notorious slum: the author Ruth Park caused a stir with her novel *Poor Man's Orange*, which offered unvarnished depictions of life in the suburb.

Some parts of Surry Hills have changed more than others. Although a gay enclave has developed near Oxford Street and fine dining has blossomed along Crown Street, the area still has plenty of hostels dotting the back streets. The warehouses of the rag trade still

Paddington Markets, held on Saturday in the grounds of the Uniting Church on Oxford Street, is the place to find the fashion stars of tomorrow. Many of Australia's most celebrated designers got their start here, including Collette Dinnigan and Lisa Ho and jewellery makers Dinosaur Designs *(see p.116)*.

The Inner-West Suburbs

While the inner-city and eastern suburbs types rejoice in their harbour views and upmarket boutiques, the dwellers of the inner-west suburbs remain convinced that theirs is the real Sydney. In suburbs such as Glebe, Newtown, Leichhardt and Haberfield, a mix of students and immigrants, New Agers and urban rebels creates vibrant communities in distinctive 'villages' that also happen to contain some of the best shopping and eating in town.

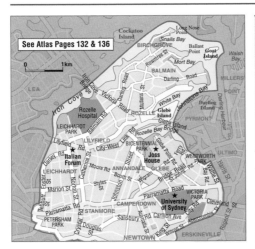

Other inner-west suburbs worth a visit are the harbour-side enclave of **Balmain**, once strictly working-class (Australia's Labor Party was formed here) but now a moneyed haunt with leafy streets and upmarket shops; and **Haberfield**, filled with heritage cottages and wonderful Italian food outlets.

Glebe

Glebe Point Road peels off from Broadway on the corner with **Sydney University**, and it is the proximity to the university that has shaped the suburb's happy hippy atmosphere. If you are looking to get your *chakras* realigned or are in the mood for some mung beans to munch on, this is the place to come.

The weekly **markets**, held at the school on Glebe Point Road, are a good place to start, with a lively selection of stalls ranging from fledgling designers to second-hand stalls and incense sellers.

From here, spend a couple of hours cruising the main strip of Glebe Point Road, which is where all the action happens. There are more than enough recycled clothing outlets, cheap ethnic eateries, CD stores and cafés to keep you occupied for an entire afternoon. One of the city's best bookshops, **Glee-books**, has not one, but two outlets on the main drag.

Architecture buffs will enjoy wandering the length of Glebe Point Road, where some of Sydney's handsomest old Victorian mansions are located. On Edward Street, just off Glebe Point Road, is a **Chinese Joss**

Right: a quick break between lectures.

Left: Sydney University.

gested, cluttered Parramatta Road is something most Sydneysiders avoid whenever possible. But Leichhardt is worth the effort.

The suburb may be named after a German explorer (who inspired Patrick White's book *Voss*), but it has become the headquarters of Sydney's Italian community. Norton Street is the place to come for potent short blacks *(see p.43)* and pasta like *nonna* used to make. The best time to come is on a weekend evening, when it seems like every single inhabitant of the suburb is out on the street, eating, drinking, or just catching up on the gossip. No-frills favourites such as **Bar Italia** do just as much of a roaring trade as newer, more up-market eateries such as **Elio**.

Recent developments on Norton Street have a mixed record. The **Italian Forum**, a shopping and apartment complex, lays it on a bit thick, with Versace in the boutiques and a Dante statue in the courtyard; but the **Palace Cinema** Norton Street is a great place to catch an art-house film.

SEE ALSO CAFES, P.44; FILM, P.61; RESTAURANTS, P.106

House, a 19th-century original that has been restored by the Chinese community.

Glebe Point Road terminates by Centennial Park on Rozelle Bay. Off Ferry Road is the suburb's other great waterside attraction: The **Boathouse at Blackwattle Bay**, one of Sydney's best seafood restaurants.

SEE ALSO LITERATURE, P.79; RESTAURANTS, P.105; SHOPPING, P.116

Newtown

While Glebe skirts the university's southern flank, Newtown runs along its western boundary. Once a student-and-immigrant ghetto, it is now one of Sydney's funkiest neighbourhoods, with a mix of sub-cultures that keeps things colourful.

What the traffic-clogged artery of King Street lacks in beauty it makes up for in cutting-edge cred. The street is home to an extraordinary array of stylish furniture and interiors shops; retro goods and pop-culture collectibles; and a virtually-unmatched array of eateries. (Thai restaurants are particularly popular; **Sumalee Thai** in the Bank Hotel is one of the best.)

Newtown's boutiques range from second-hand outlets to hip designer boutiques, which stock a good selection of up-and-coming Australian and New Zealand labels. King Street's other distinguishing characteristic is its extraordinary proliferation of bookshops, including the quality selection at Better Read Than Dead, it offers more outlets than any other street in Sydney.

SEE ALSO LITERATURE, P.78–9; RESTAURANTS, P.105; SHOPPING, P.110

Leichhardt

The least appealing thing about Leichhardt is the journey there. Travelling the con-

Below: the Chinese Joss House in Glebe.

Eastern Suburbs

When Sydneysiders sneer about 'Eastern Suburbs types', you can hear the envy in their voices. It is not surprising: the area to the east of the city is regarded by many as the most desirable part of the suburban sprawl. On one frontage is the magnificence of Sydney Harbour with its calm bays and sunny parks; on the other is the coastline where the Pacific Ocean rolls against spectacular cliffs and beaches. It is little wonder that property here fetches the highest residential prices in all Australia. Quite apart from the natural attractions, those who can afford to live here are also blessed with stylish eateries and great shopping.

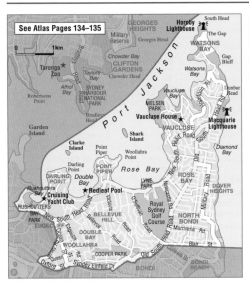

Above: Nielsen Park has a harbour beach loved by families for its wide green spaces.

Rushcutters Bay and Double Bay

The Eastern Suburbs starts where King Cross decants into **Rushcutters Bay**. The bay was named for the convicts who cut rushes here, two of whom were among the earliest Europeans killed by Aborigines in May 1788. Lined by massive Moreton Bay fig trees, the bay is home to the Cruising Yacht Club of Australia. This is the place to be on Boxing Day, when the boats set off for the annual **Sydney to Hobart Yacht Race**.

From Rushcutters Bay, the main artery of New South Head Road travels through the rather nondescript commercial centre of Edgecliff to **Double Bay**, one of Sydney's most exclusive shopping precincts.

Double Bay owes its European feel to the migrants who settled here after World War II, and its glittering array of designer boutiques and stylish cafés

to the wealthy locals who have turned shopping into an endurance sport. Those whose wallets last the distance will enjoy browsing along Knox, Guilfoyle and Bay streets.

Detour off Knox Street into tiny Transvaal Avenue, where cottages originally built to house servants are now inhabited by elegant clothing and homewares outlets. Just past the main village are the local council chambers, which also mark the entrance to **Redleaf Pool**, a popular harbour swimming spot.

SEE ALSO SPORT, P.121

no harbour access. That has
not stopped the likes of opera
diva Dame Joan Sutherland,
former prime minister Paul
Keating and radio talkback
king John Laws calling it
home. Apart from the leafy
streets and elegant Victorian
terraces, Woollahra's main
attraction is the best selection
of antiques stores and art galleries in town.

The action takes place in
the compact triangle formed
by Queen Street, Ocean
Street and Jersey Road. Here
you will find antique rarities,
exquisite fashion from the
likes of Akira Isogawa, and
provenders such as Jones
the Grocer (68 Moncur Street;
tel: 9362-1222; Mon–Sat 7.30am–
5.30pm, Sun 9am–5pm). This
is the perfect place to pick
up the makings of a picnic
to enjoy in **Centennial Park**,
which runs between
Woollahra and Randwick.
SEE ALSO PADDINGTON AND
SURRY HILLS, P.17; PARKS AND
GARDENS, P.94

For the ghoulishly-inclined, the
Eastern Suburbs contain two
rather macabre attractions: the
Gap at Watson's Bay, a sheer
cliff face that is a popular spot
for suicides; and the Stamford
Plaza Hotel in Double Bay,
where INXS singer Michael
Hutchence met his demise.

Rose Bay and Watson's Bay

The next bay along from
Double Bay is **Rose Bay**, a
wide, yacht-studded expanse
fringed by the green swathe
of Lyne Park. Two of Syd-
ney's best restaurants, **Pier**
and **Catalina**, can be found
here, along with the resident
pelicans that often surprise
diners on Catalina's balcony.

Rose Bay's shopping
precinct lies just beyond the
bay itself, and marks the
starting point for one of Sydney's most beautiful foreshore walks. The walk
continues through to **Nielsen
Park** at Vaucluse. From here
it is a short walk to **Vaucluse
House**, one of Sydney's
grandest old houses still
open to the public.

After Vaucluse, New South
Head Road terminates at
Watson's Bay, Sydney's first

fishing village, distinguished
by the lighthouse at the tip of
South Head. Most people
make the trip here by ferry
and come for just one thing:
fish and chips at **Doyle's**,
the fish specialists who have
been serving it up for over
100 years.
SEE ALSO MUSEUMS AND GALLERIES,
P.84; RESTAURANTS, P.106;
WALKS AND VIEWS, P.129–30

Woollahra

Unlike its Eastern Suburbs
neighbours, Woollahra,
located where Oxford Street
meets Centennial Park, has

Right: arriving for lunch at
Doyle's in Watson's Bay.

21

Eastern Beaches

The area to the east of Sydney is regarded by many residents and the majority of sun-seeking visitors as the best part of the city's outdoor attractions and the ultimate destination, and waterside dwellings here fetch astronomical prices compared with the rest of Australia. With good reason. The eastern beach suburbs are not just blessed with beautiful people, addictive shopping, classy bars and restaurants and the hippest cafés in town. From Bondi to Coogee each small suburb has access to its own beach, and the 8-km walk that connects them all is a popular route for tourists, walkers and runners.

Bondi

The best-known beach in all of Australia is a great place to start. Bondi – from an Aboriginal word meaning 'water breaking over rocks' – became a public beach in 1882 and there are still glimpses of its heritage. The **Bondi Pavilion**, now a venue for music and other festivals, sits comfortably on the promenade, and the **Icebergs pool**, now attached to the swanky bar and restaurant of

For more information about Sydney's beach life *see Beaches, p.38–41*

the same name, dates back to 1929, when it was established to allow the lifesavers a chance to stay fit during the chilly winter months. Today Icebergs, the bar, is where the prettiest and most famous go to eat, drink and gaze at the view, and the pool is still there if you fancy a dip. Head south and you can follow the sea path straight to Tamarama. SEE ALSO BARS, P.36

Tamarama

Small but perfectly formed, Tamarama is affectionately known by the locals as Glamarama, thanks to the abundance of beautiful people who manage to squeeze themselves onto the tiny patch of sand every weekend. Originally the site of Sydney's first amusement park in 1887, 'Tama' now helps host the annual Sculpture by the Sea exhibits, but other than that it is just a nice beach for sunbathing. Unless you seriously know what you are doing, swimming is not recommended. There are rips aplenty, so stay on dry land and people-watch instead.

Following the coastal road round the headland, you come to Bronte.

Bronte

Bronte's life-saving club was established in 1903 – they claim it is the oldest in the world – and is still going strong on what is one of the most popular beaches in the eastern suburbs. Every December the Bondi to Bronte swim brings out the most experienced swimmers from the suburbs and beyond. And even if you are not up to the challenge, it is a site not to be missed.

In recent years Bronte has added some serious cachet to its reputation thanks to the likes of Hollywood star Heath

In the late 19th century, the Police Offences Act prohibited bathing between 6am and 8pm. But in 1903 a Waverley clergyman, the Rev Frank McKeown, and a bank clerk, Frank McElhone, defied the ban at Bondi. A local newspaper reported that they had made 'a disgusting spectacle of themselves', but soon crowds of bathers were arriving at weekends and the Bondi Surf Bathers' Lifesaving Club was established three years later.

swimmers might monopolise on a hot day, but it is wiser to carry on the 10-minute walk to Coogee.

Apparently taken from an Aboriginal word meaning 'stinking seaweed', today Coogee is much sweeter. It is one of the more tightly populated areas, with houses dating back to the 1930s, but Coogee itself has been a popular seaside resort since the early 1900s, when an electric tram connected the area to the city.

Surfing is not allowed at Coogee, but the beach itself is a popular spot for local festivals and competitions, thanks to the area of grassy parkland behind it.

Coogee has made the news a few times in history. Once in 1935 when a captured tiger shark regurgitated a human arm, and again in 2003 when visitors reported seeing an apparition of the Virgin Mary. Today people still visit the site hoping for a glimpse of her.

At the northern end of the headland stands a high bronze sculpture, commemorating the local residents who perished in the 2002 Bali bombings.

Ledger and director Baz Luhrmann owning properties here. For the ordinary folk, the strip of cafés and restaurants above the beach are a main attraction.

Clovelly

Leaving Bronte and heading further south, the sprawling and stunning **Waverley Cemetery** interrupts the beaches, before you turn a corner and are greeted with Clovelly. Originally called Little Coogee, after its bigger brother beach further along the coast, Clovelly was renamed in 1913. Yet another life-saving club was established in 1906, although Clovelly soon earned its tag as 'Sydney's safest beach'. Because of the shape of Clovelly, where it stretches deeply towards the shoreline, the beach itself is a shallow and tranquil lagoon.

Today, because of this, it is popular with families and local residents. An added incentive to visit is the large car park directly above the beach, and if you are keen to venture further out into deeper waters, the snorkelling is top notch.

Coogee

Continuing on your walk will take you past tiny **Gordon's Bay**, which one or two

Right: Coogee Beach.

23

The North Shore

When the now famous Sydney Harbour Bridge was completed in 1933, it was the first time the north side of the harbour had been connected with the centre by road. Until then access had been by boat only, but that had not stopped the city's wealthier families congregating on the northern shore, and commuter ferries still provide a key transport link for office workers. Today, North Shore dwellers remain a breed apart, loving their mix of bushland, ocean views, beaches and fashionable shopping districts, and convinced that they are living in the best of all possible worlds.

Lower North Shore

Lower north shore residents can be excused for feeling slightly smug about their leafy streets and extensive harbour foreshores, all just minutes away from the CBD. Bustling **Military Road**, the main ridge-line road that winds its way through Neutral Bay and Cremorne to Mosman, is packed with shops and restaurants. A more tranquil way to get there is by following the foreshore. Stop for a dip at **Cremorne Point**, before wandering past **Mosman Bay** to the area's best attractions: the spectacularly situated **Taronga Zoo** and the leafy **Balmoral Beach**, the location of one of Sydney's best restaurants, the **Bather's Pavilion**.

Further south, skirting the edge of the Harbour Bridge, are the suburbs of North Sydney, Kirribilli and Milson's Point. North Sydney is a business district that bustles during the week and is deserted on weekends; Kirribilli, by contrast, has retained a leafy village feel. Milson's Point has two outstanding attractions in the **Luna Park** funfair and **North Sydney Olympic Pool**. This saltwater pool has stellar views of the CBD and the Harbour Bridge, as well its own casual and fine-dining restaurants.

CHILDREN, P.46–7;
RESTAURANTS, P.108; SPORT, P.122

A seaside resort may seem an unlikely setting for a revolution, but it was here at Manly that in 1902 local newspaperman W.H. Gocher defied the law banning daylight swimming, an act that helped launch Sydneysiders' love affair with a seaside lifestyle.

Left: Luna Park's dramatic entrance.

for braver souls; booking essential (tel: 9995 5000).
SEE ALSO CHILDREN, P.47; WALKS AND VIEWS, P.130–3

Northern Beaches

Manly marks the starting point of a wonderful string of surf beaches that culminate in the glossy suburbs of **Avalon** and **Palm Beach** (where *Home and Away* is filmed). The 'insular peninsula' that separates the pounding ocean surf from the tranquil waters of **Pittwater** is so popular that in summer locals rent out their luxurious beach houses for thousands of dollars.

To savour the area's splendours by yourself, catch a bus up to Pittwater and hire a kayak or a boat. Alternatively, take a ferry from Palm Beach to **The Basin**, National Parkland traced with tracks that take in Aboriginal rock carvings, secluded beaches and the landmark Barrenjoey Lighthouse. Or simply enjoy a meal at one of the area's classy eateries.
SEE ALSO BEACHES, P.40–1

> For more information about Sydney's beach life *see Beaches, p.38–41*

Manly

Manly came to fame as the seaside resort 'seven miles from Sydney, a thousand miles from care', and it is still one of the top tourist destination north of the harbour. The area has a rich history dating back to the days of Captain Cook, who named the area after the 'manly' natives he saw there.

The ferry from Circular Quay pulls up at **Manly Cove**. The neighbouring beach is perfect for quiet swimming, and nearby family attractions include **Manly Oceanworld** aquarium and **Manly Waterworks**.

Oceanworld marks the beginning of the 10-km **Manly to Spit walk**, one of Sydney's great bushland walks, taking in Aboriginal sites, hidden beaches, and some highly desirable real

estate. Or you can head in the other direction and take the steep walk up to the **Quarantine Station** on North Head.

For 150 years, the Quarantine Station was the first port of call for ships suspected of carrying infectious diseases. Fifty-seven people died here, and their spirits are said to haunt the now-unused building. The National Parks and Wildlife Service runs both daytime tours and evening sessions

Right: gazing over Pittwater.
Opposite: Manly Beach

The Blue Mountains

A magnificent World Heritage-listed wilderness, the Blue Mountains are filled with deep gorges, plunging waterfalls and expanses of bush still relatively untouched by Europeans. The mountains are one of New South Wales' most spectacular landscapes. Anyone who enjoys hiking will love its vast range of scenic bushwalks, from the eroded sandstone clifftops down into densely-wooded valleys. The less active can enjoy a more leisurely exploration of the villages and townships, which are filled with cosy guesthouses, cafés serving Devonshire teas and acclaimed restaurants that make the most of their setting and local ingredients.

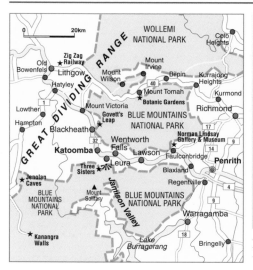

Above: Leura is well stocked with galleries and boutiques.

Reaching the Mountains

To the early settlers, the Great Dividing Range was a prison wall, the barrier isolating the fledgling colony in Sydney from the rest of the continent. Although the mountains are only around 1,100m high, their rugged folds were impenetrable, to white men, that is. Indigenous tribes had been crossing from the interior to the coast for thousands of years.

Since no one thought to ask the natives for advice, it was not until 1813 that the first European crossing was achieved. The intrepid trio who managed the feat – Blaxland, Lawson and Wentworth – gave their names to towns in the lower mountains, and today's Great Western Highway closely follows the route they took, as does the railway that provides easy access to the mountains for a growing number of commuters.

In the 1920s, Sydneysiders sweltering in the heat of the coast began to head for the mountains for relief, and many of the area's most scenic retreats date from this time. Modern visitors tend to be more adventurous. Abseilers, canyoners and bushwalkers all enjoy exploring the pockets of rainforest, ferns and hanging swamps, as well as the vast forests of eucalypts that launch their oil into the air, giving the mountains their eponymous haze. The mountains still harbour a few secrets: one recent discovery was the Wollemi Pine, a tree previously thought to have been extinct for 150 million years.

restaurants, including the indulgent **Mountain Heritage Hotel and Spa Retreat** and **Lillanfels Blue Mountains Resort and Spa**, with its acclaimed restaurant, and **Silk's Brasserie** in Leura. Leura also hosts a popular garden festival every October.
SEE ALSO HOTELS, P.77; RESTAURANTS, P.109

Blackheath and Beyond

Many visitors never make it past Katoomba, which is a pity, as the upper mountains have plenty of other townships and attractions to explore.

Blackheath has some lovely guesthouses, such as **Kubba Roonga**, and a celebrated pie shop, as well as the excellent Vulcan's restaurant. From Blackheath you can also take a breathtaking walk from **Govett's Leap** lookout to **Pulpit Rock**, which offers an awe-inspiring panorama.

Mount Wilson is famous for its landscaped gardens, which are particularly spectacular during autumn. Throughout the year, **Mount Tomah Botanic Gardens** is worth a visit. From here, the road winds through the mountains to **Lithgow**, an industrial town on the western side of the range, where you can ride the **Zig Zag Railway**, a steamline built in the 1860s.
SEE ALSO HOTELS, P.77

The Lower Mountains

Few visitors stop at the townships that dot the lower flanks of the Blue Mountains, which are less scenic and offer less to tourists than the higher towns. Definitely worth visiting is the **Norman Lindsay Gallery and Museum** at Faulconbridge. Set in beautifully landscaped gardens, this stone cottage was once the home of one of Australia's most accomplished artists. Lindsay is remembered both for his Bacchanalian nudes and for *The Magic Pudding*, a much-loved children's book.

SEE ALSO MUSEUMS AND GALLERIES, P.86

Leura and Katoomba

The two most-visited townships in the mountains are popular with shoppers, who enjoy Leura's range of galleries and boutiques, and browsing along Katoomba Street in Katoomba for vintage clothes and books.

Katoomba's most famous attraction is the **Three Sisters** rock formation at Echo Point. Some of the area's most accessible walks start from here, including the Cliff Walk to **Gordon Falls Reserve** at Leura, with panoramic views across the Jamison Valley to Mount Solitary and distant Kanangra Walls. Alternatively, walk down the **Giant Staircase** and across to the steeply-inclined **Scenic Railway**, then catch the train back to the top of the cliff.

Katoomba and Leura offer a rich choice of hotels and

Because of its altitude, winter in the Blue Mountains can be a decidedly chilly affair, by Sydney standards anyway. The regular heavy fogs and occasional flurries of snow appeal to locals who head here to celebrate Yulefest – Christmas in July – complete with a traditional English Christmas dinner.

Below: the Zig Zag Railway.

Aboriginal Culture

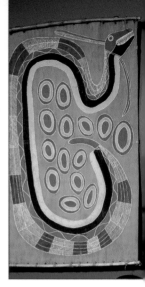

No one knows for sure how many Aborigines were living in the Sydney area before the Europeans arrived. Three groups occupied the region: the Eora, living around the harbour; the Duruk, to the north; and the Dharawal, to the south. It is estimated that the Eora numbered around 1,500. No Eora people remain; Sydney's contemporary Aboriginal population comes from all over Australia. Only place names such as Bondi, Woolloomooloo and Parramatta commemorate the original inhabitants.

Nomadic Tribes

It is thought that all Aboriginal Australians originally lived in Asia, and crossed over from New Guinea around 50,000 BC, when there was still a land bridge. They probably settled in the Sydney area around 40,000 BC, surviving on shellfish, bush food and animals. They sheltered in harbourside caves, pursuing a nomadic existence and living in tight territorial groups, with respected elders but no leader. Order was provided by family ties, language and rituals.

Below: an Aboriginal busker and *didjeridu*.

The Eora people greeted the Europeans calmly at first, but nothing in their experience could prepare them for the future. Governor Phillip was under orders to treat the natives with kindness, and he dealt severely with anyone he suspected of maltreatment. But the British settlers could not understand the Aborigines' nomadic lifestyle or the profound connection they had to their tribal lands. It seemed that they came and went without reason across the sparse landscape. The island of Australia was conveniently declared a *terra nullius* (no one's land) – effectively an uninhabited void that Europeans could occupy without concern.

The results were devastating. As white settlers arrived by the boatload, Aboriginal communities were systematically pushed from their lands, leading to the disruption and destruction of their traditional culture and communal life. Massacres of the indigenous people became common, and introduced diseases such as smallpox killed off many more.

In 1788, there were possibly more than 300,000 Aborigines in Australia; by 1900, there were 60,000. It was not until the 1970s that Aborigines began to campaign for civil rights. The Department of Aboriginal Affairs was established in 1972, followed by the Aboriginal Development Commission in 1980.

The 1990s were a decade of attempted reconciliation between white Australians and the Aborigines. A High Court decision in June 1992 declared that, contrary to the 200-year-old legal ruling, Australia was in fact an occupied country when the British arrived. This decision has had enormous implications for the seeking and granting of Aboriginal land rights, an issue which, more than any other, will determine whether or not the concept of reconciliation can be fully realised.

Aboriginal Art

Contemporary Aboriginal art covers an extraordinary range of styles, from the dot paintings of the Central Desert to the cross-hatching of the far

artists Emily Kame Knga-warreye and Gloria Petyarre.

Yiribana Gallery, Art Gallery of NSW
Art Gallery Road, The Domain; tel: 9225 1744; daily 10am–6pm (Wed until 9pm); train: Museum Station; map p.133 D2/E2
The Art Gallery of NSW contains the world's largest permanent collection of Aboriginal and Torres Strait Islander art.
SEE ALSO MUSEUMS AND GALLERIES, P.85

Aboriginal Culture

Aboriginal Heritage Tour
Royal Botanic Gardens; tel: 9231 8111; Fri 2pm; entrance charge; bookings essential; train: Martin Place, bus: 200, 441, Sydney Explorer; map p.133 D3/E2
This weekly tour covers various aspects of Aboriginal culture and includes a tour of the Royal Botanic Gardens' bush tucker and medicinal plants.

Tribal Warrior Cultural Cruise
East Pontoon, East Circular Quay; daily; entrance charge; book through Sydney Visitors Centre, tel: 9240 8788
This harbour cruise give visitors a feel for how Aborigines once lived in Sydney. Guides show you former settlements and describe traditional food gathering techniques.

north. Materials used include oil on canvas, bark paintings and Tiwi totem poles.

Aboriginal art is about more than aesthetics; it is an important form of cultural identity. Paintings that may seem abstract to Western eyes are actually documents designed to be read by other members of the tribe, conveying messages about the painter and his or her people, the relationships with the land, and the connections to the Dreaming.

Galleries

Boomalli Aboriginal Artists' Co-operative
55–59 Flood Street, Leichhardt; tel: 9560 2566; Tue–Fri 10am–5pm; bus: 435, 436, 437, 438; map p.18
Boomalli's founding members include such acclaimed artists as Tracey Moffatt and Michael Riley. It has a strong tradition of working with NSW artists, and also features non-traditional artists such as Destiny Deacon.

Coo-ee Aboriginal Art Gallery
31 Lamrock Avenue, Bondi; tel: 9332 1544; Tue–Sat 10am–5pm;

bus: 380; map p.22
Art, sculptures and artefacts from throughout Australia, particularly the Northern Territory and Western Australia.

Gavala Aboriginal Arts and Cultural Centre
Shop 131, Harbourside, Darling Harbour; tel: 9212 7232; daily 10am–9pm; train: Town Hall Station, monorail: Darling Harbour; map p.132 B1
Offers a selection of art from Queensland, northern NSW and particularly the Northern Territory, including cross-hatching, X-ray art and dot paintings.

Hogarth Galleries
Aboriginal Art Centre, 7 Walker Lane, Paddington; tel: 9360 6839; Tue–Sat 10am–5pm; bus: 389; map p.138
Australia's oldest Aboriginal fine art gallery, presenting works by established and emerging artists from around Australia.

Utopia Art Sydney
2 Danks Street, Waterloo; tel: 9699 2900; Tue–Sat, 10am–5pm; bus: 301, 302, 303, 343
Specialises in work from the celebrated Papunya Tula settlement, as well as Utopia

Take the trip to Redfern, the heart of Sydney's Aboriginal community, to get a true taste of bush tucker. **Guyna Lounge** (106 George Street, Redfearn; tel: 9690 0610; Mon–Sat 11.30am–9pm) uses traditional ingredients such as emu and crocodile, lemon myrtle and bush tomato, to create gourmet grub.

Bars

Sydney has a bar to suit every occasion. There are glam city venues and Paddington's Victorian-era pubs, loud and laidback beach barns and the quaint old-time pubs of The Rocks, discreet cocktail bars in sedate hotels and raucous halls with DJs or live music. There are a dozen different vibes to choose from. Many of the old, tiled, male-only bastions have been given a revamp, and can now look like anything from a European café to a New York nightclub. Even wine bars – traditionally a type of venue more popular in Melbourne – have started to appear around the harbour city.

Central Business District (CBD)

Arthouse Hotel
275 Pitt Street; tel: 9284 1200; Mon–Tue 11am–midnight, Wed 11am–1am, Thur 11am–3am, Fri 11am–4am, Sat 5pm–4am; train: Town Hall Station and Elizabeth Street buses; map p.133 C1
Even Sydneysiders can not believe their luck at having such a great venue in the heart of town. Urban sophisticates head upstairs for the stunning 19th-century architecture, the sleek design, the refined vibe, and, of course, the cocktails. Huge raves downstairs on Friday and Saturday nights attract a younger crowd.

Bambini Wine Room
185 Elizabeth Street; tel: 9283 7098; Mon–Fri 3–11pm; train: Town Hall, bus: George Street and Elizabeth Street buses; map p.133 D1
In the never-ending Sydney-Melbourne rivalry, Sydney-siders boast about their harbour, while Melbournites rave about their wine bars. Bambini helps tilt the balance in Sydney's favour. The flag-

stone floor, the chandeliers and flowing lamps, not to mention the selection of pleasant wines, make this intimate venue irresistible.
SEE ALSO CAFÉS P.42

Bavarian Bier Café
24 York Street; tel: 8297 4111; Mon–Thur 8am–midnight, Fri–Sat 8am–1am; train: Town Hall Station, bus: George Street and Elizabeth Street buses; map p.133 C3
This is how you target the after-work crowd. Blonde bistro interiors, a range of quality Bavarian beers and hearty schnitzel-and-sausages food. Get friendly at the communal tables, or get some privacy in a booth.

Civic Hotel
Corner Goulburn and Pitt streets; tel: 8080 7000; Tue–Thur 11am–midnight, Fri–Sat 11am–3am, Sun 3pm–midnight; train: Town Hall, bus: George Street and Elizabeth Street buses; map p.137 D4
A recent refurbishment restored the 1940s art deco splendour of this city landmark. Choose from three levels: the elegant street-level saloon with the huge, heritage-listed bar, the classy dining room upstairs, or the music venue in the basement.

Below: pizza and beer at Establishment.

Establishment

252 George Street; tel: 9240 3000; Mon–Tue 11am– 1am, Wed 11am–2am, Thur–Fri 11am–3am, Sat noon–3am, Sun 8pm–1am; train: Wynyard or Martin Place, bus: George Street buses; map p.139 D2

This beautifully-restored building houses a number of bars and clubs, including the sleek Hemmesphere upstairs *(see below)*. Walk past during the day, and you would doubt this vast space, with its 42m marble bar and airy ceilings, could ever get full; however, by 6.30 on a Friday evening, it will be packed. City girls refer to this place as The Drycleaners: it is where you go to pick up a suit.

SEE ALSO HOTELS, P.70; RESTAURANTS, P.98

Hemmesphere

Establishment, level 4, 252 George Street; tel: 9240 3040; Tue–Sat 6pm–midnight; train: Wynyard or Martin Place, bus: George Street buses; map p.139 D2

Four levels above Establishment but a world away, this lounge bar is pure delight, although you pay for the priv-

ilege. Join the charmed few savouring the cedar-scented Moroccan interiors, the chilled soundtrack, and the 26-page drinks menu.

Orbit Bar and Lounge

Level 47, Australia Square, 264 George Street; tel: 9247 9777; daily 5pm–late; train: Wynyard Station, bus: George Street buses; map p.139 D2

With floor-to-ceiling windows offering one of the city's best views, Orbit could be forgiven for not trying too hard. Fortunately, they go the extra mile anyway, with a range of quality quaffs, and a stylish fit-out right out of *2001: A Space Odyssey*.

Slip Inn

111 Sussex Street; tel: 8295 9999; Mon–Wed noon–midnight, Thur–Fri noon–2am, Sat 6.30pm–3am; train: Town Hall, bus: George Street buses; map p.139 C1

This one-stop entertainment complex – five bars, a restaurant and a nightclub – was a city favourite even before a pretty young Sydneysider

met a handsome prince here and went on to become Princess Mary of Denmark. Still popular for those with romance – or something similar – on their minds.

Wine Banq

Basement, 53 Martin Place; tel: 9222 1919; daily noon–3pm and 5pm–late; train: Martin Place, bus: Elizabeth Street buses; map p.139 E1

It's dim, moody, sophisticated but not pretentious. The subterranean Wine Banq is a very grown-up venue, with sexy banquettes, cosy armchairs and very good food. Live jazz at weekends ups the vibe.

Zeta

Hilton Hotel, 488 George Street; tel: 9265 6070; Mon–Thur and Sat, 5pm–late, Fri 3pm–late; train: Town Hall, bus: George Street buses; map p.133 C1

Designer labels get you to the top of the entrance queue; if you are looking

Right: after-work drinks in the CBD.

31

Above: the stylish Water Bar at the Blue Hotel.

particularly flash, you may even score one of the coveted semi-private sitting coves. The stellar drinks list includes concoctions such as the Mandarin and Vanilla Margarita.

The Rocks

Australian Hotel
100–102 Cumberland Street; tel: 9247 2229; Mon–Sat 11am–midnight, Sun 11am– 10pm; train: Wynyard Station, bus: George Street buses; map p.139 D3

On the fringes of The Rocks, away from the tourist clutter, this 1913 hotel is popular with locals for its extensive selection of boutique brews (90 different beers on offer) and its good-value pizzas, which include quirky toppings such as pepper kangaroo.
SEE ALSO HOTELS, P.71–2

Blu Horizon
Shangri-La Hotel, 176 Cumberland Street; tel: 9250 6013; Mon–Thur 5pm–12.30am, Fri 3pm–1.30am, Sat 5pm–1.30am, Sun 5pm–midnight; trains: Wynyard Station, bus: George Street buses; map p.139 D3

You want drinks with a view?

Take the express lift to the top and before you are even out of the lift, you will be dazzled by the stellar harbour view seen through floor-to-ceiling windows.

Firefly
17 Hickson Road; tel: 9241 2031; Mon–Sat noon–11.30pm; train, bus, ferry: Circular Quay; map p.139 D4

This is the low-key side of the harbour, and Firefly's pleasant neighbourhood atmosphere hits the spot. Order a touch of tapas and one of the two dozen wines by the glass, and watch the sun go down.

Fortune of War
137 George Street; tel: 9247 2714; Mon–Fri 9am–late, Sat 11am–2am, Sun noon–midnight; train, bus, ferry: Circular Quay; map p.139 D3

This pub opened in 1839, and one suspects that some of the regulars may have been here since the beginning. Classic old school boozer, not much bigger than a living room.

Hero of Waterloo
81–3 Lower Fort Street; tel: 9252 4553; daily 9am–11.30pm; train, bus, ferry: Circular Quay;

map p.139 D4

The title of Sydney's Oldest Pub is in dispute, but the Hero of Waterloo is definitely in the running. Legend has it that press-ganged sailors were locked up in its cellars; easy to believe once you have had a wander through the maze-like building's hidden rooms and tunnels.

Lord Nelson Brewery Hotel
19 Kent Street; tel: 9251 4044; Mon–Sat 11am–11pm, Sun noon–10am; train, bus, ferry: Circular Quay; map p.139 C3

The other contender for the 'Oldest Pub' title, but this one has a grand colonial feel, a pleasant beer garden, and six types of beer brewed in-house.

Orient Hotel
Corner George and Argyle Streets; tel: 9251 1255; daily 10am–late; train, bus, ferry: Circular Quay; map p.139 D3

If you are looking for the biggest party in The Rocks, this is it. The pub is a favourite with guys and girls who hunt in packs, and has four floors filled with pumping music.

If your idea of a good bar is one that is close to home, you will want to choose your hotel carefully. The city's best in-house bars are found at the Hilton Hotel in the CBD (Zeta, *p.31*), the Shangri-La in The Rocks (Blu Horizon, *left*), and Blue at Woolloomooloo (Water Bar, *below*).

Palisade Hotel
35 Bettington Street; tel: 9247 2272; Mon–Sat 10am–midnight, Sun 10am–10pm; train, bus, ferry: Circular Quay; map p.132 B4

Some people come here for the interiors (floorboards and stained-glass windows; some come here for the food (martini-cured salmon, anyone?); and some just come here because it is a damn good pub.

The Opera House and the Domain

Guillaume at Bennelong
Sydney Opera House, Benne-long Point; tel: 9241 1999; Mon–Sat 5.30pm–midnight; train, bus, ferry: Circular Quay; map p.139 E4

This restaurant-and-bar is one of the few places in the Opera House where you do not get a harbour view. What you do get, apart from sensu-ous chocolate-and-moss decor, is the chance to admire close-up the struts and ribs that support those fabulous sails.
SEE ALSO RESTAURANTS P.100

Minus Five
2 Opera Quays, Circular Quay East; tel: 9251 0311; daily noon–midnight; train, bus, ferry: Circular Quay; map p.139 E3

Yes, it really is minus five degrees Celsius in this bar made of ice. That is to stop

the glasses (also made of ice) melting… and the tables and the chairs (all made of ice). Despite the cold-weather gear you are issued with, there is a limit to how long you will want to stay. After-wards, warm up with a vodka in the Lenin Bar downstairs.

Opera Bar
Sydney Opera House, Bennelong Point; tel: 9247 1666; daily 10am–late; train, bus, ferry: Circular Quay; map p.139 E4

It is a restaurant, it is a bar, it has one of the best views in Sydney. There is not much that Opera Bar does not get right. Thirty Australian wines by the glass gives wine buffs a chance to explore.

Water Bar
Blue, 6 Cowper Wharf Road, Woolloomooloo; tel: 9331 9000; Tue–Sat 4pm–midnight, Sun–Mon 4–10pm; bus: 311; map p.133 E2

From the outside, the Finger Wharf does not look like the largest timber pile wharf in the world. Sit back in your sofa at the groovy Water Bar and gaze upwards, however, and the cathedral-like interior will change your mind.
SEE ALSO HOTELS, P.73

Darling Harbour and Chinatown

Cargo Bar and Lounge
King Street Wharf, Lime Street; tel: 9262 1777; daily 11am–late; map p.132 C2

After-work crowds flock here to enjoy the roomy open-air beer garden and the split-level waterfront bar. The upstairs lounge is more exclusive and more laid back.

James Squire Brewhouse and Restaurant
22 The Promenade, King Street Wharf; tel: 8270 7901; daily 11am–late; map p.132 C2

Named after the ex-convict who first grew hops in Sydney Town, this micro-brewery is the place for beer-lovers. Enjoy a schooner on the waterside promenade or watching the giant TV in the back.

Loft Cocktail Lounge and Bar
King Street Wharf, Lime Street; tel: 9299 4770; Mon–Thur 4pm–1am, Fri–Sat noon–3am, Sun noon–1am; map p.132 C2

The decor looks like some-thing Wilma Flintstone would have come up with after a trip to Morocco. Sink onto an Ottoman and be lulled by the seductive lanterns and the ambient soundtrack.

Pontoon Bar
North Promenade, Cockle Bay Wharf; tel: 9267 7099; Mon–Thur 11.30am–noon, Fri–Sat noon–3am, Sun noon–11pm; map p.132 C1

Pontoon's spacious raised dance floor is perfectly placed to catch the harbour breezes as they blow in. Along with the groove-heavy

Right: having a laugh on The Rocks.

33

Kellett Street in Kings Cross may not be particularly long, but its Victorian terrace houses have been converted into a bar strip that is unlike anywhere else in town. Most of the cosy venues sit somewhere between restaurant and bar, depending on the time of night. We like the dim lighting and intimate ambience of **Aperitif**; 7 Kellett Street; tel: 9357 4729; Wed–Sat 6pm–3am, Sun 6pm–midnight.

R&B/hip-hop soundtrack, that makes it a popular place for a weekend boogie.

Kings Cross District
The Bourbon

24 Darlinghurst Road; tel: 9358 1144; 24hrs; map p.133 E1

Originally known as the Bourbon and Beefsteak, this infamous Kings Cross institution still packs in all sorts, but feels a bit less intimidating since it was made over in 2003.

Colombian Hotel

Corner Oxford and Crown streets, Darlinghurst; tel: 9360 2151; daily 9am–6am; bus: Oxford Street buses; map p.137 E4

Are the huge windows designed to let the trendy mixed crowd inside the Colombian look out, or let the plebs on the pavement look in? Probably the latter; inside this always-packed pub, the outside world falls away.

De Nom

231 Oxford Street, Darlinghurst; tel: 0430 067 373; Tue–Sun 7pm–late; bus: Oxford Street buses; map p.137 E4

Sydney is not the sort of city that favours members' bars, but De Nom is the exception. Hidden on the top floor of the Ruby Rabbit nightclub, this Louis XIV fantasy is also open to mere mortals, as long as they book a table with the maitre d' first. You will not get to sample the members-only wine list, but the standard range of cocktails and vintage wines and bubblies is outstanding. And a visit to the toilets – the most extraordinary in town – is free.
SEE ALSO NIGHTLIFE P.91

East Village

234 Palmer Street, Darlinghurst; tel: 9331 5457; Mon–Sat noon–midnight, Sun noon–10pm; map p.137 E4

Groovy yet unpretentious, this casual pub has four floors of drinking dens. The pick is the Manhattan Roof Top bar, with its picture-postcard view over the CBD.

Gazebo Wine Garden

2 Elizabeth Bay Road, Elizabeth Bay; tel: 9357 5333; Mon–Fri 3pm–midnight, Sat–Sun noon–midnight; train, bus: Kings Cross; map p.134 A1

Serious wine buffs with serious bank accounts love the extraordinary range of wines by the glass (including the legendary Grange Hermitage), and the option of the smaller 'tasting glass'. Everybody else loves the relaxed-yet-happening vibe.

Hugos Bar Pizza

33 Bayswater Road, Kings Cross; tel: 9332 1227; daily 5pm–2am; train, bus: Kings Cross; map p.134 B1

Opened as a more casual sibling to Hugo's Lounge *(see below)*, this has become one of the grooviest drinking holes in town, and no wonder. A cosy lounge area, a cool buzz, great staff and killer pizzas. What more could you ask for?

Hugos Lounge

33 Bayswater Road; tel: 9357 4411; Tue–Sat 7pm–3am; train, bus: Kings Cross; map p.134 B1

Some people spend all weekend at Hugos. Others spend all weekend trying to get in. The interiors are luxurious, the cocktails divine, but if you do not have your glam gear with you, do not bother trying.

Jimmy Liks

186–8 Victoria Street, Kings Cross; tel: 8354 1400; daily 6pm–midnight; train, bus: Kings Cross

A seductive Asian feel pervades every aspect of this slender sliver of a cocktail lounge, from the decor to the food to the cocktail list. We love the lemongrass martinis.

Lotus Bar

22 Challis Avenue, Potts Point; tel: 9326 9000; Tue–Sat, 6pm–late; train, bus: Kings Cross; map p.134 A2

Below: an extensive menu of Australian beers.

This little hole in the wall is a hidden gem, with jewel-like interiors and comfortable banquettes, not to mention a range of exquisite cocktails.

Victoria Room

235 Victoria Street, Darlinghurst; tel: 9357 4488; Tue–Thur 6pm–midnight, Fri 6pm–2am, Sat noon–2am, Sun noon–midnight; train, bus: Kings Cross; map p.134 A1

With a deliberately eclectic decor – last days of the Raj meets Casablanca – the Victoria Room has created its own little universe. Come for dinner, come for drinks, come for high tea at the weekends; just make sure you come.

Above: and even more from the tap.

Paddington and Surry Hills

The Dome

Crown Hotel, corner Crown and Cleveland streets, Surry Hills; tel: 9699 3460; Tue–Wed 6pm–midnight, Thur–Sat 6pm–2am; bus: Crown Street or Cleveland Street buses; map p.137 E2

Finally the south end of Crown Street has a chic drinking venue to match its vibrant restaurant scene. Tucked away on the first floor, Dome cocktail lounge also brings a touch of glamour to Cleveland Street.

Fringe Bar

106 Oxford Street, Paddington; tel: 9360 5443; Sun–Thur noon–midnight, Fri–Sat noon–3am; bus: Oxford Street buses; map p.138 A3

Gets the cool-but-casual vibe just right, with its mix of upscale decor – velvet curtains, chequered floors – and laid-back atmosphere. Monday night is comedy night; at weekends the DJs take over.

SEE ALSO NIGHTLIFE, P.90

Longrain

85 Commonwealth Street, Surry Hills; tel: 9280 2888; Mon–Thur,

6–11pm, Fri–Sat 6pm–midnight; map p.136 D4

Its woven-wood decor and long banquettes are as sleek and stylish as the crowd, but the real draw here is the drinks. Longrain claims to have Sydney's best caprioskas, and we are not about to disagree; its chocolate martinis are not bad, either.

SEE ALSO RESTAURANTS P.104

Royal Hotel

247 Glenmore Road, Five Ways, Paddington; tel: 9331 2604; Sun–Thur 10am–11pm, Fri–Sat 10am–midnight; bus: 389; map p.138 B4

Ornate Victorian architecture and great food. Princess Anne's daughter, Zara Philips, hangs out here with the other rich kids when she's in town. The Royal is posh, but not snooty, and the upstairs Elephant Bar is very cosy.

Inner-West Suburbs

Bank Hotel

324 King Street, Newtown; tel: 9557 1692; bus: King Street buses; map p.18

Now armed with a 24-hour licence, this revamped favourite stays open until the party people go home,

generally around midnight early in the week, around 4am towards the weekend. The $5-million overhaul was obviously money well-spent. From the sleek black onyx bar on the ground floor, to the sumptuous interiors of the first-floor Velvet Room, it is all very smooth.

Leichhardt Hotel

95 Norton Street, Leichhardt; tel: 9569 6640; Sun–Wed 10am–midnight, Thur–Sat 10am–3pm; bus: 437, 438, 440; map p.18

This former tyre factory has become the inner west's premier pick-up joint, but it does it with style. If you find the huge piazza at the front too intimidating, there are quieter nooks and crannies to which you can retreat.

Madame Fling-Flong

Level 1, 169 King Street, Newtown; tel: 9565 2471; daily 4pm–midnight; bus: King Street buses; map p.18

There is much to love about this cosy little Newtown venue, with its sumptuous interiors, quirky soundtrack, nice range of beers and wine, and even a weekly movie night. There is only one thing not to love: at weekends, it is often booked

35

If it is past the pumpkin hour but you want one more for the road, join the diehards heading for Taylor Square off Oxford Street, where venues such as the Taxi Club and the Judgment Bar above the Courthouse Hotel carry on until well into the morning.

out for private functions, so call before dropping in.

Vanilla Room
153 Norton Street, Leichhardt; tel: 9569 9411; Mon–Thur 6pm–midnight, Fri–Sat 6pm–1am, Sun 5pm–midnight; bus: 437, 438, 440

In size, it is very New York; in attitude, it is very Sydney. While the coffee and chocolate decor is high-style, the atmosphere is decidedly relaxed. With a good range of bar food, a small cocktail list (you can have one in any flavour, as long as its vanilla), this is one of Leichhardt's hidden gems.

Eastern Suburbs

The Light Brigade
2a Oxford Street, Woollahra; tel: 9331 2930; Mon–Thur 10am–noon, Fri–Sat 10am–1am, Sun 10am–10pm; bus: 389; map p.20

Downstairs gets hot and heavy at weekends, but the Lounge Bar upstairs is a wonderfully mellow spot, with heavy armchairs to nestle into, and candles and oversized globes providing subtle and subdued lighting.

Lord Dudley
236 Jersey Road, Woollahra; tel: 9327 5399; Mon–Wed 11am–11pm, Fri–Sat 11am–midnight, Sun noon–10pm; bus: 389; map p.20

With British beers served in pints and steaming pork pies, this is a little bit of Old Blighty stranded in Woollahra. Perfect in winter, when all the

Above: the venerable Hotel Bondi has six bars.

fireplaces are blazing, and you can lie back and think of England.

Watsons Bay Hotel
1 Military Road, Watsons Bay; tel: 9337 4299; daily 10am–10pm; bus: 323, 324, 325; map p.20

Sunday afternoon at the harbourside Watsons Bay Hotel is a classic Sydney experience. The vast beer garden is thronged with people, some tucking into fish and chips, all firmly convinced there is no better place to be than right here by the harbour. They may just be right.

Eastern Beaches

Coogee Bay Hotel
Arden Street and Bay Road, Coogee; tel: 9665 0000; daily 10am–2.30am; bus: 372, 374; map p.22

This big old beer barn featured prominently in the adolescence of most Sydneysiders of a certain age, thanks to its once-legendary live music venue, Selinas (now taken over by DJs). The vast beer garden is looking reasonably sophisticated these days, while a total of six different bars means there is always something going on, from trivia nights to free wine tastings.

Hotel Bondi
178 Campbell Parade, Bondi Beach; tel: 9130 3271; Mon–Sat 10am–4pm, Sun 10am–midnight; bus: 333, 380, 389; map p.22

Scrubbed up but still smelling of saltwater, local youngsters and Brit backpackers head to the Bondi's six bars to shoot some pool, watch some sports, sink a few beers, and hopefully pick up.

Icebergs Dining Room and Bar
1 Notts Avenue, Bondi Beach; tel: 9365 9000; Tue–Sat noon–midnight, Sun noon–10pm; bus: 333, 380, 389; map p.22

Icebergs is New Bondi: glamour, money and a touch of attitude. Fortunately, it also has a stylish decor, a great cocktail list, and, of course, the million-dollar view across the beach. A must-visit.

North Bondi RSL
120 Ramsgate Avenue, Bondi Beach; tel: 9130 8770; Mon–Thur noon–11pm, Fri–Sat 10am–midnight, Sun 10am–11pm; bus: 333, 380, 389; map p.22

At the other end of the beach, here is the Old Bondi in all its glory. The view is just as glorious, but the vibe is a lot more casual: think cheap beer and spirits, rather than classy cocktails. A great place to while away an afternoon.

Shop and Wine Bar
78 Curlewis Bondi; tel: 9365 2600; Wed–Sun until 10pm; bus: 333, 380, 389; map p.22

In a city where the hippest bars tend to belong to a handful of stylemeisters, this café-cum-wine bar makes a refreshing change. It is small, it is unpretentious (the best seats in the house are on the bench out at the front) and the winelist extends to just 11 wines, but what wines!

North Shore
Commodore
206 Blue Point Road, North Sydney; tel: 9922 5098; Mon–Wed 10am–midnight, Thur–Sat 10am–1am, Sun 10am–10pm; train, bus: North Sydney; map p.24

The Commodore pulls in a typical North Shore corporate/sporty crowd with a regularly-updated roster of promotions. On footie nights, you get free beer from kick-off to first point scored; on other nights you may get the chance to win free drinks when you play the staff in rock-scissors-paper contests.

Greenwood Hotel
36 Blue Street, North Sydney; tel: 9964 9477; Mon–Wed, 11.30am–10pm, Thur 11.30am–3am, Fri noon–1.30am, Sat 2pm–1.30am, Sun 2–11pm; train, bus: North Sydney; map p.24

Thursday night is uni night at the Greenwood, so unless you are into wearing black and listening to Wolfmother, you are probably better off seeking another boozer. At other times, the three bars at The Greenwood – a gorgeous sandstone building dating back to 1878 – make this a good-value northside venue.

Living Room
Greenwood Plaza Rooftop, 36 Blue Street, North Sydney; tel: 9964 9766; Wed–Fri noon–11.30pm; train, bus: North Sydney; map p.24

If the corporate crush at the other locals is not your scene, try this hidden gem instead. To the right of the main dining room is a lovely cocktail bar complete with leather lounges and an outdoor area with a perfect view over the crowds thronging into the Greenwood.

Newport Arms Hotel
2 Kalinya Street, Newport; tel: 9997 4900; daily 10am–11.30pm; bus: L88, L90; map p.24

Up here on the peninsula, it is all about the water-lovers: young surfies, old sailors, and everyone in-between. Sooner or later, they all wind up here, soaking up the atmosphere in the sensational beer garden.

Oaks Hotel
118 Military Road, Neutral Bay; tel: 9953 5515; Mon–Thur 12.30pm–midnight, Fri 12.30pm–1.30am, Sat 10am–1.30am, Sun noon–midnight; bus: Military Road; map p.24

The perennial favourite of young North Shore types, the pub gets its name from the stunning old tree that dominates the beer garden. A favourite for weekend lunch; get in early to get a seat.

Blue Mountains
Gardner's Inn Hotel
255 Great Western Highway, Blackheath; tel: 4787 8347; Sun–Thur, 10am–10pm, Fri–Sat 10am–midnight; train: Blackheath; map p.26

A lively pub with a well-stocked bar and a roomy outdoor deck bar with table service.

Carrington Hotel
15–41 Katoomba Street, Katoomba; tel: 4782 1111; Sun–Thur 11am–9pm, Fri–Sat 11am–late; train: Katoomba; map p.26

This restored 1880s hotel has a dedicated cocktail bar, but on a cold night, you will want to take your drink into the lounge and curl up in front of the fireplace.

Lilianfels Resort and Spa
Lilianfels Avenue, Katoomba; tel: 4780 1200; daily 11am–11pm; train: Katoomba; map p.26

This luxury resort has a grand country-house feel and a wonderful terrace where you can soak up some sun while enjoying a drink or two.

Below: there are countless bars with an ocean view, but Icebergs may be the best.

Beaches

Sydney's scores of beautiful beaches are well known for the good surf, and many of them also play host to Ironman competitions, International volleyball tournaments, and, of course, thousands of tourists every year, lapping up the sun and surf or just watching the beautiful people. Not all beaches allow surfing, but boogie boarding, sailing, kayaking and snorkelling are also popular sand-side pastimes for the locals. Sydney does its best to make its beaches the safest in the world: they all have resident volunteer lifesavers, and many also have shark nets and shark-spotting helicopters.

Balmoral

Ferry: Balmoral from Circular Quay (25min); map p.24
Balmoral Beach in Mosman is one of the better family beaches on the inner harbour, and attracts many a well-heeled local. It may not have surf, but at the southern end masses of windsurfers take to the water. It is just as popular with swimmers, probably due to the fact that the northern

Below: settlements surround Balmoral Beach.

end has, like several other Sydney beaches, a shark net.

The boat-shed past the baths hires out 'trailer sailers' and windsurfers. This southern end of Balmoral was among the first beach areas on which topless bathing was the norm.

The 'island' linked to the main path by a bridge is a favourite with picnickers on summer weekends and over summer the tiny rotunda in the park is the venue for band recitals or jazz concerts, and even Shakespearian plays on occasions. There is also the divine **Bather's Pavilion Restaurant** if you want something lovely to eat. SEE ALSO RESTAURANTS, P.108

Bondi

www.waverley.nsw.gov.au lists the times lifeguards are on duty; bus: Campbell Parade from Bondi Junction, CBD; map p.22
The biggest of the city beaches, Bondi is so famous the beach even has its own TV show – *Bondi Rescue* – about the exploits of the lifeguards.

Buses stop at Campbell Parade, the main drag opposite the 1km long stretch of white sand. Stop here for restaurants, bars and anything else you could possibly need for a day at the beach.

There are people in the water here from sun-up to sundown and the beach, although big, is buzzing with tourists and locals.

Although Bondi is well patrolled, as on most Sydney beaches, it is wise to watch the waves and swim only between the flags. The first death in four years was reported at Bondi in early 2007 so it is sensible to follow the rules.
SEE ALSO EASTERN BEACHES, P.22

Bronte

Bus: 378; map p.22
Smaller than Bondi, Bronte Beach is a much loved favourite of locals, especially those with families. As well as the manicured parkland behind the beach, there is a natural rockpool and a beachside swimming pool that are both fun and safe for young children.

Picnics can be enjoyed on the lawns, there are free bar-

Left: Australia's most famous beach, at Bondi.

from the clean-up of its suburb and is finally being recognised as a beach to rival Bondi for everything but surfing. You will see only boogie boards at Coogee, but the beach itself is ideally situated close to the main drag, which has all the pubs and restaurants you will ever need. It also has a rockpool, a swimming pool and its own kiosk.

Coogee is also home to a couple of fantastic sea baths: **Wiley's Baths**, a 1900s institution sporting a modern award-winning renovation, and the **Women's Baths**, a female-only affair, popular with Muslim and lesbian communities. A visit to Coogee is not complete without a drink at the **Coogee Bay Hotel**, the local pub just across the road from the beach.

SEE ALSO EASTERN BEACHES, P.23; BARS, P.36; SPORT, P.122

There are more than 70 ocean and harbour beaches in Greater Sydney and it is easy to make the most of them: the city is only without sunshine for an average of 23 days per year.

beques complete with handy tables and chairs – popular for birthday parties and family reunions – and a decent kiosk on the promenade. There is also a line of inexpensive cafés, juice bars and restaurants up above the beach steps.

SEE ALSO EASTERN BEACHES, P.22–3

Clovelly Beach
Bus: 339; map p.22
A secret well kept by locals, Clovelly is another predominantly family beach. Thanks to the shape of the beach, which is sheltered from most of the aggressive currents or rips, parents can happily relax as their young children splash about in the shallow water. There is also a salt-water swimming pool.

As well as the obligatory kiosk – try their $5 shake, you will not regret it – there is a

larger restaurant on the beach that serves food until lunch. Just behind the beach there is also the Clovelly Pub, which serves gourmet-style food for a fraction of the cost. They also have two decks, DJs and sports screens. Not a bad place to end a day at the beach.

SEE ALSO EASTERN BEACHES, P.23

Coogee
Bus: 372, 373, 374; map p.22
Over the past decade Coogee Beach has benefited

Cronulla
Train: Martin Place, Town Hall, Sydney Central
The city's southernmost and longest surf beach with

Below: a lifesaver stands guard on the 1928 Bondi Pavilion.

Above: a refreshing day on Tamarama Beach.

10km of sand dunes stretching south from Kurnell. Unfortunately the beach is now and will always be associated with the beach riots of 2005 and many tourists and non-locals now steer clear because of the stigma. With its perfect conditions for surfing and body boarding, plus the number of pubs, bars and other nightlife, Cronulla is still popular with locals and not a beach to dismiss because of its recent history.

Manly

Ferry: Manly from Circular Quay; map p.24

'Seven miles from Sydney and a thousand miles from care', as the old sign proudly proclaimed, Manly is Sydney's main resort suburb. Permanently bustling with tourists and buskers, the Corso is lined with souvenir shops with 1930s façades and cheap snack bars. Try the local fish and chips, sold in takeaway packages to eat on the beach. Swim in the harbour, surf the ocean beaches, walk the sands of either; just browse along the shops of the Corso and have a pie on a bench in the mall; eat in one of the cafés or restaurants along the Esplanade, or down a beer in one of Manly's many pubs. There is no shortage of things to do here, and the bustle of the city seems distant indeed.
SEE ALSO NORTHERN SHORE, P.25

Freshwater Beach can claim the distinction of being the first in Australia to witness surfing. The American swimming champion Duke Kahanamoku, originally from Waikiki, toured the world giving swimming exhibitions and demonstrating the Hawaiian sport of surfboard riding. The board he used here in 1914 is kept by the Freshwater Surf Club and there is a statue of Kahanamoku *(right)* on the headland at Freshwater.

Northern beaches

Map p.24

Get out of the city for a day and explore the northern beaches: Freshwater, Curl Curl, Dee Why, Long Reef, Collaroy, Narrabeen, Warriewood, Mona Vale, Bungan, Newport, Bilgola, Avalon, Whale and Palm. You have got a few to choose from.

They are easy to navigate from the city, but you will need a car. The reason why only the rich and famous (who do not have to com-

Right: reading on the beach.

Right: reading on the beach.

mute daily) live this end of Sydney is because there is no public transport. Be warned: this leads to long traffic queues on long week-ends and sunny days.

One of the most pictur-esque beaches is **Freshwater** in the suburb of Harbord, which also has a restaurant in a wonderful location in the park overlooking the beach. Another is **Bilgola** right up on the peninsula, where a small community is snuggled into a diminutive cove far below the main Barrenjoey Road.

En route to the northern tip, the road passes the very exclusive suburb of **Palm Beach**. This is the favoured address of media types and film industry folk. Chic restaurants and cafés line the waterfront, and there are plenty of gorgeous houses to gawk at. Windsurfing and surfing are particularly popular here.

At the very tip of the peninsula stands **Barrenjoey Lighthouse**, reached via a one-hour walk from Palm Beach. The views at the end make the effort worthwhile.
Palm Beach Ferry Service Barrenjoy Road; tel: 9974 2411; www.palmbeachferry.com.au Offers tours of the glittering

waterways on the inland side of the peninsula.

Nudist Beaches

Lady Jane Beach
Bus, ferry: Watsons Bay from Bondi Junction, then a short walk north along the sands; map p.22
Below South Head, on the harbour side, is the univer-sally misnamed Lady Bay. Ask for directions to it and the response will be a blank stare. However, ask for Lady Jane Beach and most will respond with a knowing look, for this is Sydney's best-known nudist beach. Tour boats cruise past throughout the weekend. It is the perfect symbiotic balance: voyeurs watching exhibitionists. If more modest bathing is your scene, stay away, but it is quite a sideshow for those who love to people-watch.

Royal National Park's coastline
Visitor Centre: Farnell Avenue, Audley; tel: 9542 0648; 8.30am–4.30pm school holidays, week-ends and public holidays; 9.30am–4.30pm at other times; train: Engadine, Heathcote, ferry: Bundeena from Cronulla
The Royal National Park has 21km of beautiful coastline: surfing beaches interspersed by rugged sandstone head-

lands, eroded by centuries of wave activity.

Era Beach and **Garie Beach** are the most popular surfing spots and the small town of **Bundeena**, within the sheltered waters of **Port Hacking**, is a renowned windsurfing area. The well-appointed camping area of **Bonnie Vale** nearby is adja-cent to a sandy spot with good swimming. **Wattamolla**, although it is on the ocean side, has a good swimming lagoon and attracts snorkellers and divers explor-ing the inlet. Just below the southern border of the park, the foreshore road leading down to **Wollongong** has some of the best coastal views in Australia.

Tamarama
Bus: Bondi Explorer; map p.22
Located just south of Bondi, 'Tama' is another beautiful stretch of warm waters and white sand and a popular spot for Sydney's beautiful people. Although it looks safe and protected, the surf at Tamarama is notoriously dan-gerous, so this is definitely not a great choice for families with young children.

Tama has its own surf lifesaving club, and a decent café selling basic beach fare and ice creams.

SEE ALSO EASTERN BEACHES, P.23

Cafés

Sydneysiders adore their cafés. Whether that means grabbing a quick espresso on the way to work, or settling in for Sunday morning breakfast with a long latte and the weekend papers, café culture is an essential part of Sydney lifestyle. A café in Sydney is anything from an outdoor pie stall to a corner coffee stop to something not far short of a restaurant, where you can have a sandwich or a full meal. Indeed, many upmarket restaurants now include a separate café. And in a city where being a 'barrista' in a coffee shop is a well respected profession, you can always be sure of a good coffee.

Central Business District
Bambini Trust Café
185 Elizabeth Street; tel: 9283 7098; Mon–Fri 7am–10pm, Sat from 5.30pm; train: Town Hall, bus: George Street and Elizabeth Street; map p.133 D1

This upmarket spot feels like a café-bar in Paris, Rome or Florence, and attracts Sydney's food and wine sophisticates. The lighting is muted and the atmosphere is intimate: this is the kind of place to fall in love. Next door, there is the new Bambini Wine Room, which has French chandeliers, ornate wallpaper and an exquisite bar food menu.
SEE ALSO BARS, P.30

GG Espresso
175 Pitt Street; tel: 9332 1644; Mon–Fri 6.15am–5pm; train, bus: Town Hall; map p.139 D1

The coffee stop for Sydney regulars, this casual place serves great coffee of all breeds, delicious sandwiches in a hurry, and fresh juices. The café takes its name from the initials of Rugby Union star and part-owner George Gregan.

The Tearoom
Level 3, Queen Victoria Building, George Street; tel: 9269 0774; daily 11am–5pm, Sat 11am–3pm; train: Town Hall, bus: George Street; map p.133 C1

In what was once the Ballroom of the Queen Victoria Building, the Tearoom is the spot for morning or afternoon tea in Sydney. Choose from 40 different teas served in beautiful china, and savour delicate morsels from tiered silver trays. The Tearoom is decorated with plush velvet and ornately carved wood panelling under a lofty moulded ceiling. Light lunches are also served.

Opera House and The Domain
Art Gallery of New South Wales
Art Gallery Road; tel: 9225 1744; daily 10am–4.30pm (Wed until 8.30pm); train: Museum Station, 10 minutes' walk; map p.133 D2/E2

Coffee and snack outlets are in short supply in this area. Luckily, the art gallery offers a comfy upstairs restaurant and deli-café for gallery visitors and passers-by. Both get busy at weekends. The café stays open Wed evening in conjunction with the gallery's Art After Hours programme.
SEE ALSO MUSEUMS AND GALLERIES, P.85

Harry's Café de Wheels
Cowper Wharf Road, Woolloomooloo; tel: 9211 2506; daily until late; map p.133 E2

Harry's is a classic stop after a big night out on the town. It is most famous for its pies – preferably with peas and gravy – but there is more than just this traditional Aussie staple. Get your late-night chips, hot

Left: a perfect creation.

Left: the upmarket Bambini Trust Café.

Café Hernandez

60 Kings Cross Road; tel: 9331 2343; 24 hours; train, bus: Kings Cross; map p.133 E1

Coffee roaster Joaquin Hernandez immigrated from Spain to Sydney and set up this landmark Kings Cross coffee spot in 1972. He still roasts his own coffee for that perfect cup. Exotic varieties include Nicaraguan and Ethiopian.

Dean's Café

5 Kellett Street, Kings Cross; tel: 9368 0953; daily until late; train, bus: Kings Cross; map p.133 E1

A quirky place that has been going for years. Psychedelic and kitsch decor attracts an array of arty types. Good coffee, interesting crowd and tasty, affordable snacks.

Ecabar

128 Darlinghurst Road; tel: 9332 1433; daily breakfast until late; bus: Oxford Street; map p.137 E4

Some say this is the best coffee in Sydney. Ecabar also does great breakfasts: the bircher muesli is to die for.

Le Petit Crème

118 Darlinghurst Road; tel: 9361 4738; Mon–Sat 7am–3pm, Sun 8am–3pm; bus: Oxford Street; map p.133 E1

This is an unpretentious French café, renowned for its

> Australians have some peculiar ways of describing their coffees. A 'short black' is an espresso, while a 'long black' is a coffee without milk. A 'flat white' is coffee with milk, not to be confused with a cappuccino, or a café latte, which here is simply known as a latte.

dogs and hamburgers here. At least one post-pub visit to this Sydney institution is obligatory.

SEE ALSO FOOD AND DRINK, P.62

MOS Café

Museum of Sydney, Corner of Bridge and Philip streets; tel: 9241 3636; Mon–Fri 6.30am–9pm, Sat–Sun 8.30am–5pm; train, bus, ferry: Circular Quay; map p.139 E2

Serving meals or just a coffee and cake, this popular spot is only moments from Circular Quay, and pulls a buzzy city crowd, which spills out onto the sandstone forecourt at lunchtime. Sassy Modern Australian food, with desserts to die for: the amaretto and coffee semifreddo is a must.

SEE ALSO MUSEUMS AND GALLERIES, P.82–3

Kings Cross

Bar Coluzzi

322 Victoria Street, Darlinghurst; tel: 9380 5420; daily breakfast until late; train, bus: Kings Cross; map p.133 E1

A local landmark. The outdoor seating on the wide Victoria Street footpath makes this tiny coffee shop a lot larger.

Bill and Toni's

74 Stanley Street, East Sydney; tel: 9360 4702; daily 7am–midnight; train: Museum Station; map p.133 D1

Ever-popular coffee house in Little Italy. Economical coffee and snacks like *focaccia*. There is also a cheap no-frills spaghetti place upstairs.

Below: the Tearoom at the Queen Victoria Building.

Sydney owes its café culture to post-war immigration from Southern and Eastern Europe from the 1950s. Before that, a café was a tearoom, and Anglo-Saxon tea-and-sandwiches was about as far as it went.

excellent omelettes, filled baguettes, home made pâté and steak and frites. Popular with locals and those in the know, Le Petit Crème is the perfect place to sit and enjoy the Sunday newspapers with a bowl-sized café au lait.

Piccolo Bar
6 Roslyn Street, Kings Cross; tel: 9368 1356; early morning to late; train, bus: Kings Cross; map p.133 E1
A tiny place in the thick of Kings Cross street activity, and something of an institution. Neapolitan owner Vittorio Bianchi has been brewing coffee for the local Bohemians for 40 years.

Tropicana Caffe
227 Victoria Street; tel: 9360 9809; Sun–Thur 5am–11pm, Fri–Sat 5am–midnight; train, bus: Kings Cross; map p.133 E1
This is the home of Sydney's independent film festival, Tropfest, which had its roots here, and this café is still the hangout of the film-making crowd. Good value food, served fast, in a lively atmosphere. There are music videos on wide screens and pictures of the clientele on the walls.

Inner-West Surburbs

Alexander's
238 Church Street, Parramatta; tel: 9687 1230; daily 9am–11pm; train: Parramatta or Harris Park; map p.18
A busy coffee house on Parramatta's main street that also serves up pizza and seafood selections.

Badde Manors
37 Glebe Point Road, Glebe; tel: 9660 3797; daily 7.30am–midnight; bus: Glebe Point Road; map p.136 A4
A grungy and eclectic Glebe coffee house with funky decor and friendly service. Try the *sahlep* – aromatic Turkish milk – with a wholesome veggieburger, while you take a break from browsing at the Glebe markets opposite.

Bar Italia
169–171 Norton Street, Leichhardt; tel: 9560 9981; Sun–Thur 9am–11pm, Fri–Sat 9am–midnight; bus: 437, 438, 400, 470; map p.18
A long-established Italian coffee shop, noted for its delicious *gelati*. Open long hours and also serves basic Italian fare like pasta.

Danks Street Depot
1–2 Danks Street, Waterloo; tel: 9698 2201; Mon–Wed 7.30am–4pm, Thur–Fri 7.30am–11pm, Sat 8am–11pm, Sun 9am–4pm; bus: 301, 302, 303, 343; map p.18
This converted warehouse in a quiet backstreet is a serene place for a quiet coffee in the morning, and is all abuzz come lunchtime. Try the Fremantle sardines on sourdough for breakfast, or the pea and lettuce risotto for dinner (Thur–Sat only).

With soaring ceilings and natural light, this café is as beautifully designed as its excellent food.

Inside Out Café
99 Phillip Street, Parramatta; tel: 9687 9045; Mon–Fri noon–3pm and 5.30–9.45pm, Sat 5.30pm–late; train: Parramatta; map p.18
A coffee shop-cum-restaurant with a wide menu, ranging from modern Australian to seafood and Italian.

Mado Café
63 Auburn Road, Auburn; tel: 9643 5299; daily 8am–11pm; map p.18
A Turkish coffee house with pavement eating in the heart of Sydney's Turkish community. Also serves up interesting Turkish ice cream and *baklava*.

Eastern Suburbs

Café Zigolini
107 Queen Street, Woollahra; tel: 9326 2337; Tue–Sat 6.30am–11pm, Sun–Mon 6.30am–6pm; bus: Oxford Street; map p.138 B3
Down-to-earth food and friendly service in this pretty Woollahra setting. The BBQ octopus is recommended, and the atmosphere is pleasingly tranquil.

Jones the Grocer
68 Moncur Street, Woollahra; tel: 9362 1222; Mon–Sat 7.30am–5.30pm, Sun 9am–

Right: Danks Street Depot.

Above: French style in Darlinghurst, Le Petit Crème.

5pm; bus: Oxford Street buses; map p.138 C3
Stylish café meals as well as grocery treats and upmarket kitchenware: Jones is definitely top-notch cool. There is a walk-in cheeseroom, and communal long table where locals meet to chat over lunch. There is a tempting range of sweets and pastries too.

Eastern Beaches
The Bogey Hole
473 Bronte Road, Bronte; tel: 9389 8829; daily 7am–4pm; bus: 378; map p.22
Named after a rugged natural pool on the southern end of Bronte Beach, this is a local favourite for killer breakfasts or quick lunchtime snacks.
Catch Seafood Café
Corner of Alfred and Ramsgate roads, Ramsgate Beach; tel: 9529 2589; bus: 303; map p.22
A licensed, modern Australian and seafood café with affordable snacks and an economical set menu. You get a free bottle of wine for bookings of four or more.
Cozzi Café
233 Coogee Bay Road, Coogee; tel: 9665 6111; daily 7am–6pm; bus: 372, 373, 374; map p.22
A bright and breezy beachside coffee shop. Attentive

staff and a convenient central Coogee location.
Grind Espresso Bar
Rydges Hotel, Kings Way, Cronulla; tel: 9527 3100; Mon–Fri 7am–7pm, Sat–Sun 8am–6pm; train: Martin Place to Cronulla; map p.22
A popular coffee shop in an otherwise café-deprived area. Serves breakfast and a selection of budget-priced meals. Outdoor tables.

North Shore
Electric Bean
Shop 6, 90 Mount Street, North Sydney; tel: 9956 7703; Mon–Fri 7.30am–6pm, Sat 8.30am–3pm; train: North Sydney, bus: 202, 290; map p.24
This café stands out in busy North Sydney for wonderfully friendly service, and coffee that is just as good. They serve good value Mediterranean-influenced food, and also have a great selection of handmade chocolates: try the chilli or the strawberry ganache.
Ground Zero
18 Sydney Road, Manly; tel: 9977 6996; Mon–Fri 7.30am–9pm, Sat–Sun 7.30am–4pm; ferry: Manly; map p.24
Hang out on one of the comfy couches by the fire-

place on a Sydney winter's day, or the sunny courtyard in summer. The excellent coffee is the drawcard, as are the breakfasts.

Blue Mountains
Café Bon Ton
192 The Mall, Leura; tel: 4782 4377; daily 8.30am–9.30pm; train: Leura (from Central Station); map p.26
A relaxed café in the heart of the Mall, with courtyard tables, an attached coffee shop and economical prices. It is a good place for weekend breakfasts.
Isobar
40 Katoomba Street, Katoomba; tel: 4782 4063; daily 7am– 10pm; train: Katoomba (from Central Station); map p.26
Cool, modern place that is great for coffees and snacks, or a simple meal at any time of the day.
Paragon Café
65 Katoomba Street, Katoomba; tel: 4782 2928; Tue–Sat 4–10pm, Sat and Sun noon–2pm; train: Katoomba (from Central Station); map p.26
Famous café with 1930s art deco interior, serving home-cooked foods, great coffee and delicious chocolates.

Below: the 1930s art deco of the Paragon in Katoomba.

Children

With Sydney's outdoor lifestyle, there is always something to keep kids occupied. Areas such as The Rocks, Circular Quay and Darling Harbour offer plenty of free entertainment, some museums go out of their way to attract young visitors and, of course, there is the water. Beaches like Bronte and the calmer Nielsen Park are perfect for picnics, with plenty of parkland and barbecues, while many surf beaches host learn-to-surf classes for children. Kayaking is available at Rose Bay, Manly and The Spit, and Centennial Park is the place to hire bicycles, roller-blades or even a horse.

Museums

Australian Museum

6 College Street; tel: 9320 6000; daily 9.30am–5pm, entrance charge; train: Museum; map p.133 D1

Highlights include the hands-on 'Search and Discover' section, the skeleton gallery and the dinosaurs. Younger children are catered for with toys, animal models and props at Kids' Island.

SEE ALSO MUSEUMS AND GALLERIES, P.84

Powerhouse Museum

500 Harris Street, Ultimo; tel: 9217 0111; daily 10am–5pm,

Below: snapping up memories at Bondi.

entrance charge; train: Central Station, monorail: Darling Harbour; map p.137 C4

The Kids Interactive Discovery Spaces feature a range of games and hands-on activities exploring subjects such as music, machines, life in the home, film and television. There are also more than 100 interactive demonstrations on topics as diverse as the chemistry of smell and computer animation.

SEE ALSO MUSEUMS AND GALLERIES, P.85

Events

Opera House

Bennelong Point; tel: 9225 1700; bus, train, ferry: Circular Quay; map p.139 E4

The Opera House runs regular children's events such as the Babies Proms, which lets toddlers get close to the musical instruments.

Art Gallery of New South Wales

Art Gallery Road, The Domain; tel: 9225 1700; daily 10am–5pm (Wed until 9pm); train: Museum; map p.133 D2/E2

Holds special family events on Sundays, such as renditions of

Aboriginal Dreamtime stories.

SEE ALSO MUSEUMS AND GALLERIES, P.85

Playgrounds and Funfairs

EQ

Lang Road, Moore Park; tel: 9383 4333; bus: Anzac Parade; map p.138 A1

This entertainment precinct has two state-of-the-art playgrounds, one for under-fours, the other for 4–12-year-olds: ball pits, giant mazes, tunnels, cargo nets, climbing, jumping, sliding and exploring. It is a multistorey funhouse for kids of all ages. There are tables and shaded seating for parents, along with a huge grassed area where the kids can run and play.

Tumbalong Park

Darling Harbour; train: Town Hall, monorail: Darling Harbour; map p.132 B1/C1

This venue close to the centre of town has a playground and a stage for free concerts. It is also a regular venue for colourful festivals of all kinds.

Luna Park

1 Olympic Drive, Milsons Point; tel: 9922 6644; Mon and Thur 11am–6pm, Fri 11am–11pm,

koalas. The park also contains emus, kangaroos, wallabies, wombats and native Australian birds.

Sydney Aquarium

Darling Harbour; tel: 9262 2300; daily 9am–10pm; entrance charge; train: Town Hall, monorail: Darling Harbour; map p.139 C1

This modern aquarium has a good selection of creatures from Australian waters, including man-eating salt-water crocodiles and toothy sharks. The transparent tunnels that go through the tanks allow you to get eerily close to the sharks and stingrays.

Taronga Zoo

Bradleys Head Road, Mosman; tel: 9969 2777; daily 9am–5pm; entrance charge; ferry: Mosman (from Circular Quay), bus: 247; map p.24

This zoo with superb harbour views has animals from every continent, with favourites including Asian elephants and the Sumatran tiger. Of course there are plenty of kangaroos, wombats and echidnas, as well as the country's seven most poisonous snakes. This is the only place in Sydney where you will get to see a duck-billed platypus.

Supplies and Illness

Basic children's supplies, from nappies to formula, are widely available at supermarkets and chemists. In case of illness, call the KidsNet service (tel: 9845 2431) to obtain advice from a qualified medical practitioner. For serious cases, the Children's Hospital in Randwick (Randwick High Street, tel: 9382 1111) has an emergency room.

Sat 10am–11pm, Sun 10am–6pm; ferry: Luna Park (from Circular Quay), train: Milsons Point; map p.24

Generations of Sydneysiders have fond memories of this harbourside funfair with its famous laughing face. Buy an unlimited pass to enjoy your fill of the dodgem cars, Coney Island and the Ferris Wheel (amazing close-ups of the Harbour Bridge).

Manly Waterworks

West Esplanade, Manly; tel: 9949 1088; Sept–Apr: weekends and school holidays 10am–5pm, also Dec–Feb Sat 6–9pm, entrance charge; ferry: Manly; map p.24

Giant water-slides for kids (taller than 120cm) and a large spectator viewing area for their parents.

Sydney's picturesque harbour islands are the setting for exciting school-holiday adventure tours, with outings including Bare Island's Military Madness, Fort Denison's Convicts, Cannons and Critters, and Treasure Hunts on Goat Island. For details tel: 9247 5033.

Wildlife

Featherdale Wildlife Park

Kildare Road, Doonside; tel: 9622 1644; daily 9am–5pm; entrance charge; train: Blacktown, then bus 725

The largest private collection of Australian animals, including 230 species of birds. See crocodiles, Tasmanian devils and dingoes, or get close to a koala.

Manly Oceanworld

West Esplanade, Manly; tel: 8251 7877; daily 10–5.30pm, entrance charge; ferry: Manly; map p.24

A moving walkway takes you through a transparent underwater tunnel with sharks, stingrays and other fish swimming around you. For the brave, there is also a chance to dive with sharks. The beach and Waterworks (*see above*) are right next-door.

Koala Park Sanctuary

Castle Hill Road, West Pennant Hills; tel: 9484 3141; daily 9am–5pm; entrance charge; train: Pennant Hills

The highlight of this koala research centre and sanctuary is the opportunity to pet

Environment

Like the Americans, the Australian government refused to sign the Kyoto Protocol and tough measures to cut emissions have yet to be adopted. Instead, 'creative' measures – from free energy-efficient lightbulbs to solar-powered parking meters – have been employed to cut the city's dependancy on energy. Sydneysiders themselves have a history of campaigning for a cleaner world, from the builders who influenced today's landscape by refusing to destroy historic neighbourhoods in the 1970s to the recent campaign that saw Sydney turn out its lights for one night in 2007.

The Natural Environment

Sydney is one of the greenest cities of its size in the world – literally as well as metaphorically – with about 23sq. m of parks and open space for every resident.

In the city itself, there are 248 parks and open spaces, comprising around 374 hectares (equal to 14 per cent of the land area). There are about 34,000 trees (around half of them native species) in streets and parks that are managed by the city, and many more in the Royal Botanic Gardens, the

Below: the rainbow lorikeet is common in the national parks.

Domain, Moore Park, Sydney Harbour Foreshore Authority and other Government land.

The region also has more than its fair share of national parks. Sydney Harbour, Garigal and Lane Cove national parks are in the city itself; Kurring-gai Chase National Park is just to the north; and Botany Bay and Royal national parks are just to the south.

As a result of all this green space, the Sydney area contains an astonishing variety of wildlife: around 285 bird species, 90 or so mammals, 70 reptiles and 35 amphibia.

Australia has a deserved reputation for dangerous creatures, including spiders, scorpions, jellyfish and at least 30 venomous snakes. But you are unlikely to encounter any of them in Sydney, with the possible exception of the Sydney funnel-web spider, which often sets up home in rockeries and shrubberies in suburban gardens. The funnel-web's venom can be lethal, and if you are bitten you should go straight to hospital.

SEE ALSO PARKS AND GARDENS, P.94–7

Greenhouse Action

Although Australia refused to ratify the Kyoto Protocol on global warming, Sydney is doing its bit to reduce carbon emissions in the city. The Greenhouse Action Plan seeks to achieve energy savings in buildings and transport, to encourage the use of renewable energy, and to reduce air pollution.

The target of the ambitious $1million programme is an 11 per cent reduction in Sydney's total energy consumption and a 15 per cent reduction in greenhouse emissions. The city's long-term aim is to become carbon-neutral through

An unusual-looking passenger ferry in Sydney Harbour is *Solar Sailor*, a revolutionary low-energy boat developed with support from the Australian government. It is powered partly by a combination of sunlight and wind, with solar panels that double as sails, and uses half as much diesel as a conventional ferry.

Left: Sydney has more green space than most cities this size.

The first green ban, in 1971, was not to save historic buildings but to preserve Kelly's Bush, the last remaining piece of native bushland on the foreshore of the Parramatta River. The action was spearheaded by a group of 13 local women, known as the 'Battlers for Kelly's Bush'. When their protests were ignored by the local council, the mayor of Sydney and the nsw government, they appealed to the Builders Labourers' Federation, who threatened to down tools on all the developer's sites in the city. Kelly's Bush was saved, and set the pattern for future cooperation between the union and residents' action groups.

energy efficiency and greenhouse gas offsets.

Initiatives already under way include using more 'green power' for City of Sydney buildings and street lighting; introducing biofuel vehicles to the Corporation's fleet; a 'Cycling in the City' programme, encouraging people to ride to work; providing energy-efficient light bulbs free for all citizens; and a host of other measures, ranging from treeplanting schemes to solarpowered parking meters.

The 'Green Games'

The 2000 Olympic Games were an opportunity for the city to display its green credentials. The sports venues at Olympic Park were designed for low energy use, to reduce greenhouse gas emissions. Stadium Australia has some unique environmental features, including a system to collect rainwater from its arched roofs, which is used to irrigate the pitch. Recycled water is also used to flush toilets at venues throughout Olympic Park.

Spectators used public transport and dined on food and beverages sold in new recycled packaging developed especially for Sydney 2000. Tables, bookcases, desks and bins in numerous Games venues were made from 100 per cent recycled materials, and were recycled again after the Games. The Athletes Village, now converted for residential use, is part of one of the world's largest solarpowered suburbs.

Environmental Campaigns

Much of the historic Sydney that visitors enjoy today would have been replaced by concrete-and-steel office developments three decades ago if it had not been for opposition from the unlikely source of a building workers' trade union.

Jack Mundey was a union leader who spearheaded the 'green bans', under which members of the NSW branch of the Builders Labourers Federation (BLF) would refuse to work on sites that threatened historic or environ-

mentally sensitive areas of the city. In the early 1970s they placed bans on 42 developments worth $3 billion, and in the process stopped developers razing the historic Rocks and much of Victoria Street in Kings Cross, as well halting developments in the inner suburbs of Glebe, Pyrmont and Woolloomooloo.

The green bans led to the New South Wales government bringing in tighter demolition laws. Between 1971 and 1975 there is no doubt that they saved The Rocks from being developed as 'a Manhattan on the Pacific', prevented Centennial Park being turned into a concrete sports stadium, and stopped the Royal Botanic Gardens becoming a car park for the Opera House. The National Trust considers that more than 100 buildings worthy of preservation were saved by the BLF's green bans.

Essentials

This chapter contains listings of the practical information that you may need when planning your visit to Sydney, or during your stay. The right knowledge should permit you to sail through on arrival and get on with the business of enjoying your stay. There is advice on staying safe and healthy, on taking care of money matters, and how to keep in touch by phone and mail. For more information on visiting Sydney, these are some of the most comprehensive and reliable websites: www.australia.com; www.atn.com.au; www.sydneyaustralia.com; www.sydney.com.au; www.visitnsw.com.au

Admission Charges

Several of Sydney's cultural sites are administered by the **Historic Houses Trust** (tel: 9692 8366), who also look after the Museum of Sydney. Admission to such buildings as Vaucluse House, Elizabeth Bay House and the Justice and Police Museum costs the same: $8 for adults, $3 children/concessions and $17 for a family ticket. (The Museum of Sydney and Hyde Park Barracks cost $10 adult, $5 child, $20 family.) A few of the Trust's properties, including The Mint and Government House, are free to enter.

General admission to the National Maritime Museum, the Art Gallery of New South Wales and the Museum of Contemporary Art is also free, but they all charge for temporary exhibitions. Entry to the Australian Museum costs $10 for adults, $5 for children, $25 for a family.

Business Hours

Banks generally open 9.30am–4pm Monday to Thursday, and 9.30am–5pm on Friday. Currency exchange facilities at the airport are open all hours.

Most shops are open 9am–6pm Monday to Friday and until 5pm Saturday. Many of the large city and suburban centres now open all day Sunday as well, although often with slightly shorter hours (generally 10am–4pm).

Thursday night is late-night shopping, when some shops stay open until 8 or 9pm. However, visitors will find plenty of late-night shops operating all week including chemists, gift stores and bookshops, particularly around the major tourist centres. There are many 24-hour outlets for grocery items, including major supermarkets.

Climate

Sydney is usually mild and sunny with beautifully warm (though often quite humid) summer days, cooled in the evenings by southerly breezes. The average maximum temperature for January and February, Sydney's

Left: admission is free to the Art Gallery of New South Wales.

Left: the well-stocked Sydney Visitors' Centre in The Rocks.

on public transport is safe at any time in the inner-city area. Avoid longer, quieter trips after 10pm.

Customs

Australia has extremely strict regulations about what can and cannot be brought into the country. Before disembarking from the plane, visitors are asked to fill in an Incoming Passenger Card. Customs officers check the information on the cards when passengers disembark, and may initiate a baggage search. It is always best to declare an item if in doubt.

Strict quarantine laws apply in Australia to protect the agricultural industries and native Australian flora and fauna from introduced diseases. Animals, plants and their derivatives (feathers, untreated wood, fur, etc.) must be declared on arrival. The import or export of protected species, or products made from protected species, is a criminal offence.

All food products, no matter how well packaged, must be declared on arrival.

Customs Information Centre

Tel: 1 300 363 263 (in Australia), tel: 61 2 6275 6666 (outside Australia); www.customs.gov.au

DUTY-FREE ALLOWANCES
Anyone over the age of 18 is allowed to bring into Australia A$400-worth of goods, not

hottest months, is 26°C and the minimum is 19°C. The average maximum for July, Sydney's coldest month, is 16°C and the minimum, 8°C.

The wettest months are March and June. During the peak season in summer, travellers can expect rain on about 12 days a month, although this is likely to be little more than a brief shower.

Crime and Safety

Common-sense rules apply when visiting Sydney. Because of its high tourist

Below: expect rain – or at least showers – in March and June.

profile, crimes against tourists have become something of an issue. Most often, these offences are in the order of petty thefts in popular visitor locations. Keep wallets out of sight, do not leave valuables visible in the car or luggage unattended.

Kings Cross has a fairly unsavoury reputation, but unless you get involved in something you should not, the crime there is not likely to affect you directly. In fact, Kings Cross, with its constant urban buzz, is probably a lot safer than the average suburban street come midnight. It is best to avoid Hyde Park after dark, particularly if you are on your own.

Many city and suburban railway stations are either unstaffed or run with a skeleton staff during off-peak periods. Some stations have 'night safe' areas on the platforms, with security cameras and an intercom for contacting staff, and trains have a blue light on one of the front carriages, indicating that there is a guard travelling in the carriage. Generally, travel

---

Emergency Numbers
Police, Fire, Ambulance:
Tel: 000
Doctor Services (for hotels)
Tel: 9962 6000
Dental Services
Tel: 9692 0333

including alcohol or tobacco; 1,125ml (about 2 pints) of alcohol (wine, beer or spirits); 250 cigarettes, or 250g of cigars or tobacco products other than cigarettes.

Disabled Travellers

Sydney caters reasonably well for people with disabilities, but you would be wise to start making enquiries and arrangements before leaving home. A good place to begin is with the **National Information Communication Awareness Network** (NICAN), a national organisation that keeps a database of facilities and services with disabled access, including accommodation and tourist sights. They also keep track of the range of publications on the subject.

The **Australian Quadraplegic Association** (AQA) publishes *Accessing Sydney*, which lists a wide variety of places with disabled access, as well as various services. You can also phone for information.

The **State Library of NSW** offers a good telephone service, where operators deal promptly with queries on topics such as equipment hire and access to medical and other services.

AQA
1 Jennifer Street, Little Bay, NSW 2036; tel: 9661 8855
NICAN
PO Box 407 Curtain, ACT 2605; tel: 1 800 806 769
State Library of NSW Disability Service
Tel: 9273 1583

Embassies and Consulates

IN SYDNEY
British Consulate General
Level 16, 1 Macquarie Place; tel: 9247 7521; map p.139 D2

Above: for most visitors, excessive exposure to the sun is the biggest health risk.

Canadian Consulate General
Level 5, 111 Harrington Street; tel: 9364 3000; recorded information: 9364 3050; map p.139 D3
Consulate General of Ireland
Level 30, 400 George Street; tel: 9231 6999; map p.139 D1
US Consulate General
MLC Centre, 19–29 Martin Place; tel: 9373 9200; after-hours emergencies tel: 4422 2201; map p.139 D1

OVERSEAS MISSIONS
Canada
Australian High Commision, Suite 710, 50 O'Connor Street, Ottawa, Ontario K1P 6L2; tel: (613) 236 0841 (plus consulates in Toronto and Vancouver)
Ireland
Australian Embassy, Fitzwilton House, Wilton Terrace, Dublin 2; tel: (01) 664 5300
United Kingdom
Australian High Commision, Australia House, The Strand, London WC2B 4LA; tel: (020) 7379 4334; www.australia.org.uk, (plus consulates in Manchester and Edinburgh)
United States
Australian Embassy, 1601 Massachusetts Avenue, Washington DC NW 20036-2273; tel: (202) 797 3000; (plus consulates in New York, Los Angeles, San Francisco, Miami, Detroit).

Health

Australia has excellent medical services. For medical attention out of working hours go to the casualty department in one of the large hospitals or, if the matter is less urgent, visit a 24-hour medical centre, listed in the Yellow Pages, or ask at your hotel.

New Zealand, Finland, Italy, Malta, the Netherlands, Norway, Sweden, the UK and Ireland have reciprocal health-care agreements with Australia, so visitors are entitles to free hospital treatment and GP treatment benefits. It is recommended, however, that visitors from all countries take out a travel insurance policy that covers health.

No vaccinations are required for entry to Australia, unless you have been in an epidemic zone or a yellow fever, cholera or typhoid-infested area in the six days prior to your arrival.

LOCAL HEALTH HAZARDS
The biggest danger for travellers in Australia is the sun. Care should also be taken while swimming in Sydney. Rip tides resulting in dangerous conditions are fairly common, so the best advice is to swim only at beaches that are patrolled, and between

Chemist shops are a great place to go for advice on minor ailments such as bites, scratches and stomach trouble. If you have a prescription from your doctor, and you want to take it to a pharmacist in Australia, you will need to have it endorsed by a local medical practitioner.

Electricity

The Australian power supply is 220–240 volts AC. Sockets are three flat pin plugs and electrical items from the US and Europe, including the UK, will require an adaptor plug.

the yellow and red flags. Never swim at night after drinking.

The shark bells along the beaches do ring occasionally, but it is usually a false alarm. Some of the harbour beaches have shark nets, so if you are nervous, swim there.

SNAKES AND SPIDERS

Sydney is home to two dangerous spiders, the funnel-web and the redback. Because you will not necessarily be able to identify these creatures, seek medical help for any spider bite. Dangerous snakes are also part of the Sydney landscape, but most will not attack unless directly provoked. Again, seek medical advice for any bite.

Holidays

Banks, post offices, offices and most shops close on the following public holidays:

1 Jan	New Year's Day
26 Jan	Australia Day
Mar/Apr	Good Friday
	Holy Saturday
	Easter Monday
25 Apr	Anzac Day
Jun (2nd Mon)	Queen's Birthday
Aug (1st Mon)	Bank Holiday
Oct (1st Mon)	Labour Day
25 Dec	Christmas Day
26 Dec	Boxing Day

There are four school holidays a year: mid-December to the end of January, two weeks

over Easter, two weeks in July and two weeks at the end of September. It can be difficult to get discounted air fares and accommodation during these peak periods.

Money

BANKS

The four big banks in Australia are the National, the Commonwealth, Westpac and ANZ. Trading hours are generally 9.30am–4pm Monday to Thursday and 9.30am–5pm Friday. A few of the smaller banks and credit unions open on Saturday mornings. Most banks will have a board on display advertising exchange rates; if not, ask a clerk.

CURRENCY

The local currency is the Australian dollar (abbreviated as A$ or simply $), made up of 100 cents. Coins come in 5, 10, 20 and 50 cent units and 1 and 2 dollar units. Notes come in 5, 10, 20, 50 and 100 dollar units. Single cents still apply to many prices, and in these cases the amount will be rounded up or down to the nearest 5 cent.

There is no limit to the amount of foreign or Australian currency that you can bring into or out of the country, but cash amounts of more than A$10,000 (or its

equivalent) must be declared to customs on arrival and departure.

CREDIT CARDS AND ATMS

There are literally hundreds of Automatic Teller Machines (ATMs) around the city, allowing for easy withdrawal of cash. Many small businesses still accept cash only.

EXCHANGE

Most foreign currencies can be cashed at the airport's exchange outlets. Sydney has many bureaux de change, but you will usually get a better rate at one of the big banks.

TRAVELLERS' CHEQUES

All well-known travellers' cheques can be cashed at airports, banks, hotels and similar establishments, and are as good as cash at many of the larger retail outlets and shops in major tourist areas.

Banks offer the best exchange rates on cheques in foreign currencies; most banks charge a fee for cashing cheques. Travellers' cheques can also be purchased at the larger banks.

LOST CARDS AND CHEQUES

If you lose your travellers' cheques or need replacements, contact the following:

Right: ATMs are located throughout the city and near the beaches.

Above: the General Post Office in Martin Place.

American Express
tel: 1 800 688 022
**Thomas Cook/
MasterCard Travellers'
Cheques**
tel: 1 800 127 495
If you lose your credit card:
American Express
tel: 1 300 366 105
Diners Club
tel: 1 300 360 060
MasterCard
tel: 1 800 12 0113 (world service puts you in contact with local authority)
Visa
tel: 1 800 621 199

Post

Post offices are open 9am–5pm Monday to Friday, with some branches opening Saturday morning. The General Post Office (GPO) is located in Martin Place in the City and is open 8.15am–5.30pm weekdays and 8.30am–noon on Saturday .

OVERSEAS POST
Standard overseas mail takes about a week to most destinations. There are two types of express international mail. Express Mailing Service (EMS) will reach the UK in three or four days. The minimum cost for a package is $35. Express Post International (EPI) will arrive in the UK within four to five working days and is priced according to weight and size.
EMS AND EPI
Tel: 13 13 18

Telephones

Calling from hotel phones is very expensive. Using public phones is easy and cheap with a phonecard. These are widely available from newsagents and other outlets displaying the Telstra logo.
Numbers beginning with 1 800 are toll-free. Numbers beginning with 13 are charged at a local rate, Numbers beginning with 018, 041, 015, 019 are mobile phones.
Directory enquiries: 1223
Overseas assistance: 1225
International calls: 0011 followed by the national code of the country you are calling.

MOBILE PHONES
Most of the large urban areas and major rural centres are covered by a telecoms 'net'. Smaller towns and remote regions are not covered, which means that mobiles have virtually no use as a safety communications device when travelling in the Outback.
Many visitors will find that they can use their own

Below: public telephones are cheap and easy to use.

phones from home. Contact your provider before leaving home to find out what is involved.

FAXES
There are many places from which you can fax documents, including hotels, video stores, newsagents, a variety of small businesses, and also post offices, where the rates are very reasonable.

Time Zone

Sydney is on Eastern Standard Time (along with the rest of New South Wales, Queensland, Victoria and Tasmania). This is GMT +10.
During the summer, New South Wales observes Daylight Saving Time, moving the clock forward by one hour between the last Sunday in October and the last Sunday in February.

Tipping

Tipping is not obligatory but a small gratuity for good service is appreciated. It is not customary to tip taxi-drivers, hairdressers or porters at airports. Porters have set charges at railway terminals, but not at hotels. Restaurants do not automatically include service charges, but it is customary to tip waiters up to 10 per cent of the bill for good service.

Toilets

Australians manage without euphemisms for 'toilet'. 'Dunny' or 'Thunder Box' is the Outback slang, but 'washroom', 'restroom', 'Ladies' and 'Gents' are all understood. In Sydney, public toilets are often locked after certain hours, but you can generally use the facilities in any pub or cinema without making a purchase.

Above: tipping is not obligatory, but always appreciated.

Toilets are generally clean, even in the Outback. Sydney's most ornate toilets are located on the ground floor of the State Theatre on Market Street.

Tourist Information

Australian Tourist Commission
Level 4, 80 William Street, East Sydney; tel: 9360 1111; www.australia.com; 9am–5.30pm; map p.133 D1
There are also ATC offices in Britain and the USA.
United Kingdom
Gemini House, 10–18 Putney Hill, London SW15 6AA; tel: (020) 8780 2229
USA
2049 Century Park East, Suite 1920, Los Angeles CA 90067; tel: (310) 229 4870

TOURIST CENTRES
In the excellent tourist centres/kiosks dotted around the city, you will find maps, accommodation guides, brochures and well-informed staff to help with any queries, including information about combined tickets to many of the attractions.
Sydney Visitors' Centre
106 George Street, The Rocks; tel: 9255 1788; map p.139 D3
Blue Mountains
Echo Point, Katoomba and Great Western Highway, Glenbrook; tel: 4739 6266, or 1 800 641 227; map p.26
Bondi
Bondi Beachside Inn, corner of Campbell Parade and Roscoe Street, Bondi Beach; tel: 9130 5311; closed Sat–Sun; map p.22
Darling Harbour
Palm Grove, between Cockle Bay and Tumbalong Park, Darling Harbour; tel: 9240 8788; map p.132 C1
Manly
Manly Wharf, Manly; tel: 8966 8111; map p.24

Visa Information

Visitors to Australia must have a passport valid for the entire period of their stay. Anyone who is not an Australian citizen also needs a visa, which must be obtained before leaving home, except for New Zealand citizens, who are issued with a visa on arrival in Australia.

ETA VISAS
The Electronic Transfer Authority (ETA) enables visitors to obtain a visa on the spot from their travel agent or airline office. The system is in place in over 30 countries including the UK and the USA. ETA visas are generally valid over a 12-month period, during which you can make return trips, but no stay can exceed three months. ETAs are issued free, or you can buy one online for A$20 from: www.eta.immi.gov.au.

TOURIST VISAS
These are available for continuous stays longer than three months, but must be obtained from an Australian visa office, such as an Embassy or Consulate. A $20 fee applies. Those travelling on tourist visas and ETAs are not permitted to work while in Australia. Travellers are asked on their applications to prove they have funding for their time in Australia (around $1,000 a month).

TEMPORARY RESIDENCE
Those seeking temporary residence must apply to an Australian visa office, and in many cases must be sponsored by an appropriate organisation or employer. Study visas are available for people who want to undertake full-time courses. Working holiday visas are available to young people from a list of 19 countries, including the UK and Canada.
Department of Immigration and Multicultural Affairs
tel: 13 18 81; www.immi.gov.au

Below: visit The Rocks for tourist information.

55

Fashion

A few decades ago it would have been almost unthinkable that Aussie fashions would strut down the catwalks of Paris and London during the elite Fashion Weeks. But some major breakthroughs in fashion have occurred in the last decade, and most of the brains behind the collections started here in Sydney. The city is great for cheap, chainstore steals, as is Bondi Junction's Westfield Mall. For your designer flagship stores look on the top end of Oxford Street, and on William Street, fast becoming the favourite spot for new shops. And for something different head to any of the outer suburbs or city markets.

Cheap Chic

Sydney is starting to get to grips with the idea of mixing and matching inexpensive, disposable fashion with high-end designer togs. It is not unusual to see a fashionista clutching her *Vogue* magazine and sporting a pair of Prada heels, while also wearing a $60 dress. Cheap chic is the name of the game in Sydney this decade.

For High End...

Lisa Ho
2a–6a Queen Street, Woollahra; tel: 9360 2345; Mon–Fri 10am–6pm (Thur until 7pm),

Sat 9.30am–6pm; bus: Oxford Street; map p.138 B3
Like many other Aussie success stories in fashion, Lisa Ho started out by selling her pieces at the local markets. Today she is sold worldwide and appeals to the moneyed, mature customer. Her dresses also attract a younger clientele, who tend to wait for the end-of-season sales when prices are slashed to the point of affordable.

Sass and Bide
Shop 4, 132 Oxford Street, Paddington; tel: 9360 3900; Mon–Sat 10am–6pm (Thur until 8pm), Sun 11am–5pm; bus: Oxford Street; map p.138 C2
Sarah Jane Clark (aka Sass) and Heidi (Bide) Middleton's unique low-sitting, 2-in-zip jean catapulted them into international stardom in the late 90s. They were the first Aussie duo to show in New York and their range is now sold in high-end stores such as Selfridges in London and Bloomingdales in New York. Jeans start at around $200,

Left: at Scanlan and Theodore in Oxford Street.

and if you are bigger than a UK size 12 you will struggle to find anything that fits, but the jeans are famous for their stretch so it is worth having a go.

Scanlan and Theodore
122 Oxford Street, Paddington; tel: 9380 9388; Mon–Fri 10am–6pm (Thur until 8pm), Sat 10am–5.30pm, Sun noon–5pm; bus: Oxford Street buses; map p.138 B3
A sophisticated designer option with beautiful tailored skirts, suits and jackets for the career professional. S&T have an outlet store on Oxford Street, where you can get as much as 75 per cent off last season's wares.

Zimmerman
Shop 1/387 Oxford Street, Paddington; tel: 9357 4700; Mon–Sat 10am–6pm (Thur until 8pm), Sun noon–5pm; bus: Oxford Street; map p.138 B3
Dresses, dresses, everywhere! If you want the most on-season style, colour and fabric (or just a very hot little number to take your date's breath away), head straight to Zimmerman. A lot of their styles, although perfect for

Left: Sass and Bide reveal their latest line.

With sizes ranging from XXXs to large, this store caters for the teeny-boppers who want to look older, and the older customer who wants to look hot in the summer months. Mostly cheap and cheerful, the loud music in every store is enough to keep you away. But it is worth a look for cheap belts and the occasional pretty beach dress.

For One-Off Finds...
Bondi Beach Market
Campbell Parade; tel: 9315 8988; Sun 10am–5pm; bus: 333, 378, 380, Bondi Explorer; map p.22

If you see a Sydney girl wearing a vintage belt or unique 1960s style dress, chances are she bought it here. The Bondi Beach Market, held in the grounds of the Bondi Beach public school, have helped establish more than a few of the most successful Sydney designers. Young hopefuls set up stalls each week in hope of being discovered. Get there early to avoid the crush and bag the bargains first.

SEE ALSO SHOPPING, P.116

Kirribilli Markets
Burton Street Tunnel and on Bradfield Park; tel 9936 8197; fourth Sat of each month (first and third Sat, Dec) 7am–3pm; bus, train, ferry: Milson's Point; map p.24

If there is one reason to get up early on a Saturday, this is it. Here are over 300 stalls full of vintage clothes and accessories. The dedicated followers of fashion in Sydney prowl this venue so get there early and be prepared to grab whatever you can lay your hands on, especially at the $5 dress stall.

---

the Size 6 model within us all, flatter even the most curvy shape.

David Jones
65–77 Market Street; tel: 9266 5544; Mon–Wed 9.30am–6pm, Thur 9.30am–9pm, Fri 9.30am–7pm, Sat 9am–6pm, Sun 10am–6pm; train: Town Hall, bus: 441; map p.133 C1

Your one-stop shop for almost every local and international designer you could wish for. As well as all of the above, DJs stock other local names such as Willow and Wish, as well as the veterans Prada, Dior, Burberry et al.

SEE ALSO SHOPPING, P.114

For Budget Beauties...
Sportsgirl
18–20 Oxford Street, Paddington; tel: 9360 4077; Mon–Fri 10am–6pm (Thur until 7pm), Sat 9.30am–6pm; train: Museum, bus: Oxford Street; map p.137 E4

Following in the footsteps of Topshop in the UK, Sportsgirl has a new vintage range and chic affordable glamour wear. Their reputation for quality goes up and down, but they remain a solid favourite.

SES
500 Oxford Street, Bondi Junction; tel: 9389 5642; Mon–Fri 9.30am–7pm (Thur until 9pm), Sat 9.30am–6pm, Sun 10am–6pm; train: Bondi Junction, bus: 378, 389

Fast replacing Supré as the place to kit yourself out for the season for less than $100, SES prices start at the almost ridiculously low. They are quick to turn out the latest catwalk trends, and it is a great place to find hidden gems, but you will not want to rely on the clothes lasting more than a few wears.

Supré
54 Imperial Arcade, Pitt Street; tel: 9233 3731; Mon–Fri 9am–6pm (Thur until 8pm); Sat 9am–5pm, Sun 11am–4pm; train: Town Hall; map p.133 C1

With the shopping-obsessed Sydneysiders, it is no surprise that the massive mall at Westfield Parrammatta is the largest of its kind of the southern hemisphere, with more than 500 stores

---

Festivals

Sydney is the events capital of Australia. If you can, try to time your visit to the city to coincide with one of the big party days on the calendar, such as the magnificent spectacle of the Sydney to Hobart Yacht Race, which leaves from Sydney Harbour on Boxing Day each year, January's hugely popular Concerts in the Domain, or the spectacular Gay and Lesbian Mardi Gras in February or March. But scarcely a week goes by without some major cultural or sporting event taking place: whenever you vist, you will find something to celebrate. Here is a list of some of the festival highlights.

Spring (Sept–Nov)

Royal Botanic Gardens Spring Festival
September
Spectacular seasonal displays, complete with brass bands, art shows and food stalls.

Spring Racing Carnival
Randwick Racecourse, September
Sydney's top horse racing event, culminating in the Sydney Cup.

Australian Rugby League Grand Final
Telstra Stadium, late September
One of the country's great sporting rituals.

Manly Jazz Festival
October
Music at Sydney's other favourite seaside venue.

Good Food Month
October
Look for major discounts at Sydney's best restaurants, as well as food festivals and cooking classes, during this culinary celebration.

Australian International Motor Show
Darling Harbour, October
A must for the car-lover.

Sculpture by the Sea
Bondi to Bronte Walk, November
A two-week display of sculpture in one of the city's most scenic locations.

Summer (Dec–Feb)

Carols in the Domain
December
Share the spirit of Christmas at this family event.

Sydney to Hobart Yacht Race
26 December
Thousands of Sydneysiders flock to the foreshore to watch the start of the race.

New Year's Eve
31 December
If you are not invited to a party, do not despair: the biggest party happens right

> January is the month for the much-loved Concerts in the Domain series. Part of the Sydney Festival, these free events are held on consecutive Saturday nights, and are devoted to jazz, symphonic music and opera respectively. Get there early and bring a picnic, or buy food there.

on the harbour. An estimated one million people watch the two major firework displays, one at 9pm and another at midnight. Both are launched from city skyscrapers, barges anchored in the harbour, and from the Harbour Bridge itself.

Sydney Festival
January
Sydney gets into the summer spirit with a three-week festival of local and international arts, including music, dance and theatre.

Sydney International Tennis
Sydney Olympic Park Tennis Centre, January
See the best tennis players from Australia and overseas in action.

Open-Air Cinema
Royal Botanic Gardens, January–February
Tickets sell out quickly to this glamorous event, where on-screen action has to compete with one of the best views in Sydney.

Moonlight Cinema
Centennial Park, December–March
A more relaxed outdoor cinema experience. Bring a

Left: New Year's Eve fireworks light up the harbour.

Sydney's autumn horse racing carnival is a chance to frock up and get festive.

Royal Easter Show
Sydney Showground, Olympic Park
The country comes to town: wood-chopping and cattle contests, along with sideshows and plenty of free entertainment.

Archibald Prize
March–April, Art Gallery of NSW
This annual portrait prize is a favourite with the crowds; coincides with the Wynne and Sulman Prizes.

St Patrick's Day Parade
17 March
Celebrated by the many Sydneysiders of Irish descent, and by the even more numerous Sydneysiders who just like a drink.

Sydney Writers Festival
May
A varied programme of bookreadings, public lectures and panel events, many of which are free.

Rugby League State of Origin Series
May–June
Tribal passions flair as NSW and Queensland go head to head.

Winter (June–Aug)

Sydney Film Festival
June
Includes over 250 screenings in two weeks, many of which are held in the grand old State Theatre.

Biennale of Sydney
Mid-July (even-numbered years)
Celebrates the best of international contemporary art.

City to Surf Race
Early August
Athletes and couch potatoes alike take part in the celebrated race from the city to Bondi.

blanket and a picnic.

Australia Day
26 January
Celebrations include the Surfboard Challenge (1,000 surfers paddle from the Opera House to Blues Point), the Ferrython race, and the Royal Sydney Yacht Squadron's Regatta, the world's oldest continuous regatta.

Sydney Fringe Festival
Late January–early February
A film and arts festival with an alternative bent.

Gay and Lesbian Mardi Gras
February/March
More than just a colourful street parade and party, the Mardi Gras is also an arts festival with a varied programme.
SEE ALSO GAY AND LESBIAN P.66

Chinese New Year
Mid-February
Three weeks of festivities based in Chinatown and Darling Harbour. Look for food stalls and extravagant banquets, lion processions and dragon-boats races, as well as a variety of arts events.

Tropfest
The Domain, February
What started out as a short-film screening session in a Kings Cross cafe has become the world's largest short-film festival.

Autumn (Mar–May)

Harbour Week
March
A varied programme of events including tours of the harbour islands and of the foreshore.

Golden Slipper Festival
March, Sydney Turf Club

Below: dragons on George Street at Chinese New Year.

Film

For such a small nation, Australia has made a remarkable impact in Hollywood, and many of the most in-demand talents – from director Peter Weir to actors such as Nicole Kidman, Cate Blanchett, Naomi Watts and Hugh Jackman – are true-blue Sydneysiders. Sadly, it is the lack of opportunities locally that convinces many of them to head overseas, although initiatives such as Tropfest, the world's largest short-film festival, are trying to redress the balance. The city itself has a splendid diversity of cinemas, from multiplexes showing blockbusters to small independent houses screening obscure films.

A Late Bloomer

Australia was one of the pioneers of cinema, producing films, or parts thereof, in the late 19th century. However, the local industry remained relatively quiet until a sudden explosion of output in the 1960s and 1970s, prompted by the setting up of the Australian Film, Television and Radio School and the introduction of tax breaks for investment in the local product. Films such as *My Brilliant Career* (1979) helped launch the careers of actors Judy Davis and Sam Neill, as well as director Gillian Armstrong.

Perhaps the era's biggest success was Sydney-born director Peter Weir. After creating two pieces of classic Australian cinema – *Picnic at Hanging Rock* (1975) and *Gallipoli* (1981), the latter starring a young Mel Gibson – Weir headed for Hollywood, to direct a string of commercially and critically successful movies. These included *Witness* (1985), *Dead Poets Society* (1989), *The Truman Show* (1998) and the seafaring adventure *Master and Commander* (2003), starring his compatriot Russell Crowe.

Meanwhile, local feature film production has ebbed and flowed. A huge boost was provided by the setting up of **Fox Studios** at Moore Park, where

international productions such as *The Matrix* trilogy and the *Star Wars* prequels were filmed. More recently it has declined, with Hollywood now favouring alternative destinations such as Canada.

Australian films that make it big internationally tend to share a certain flamboyance. *The Adventures of Priscilla, Queen of the Desert* (1994) tells the tale of three drag artists on tour across the Outback in a bus; *Muriel's Wedding* (1994) is a deceptively simple tale of one girl's dream to get married; and Baz Luhrmann's over-the-top creations include *Moulin Rouge* (2001), *Romeo + Juliet* (1996) and *Strictly Ballroom* (1992).

However, there is another side to Australian cinema. From the late 1990s on, attention began to focus on indigenous themes, with films such as *Rabbit-Proof Fence* and *The Tracker* (both 2002) putting indigenous stories in the spotlight. The director of *The Tracker*, the acclaimed

Left: Rolf de Heer, director of the acclaimed *Ten Canoes*.

Left: Priscilla, Queen of the Desert is now a stage show, based on the cult film.

Chauvel Cinema
249 Oxford Street, Paddington; tel: 9361 5398; bus: Oxford Street; map p.137 E4
Innovative programmes, with classics each Monday night.

Dendy Cinemas
Opera Quays, 2 East Circular Quay; tel: 9247 3800; train, bus, ferry: Circular Quay; map p.139 E3
261–263 King Street, Newtown; tel: 9550 5699; train: Newtown, bus: King Street
Varied cinema programmes, just to the left of mainstream.

IMAX Theatre
Southern Promenade, Darling Harbour; tel: 9281 3300; metro: Convention station, ferry: Darling Harbour; map p.132 B1/C1
Mega movies on a giant screen.

Palace Cinema Norton Street
99 Norton Street, Leichhardt; tel: 9550 0122; bus: Norton Street
Art-house and foreign films in the heart of Little Italy.

The Verona
17 Oxford Street, Paddington; tel: 9360 6099; bus: Oxford Street; map p.137 E4
Part art-house, part Hollywood, showing crossover product.

Even movies go outdoors in Sydney summers. The most glamorous venue is the Open-Air Cinema in the Royal Botanic Gardens (www.stgeorgeopenair.com.au). Bookings for its January–February season sell out very quickly. The more relaxed Moonlight Cinema at Centennial Park runs from December to March (www.moonlight.com.au).

innovator Rolf de Heer, went on to work with the people of Ramingining of Arnhem Land on *Ten Canoes* (2006), the first Australian film made in indigenous language.

Festivals
Sydney's biggest movie moment comes in June, with the annual two-week Sydney Film Festival. The programming includes low-budget gems, documentaries and features from around the world, as well as artist retrospectives. The principal venue is the State Theatre *(see p.125)* on Market Street, with a beautiful baroque interior dating from 1929.

The other highlight on the local film calendar is Tropfest (www.tropfest.com). The world's largest short-film festival takes place every February in The Domain.

Cinemas
Check the daily papers for cinema listings, and the weekend papers for the best film reviews. ABC-TV, Australia's national broadcaster, runs an excellent half-hour film review programme on Wednesday evenings, which covers most of the major releases.

The city's largest multi-screen complex, where you will find all the big blockbuster movies and latest releases, is located on George Street. Sydney also has plenty of small art-house and foreign-language cinemas in the city and inner suburbs. Foreign-language films all carry English subtitles.

Academy Twin Cinema
3a Oxford Street, Paddington; tel: 9331 3457; train: Kings Cross, bus: Oxford Street; map p.137 E4
Long-established non-mainstream release cinema.

Below: the massive IMAX cinema at Darling Harbour.

Food and Drink

Sydney is one of the world's great dining capitals. With quality produce, including sensational seafood, and a diverse immigrant population adding a rich range of culinary influences, it's no wonder the food is so good. Add to that a climate that favours al fresco eating, a harbour and beaches offering meals with a view, and an informal culture that stops even the most sophisticated restaurants from being too stuffy, and you have a gastronomic combination that is hard to beat.

Ethnic Cuisines

Perhaps the most surprising thing about Sydney's internationally-acclaimed restaurant scene is how recent it is. The first ethnic restaurants opened in the 1950s, and were run by immigrants for immigrants, Australians being highly suspicious of these foreigners who did not eat at home like respectable folks.

But once they tried it, Sydneysiders discovered that they loved dining out, and a local cuisine quickly evolved based on fresh local ingredients and techniques that married European and Asian traditions. 'Modern Australian' cooking is a fusion of the world's great traditional cuisines, particularly French,

Italian, Chinese, Japanese, Vietnamese and Thai. The food tends to be fresh, light, low in fat, simply presented and reasonably priced.

Sydney's hundreds of ethnic restaurants offer constantly changing variety, originality and, above all, value for money. While Italian and Lebanese restaurants remain popular, it is not surprising that Asian establishments dominate the casual dining scene.

Chinatown's dozens of restaurants provide meeting-places for the large Chinese community living in nearby high-rise units, as do similar enclaves in suburbs such as Chatswood. *Yum cha*, similar to *dim sum*, is a very cheap and popular choice for

people meeting friends. Diners can choose from up to 250 dishes consisting of small servings of dumplings, won tons, noodles and vegetables off circulating trolleys.

Japanese restaurants and sushi bars arrived in Sydney with the waves of Japanese tourists and business travellers in the 1980s, and are particularly popular in the city and inner suburbs. No visitor to Sydney should miss the cornucopia of the seas on display at the **Fish Markets** *(see p.65)* at Pyrmont, or Sydney's freshest sushi and sashimi at the **Fish Markets Sushi Bar**.

Indian restaurants can also be found throughout the suburbs, but Sydneysiders' most passionate love affair has been with Thai cuisine, partly for its rich complexity of flavours, and partly because most restaurants tend to be modestly priced and unpretentious. Recently Vietnamese cuisine, which shares a similar lightness and freshness, has been catching up fast.

SEE ALSO RESTAURANTS P.101

Japanese sushi, Italian foccaccia and Turkish pide are all popular, but the quintessential Aussie snack remains the meat pie. For a true taste of Sydney, visit Harry's Café de Wheels near the Finger Wharf in Woolloomooloo, a pie vendor that is one of the city's oldest institutions *(see p.42)*.

Left: quandongs are similar to peaches, but have a rhubarb-like tang.

and chilli sauce), sandwiches and pastas to three-course meals.

Cafés tend to cluster together. The best-known strips include: Victoria Street between Craigend and Liverpool Streets and the corner of Macleay Street and Challis Avenue in Kings Cross; Stanley Street in East Sydney; along Oxford Street in Paddington; King Street between Missenden Road and Newtown Station in Newtown; Knox and Bay Streets in Double Bay; and Norton Street in Leichhardt.

Bush Tucker

For tens of thousands of years, the indigenous Australians survived on the fruits, seeds, nuts, fungi, mammals, reptiles, fish and birds, collectively referred to as 'bush tucker'.

Apart from the macadamia nut, most native plants have resisted cultivation, so the place you are most likely to see ingredients such as muntari berries, bush tomatoes, Illawarra plums, lemon myrtle and lilli pillies, is on a restaurant menu. Popular ingredients include quandongs, wattle seeds (sometimes used to give ice cream a coffee-like flavour), Kakadu plums (less sweet than the usual variety) and bunya bunya nuts (delicious in satay sauces).

Among native meats, kangaroo, crocodile and emu are slowly growing in popularity. Only kangaroo can be found in the supermarket, but all three are commercially

Right: sushi arrived in Sydney in the 1980s and remains stylish and popular.

farmed and are low in fat.

Two indigenous foods unlikely to appear on a menu near you are witchetty grubs (large larvae found in the trunks and roots of wattle trees) and bogong moths (a hefty migratory moth, usually roasted in a fire and eaten like peanuts).

Café Life

Sydney has hundreds of cafés, many with outdoor tables on the pavement, offering very good espresso coffee, together with food ranging from snacks (such as potato wedges, deep-fried and served with sour cream

Australian Wines

Australian wines are among the world's best, a judgement regularly confirmed at international wine shows. The Australian wine industry is aiming to become the world's most profitable and influential supplier of branded wines within 30 years, a target that assumes a massive increase in the value of Australia's wine exports. Wine is produced in every state in Australia over a great range of climatic and soil conditions. Riesling, Chardonnay and Semillon are the most favoured white varieties,

Above: Coopers, a strong ale brewed in Adelaide.

while popular reds include Cabernet Sauvignon, Merlot, Pinot Noir and Shiraz (known in Europe as Syrah).

Many of Sydney's less expensive restaurants are BYO (bring your own wine). Bottle shops (off licences) are not hard to find, and most offer a wide selection at very moderate prices. A number of fully-licensed restaurants have very well chosen wine cellars.

Food and Wine Tours

FOOD TOURS
Gourmet Safari
tel: 9960 5675
Offers a broad range of tours taking in the diverse flavours of Sydney, such as a Greek walking tour of Marrickville, a Vietnamese walking tour of Cabramatta and a Lebanese walking tour of Punchbowl. 'World In A Day' shopping tours take in everything from Indian samosas to Italian butchers.
Chocolate Espresso
tel: 9960 5675
Walking tours in the CBD focusing on the best of Sydney's chocolate and coffee outlets. Plenty of sampling included.

WINE TOURS
The Hunter Valley, one of Australia's premium wine-growing regions, lies about 2hrs from Sydney, and is famous for its full-bodied Shiraz and fruity Semillons and Chardonnays. Many companies offer day tours to the Hunter for around $100, including visits to some of the 120 wineries and cellar doors in the district.
Boutique Wine Tours
Tel: 9499 5444;
www.visitours.com.au
Hunter Valley Wine Tasting Tours
Tel: 8920 1141; www.hunter valleywinetastingtours.com.au;

Wine Shops

Australians are passionate wine consumers; the following wine shops have good selections and helpful staff.
Best Cellars
91 Crown Street, East Sydney; tel: 9361 3733; Mon–Wed 9am–9pm, Thur–Fri 9am–10pm, Sat 11am–10pm, Sun noon–8pm; bus: Oxford Street; map p.133 D1
Small wine shop with a good range, including a strong selection of New Zealand wines.
Five Way Cellars
4 Heeley Street, Paddington; tel: 9360 4242; Mon–Sat 9am-9pm, Sun 11am–7pm; bus 389; map p.138 A3
Tiny terrace house filled to the brim with a range of rarities from around the world.
Kemeny's
137–47 Bondi Road, Bondi; tel: 13 88 81; open Mon–Sat 8am–9pm, Sun 9am–8pm; bus: 333, 380, 389, Bondi Explorer; map p.22
Warehouse-type store with

Right: Sydney's Fish Markets, on Blackwattle Bay, have fresh fish and seafood seven days a week.

a vast range at excellent prices.
Vintage Cellars
396 New South Head Road, Double Bay; tel: 9327 1333; www.vintagecellars.com.au; bus 323, 324, 325; map p.135 D1
Vintage Cellars has outlets throughout Sydney (see their website for locations), but this is its flagship store. Especially good on Italian and French wines, particularly Champagne.

The Amber Nectar

Beer is served cold, sometimes very cold. Although Fosters lager is the best-known Australian beer internationally, Sydneysiders consider it a beer for tourists. Tooheys and VB (Victoria Bitter) are big-selling brands in Sydney bars, along with imports such as Stella and Corona. Some beers are sold in 'new' and 'old' varieties, the first being lager, the latter darker in colour.

The alcoholic strength of Australian beer must by law be displayed on the can or bottle. Full-strength draught beer is around 4.9 per cent alcohol, 'mid-strength' beer

will be around 3.5 per cent and beers marked 'light' will be no more than 2.7 per cent alcohol.

'Boutique' beers, brewed in smaller batches, are increasingly popular. Commercial premium brands include Hahn, James Boag and Cascade. Coopers Ale, brewed in South Australia, has a loyal following. Coopers is more like a British beer (but colder) and pretty strong, at 5.8 per cent alcohol.

A 285ml beer glass is called a 'middie' in New South Wales and a 425ml glass is a 'schooner'. A small bottle of beer is known throughout Australia as a 'stubbie'. An off licence is called a bottle shop, or 'bottle-o'. To 'shout' someone a drink means to buy them one, as in, 'Can I shout you a drink?' Pub patrons may be 'in a shout', which means they are with a group of drinkers who take turns to buy drinks for the whole group.

Shopping for Food

Local delicacies include macadamia nuts, bush honey, royal jelly, chocolates and the inevitable Vegemite,

Above: Australia's favourite savoury spread.

a savoury spread that is equivalent to Marmite (of course, many will strongly refute this statement) and an Aussie favourite.

Sydney Fish Markets
Bank Street, Pyrmont; tel: 9660 1611; daily 7am–4pm; bus, metro, ferry: Blackwattle Bay; map p.132 A1

These bustling daily markets offer a vast range of fish, either live or prepared for cooking, all fresh each day from the nearby ocean, and are popular with both restaurateurs and home chefs. There are also seafood restaurants, sushi bars and even a cookery school above the market, offering lessons on the preparation of fresh seafood.

David Jones Food Hall
65–77 Market Street; tel: 9266 5544; Mon–Wed 9.30am–6pm, Thur 9.30am–9pm, Fri 9.30am–7pm, Sat 9am–6pm, Sun 10am–6pm; train, bus: Town Hall; map p.133 C1

In the heart of the city, Sydney's best one-stop food shop has an oyster bar, a sushi bar, a butcher, a baker, a pasta bar, and plenty more besides. Pick up delicacies from around the world, or enjoy half a dozen oysters with a glass of bubbly.

SEE ALSO SHOPPING P.114

Paddy's Market
9 Hay Street, Haymarket; open Thur–Sun (and Public Holiday Mon) 9am–5pm; train, bus: Capitol Square; map p.137 C4

A corner of this undercover market is devoted to fruit and vegetables, with another section selling fresh seafood. Noisy, sometimes smelly, but always packed with bargains.

SEE ALSO SHOPPING, P.117

Farmers Markets
With Sydney's main produce market at Flemington, a long way from the city centre, local farmers' markets have increasingly become the place to buy the wide range of gourmet produce, from boutique cheesemakers to organic fruit and veg. Names to watch out for include Willowbrae cheese, Mandalong lamb and Jannei goat dairy.

EQ Farmers Market
EQ, Moore Park; Wed and Sat 10am–3.30pm, Sun 10am–5pm; bus: Anzac Parade; map p.138 A2

Good Living Growers Market
Pyrmont Bay Park (opposite Star City Casino); first Sat of each month, 7–11am; metro: Pyrmont Bay; map p.132 B2

Leichhardt Farmers Market
Orange Grove Public School, corner Balmain Road and Perry Street; Sat 8am–1pm; bus: 440, 445; map p.18

Sydney's love affair with local seafood – from fish such as snapper and John Dory to crustaceans including blue swimmer crabs and Balmain bugs – is nothing new. Archaeologists investigating Aboriginal middens have found deposits from Sydney rock oyster shells dating back to 6000 BC.

Gay and Lesbian Sydney

Few cities in the world are more beautifully muscled, tanned and gay as Sydney. Sydney's gay crowd is hot, and they know it. To cater for this demanding posse there are no end of bars, clubs and hot spots open day and night, seven days a week – most of which are on Oxford Street around Taylor Square. Fag Tag is a fairly new phenomenon where gay men and lesbians take over a mainstream straight bar for the night, often complete with drag shows and other entertainments.

Mardi Gras

The culmination of all the gay community's efforts to be a seen-and-heard element in Sydney's mainstream is the annual Mardi Gras, a week-long party of events, ending in a parade and huge ticket-only all-night dance party. The parade attracts around half a million spectators who line Oxford Street to see the various themed floats.

However, it is wise to not be naïve. The city still has its prejudices. Although Mardi Gras attracts many straight fans who love the glamour and excess of the parade, and Sydney has come a long way since the first event – a protest march in June 1978, when many protesters were arrested – there is still a clear divide. Despite being one the most visible gay parades in the world, the Mardi Gras rarely makes it on to the front pages and if you did not know any better it would be easy to mistake the increased traffic and crowds in town, who come from all over the world, for end-of-summer tourists.

There are other top-notch events as well, notably the Sleaze Ball in early spring, which started as a fundraiser for the Mardi Gras in the years when the parades were still seeking acceptance. Now it is an excuse for all sexualities to show off their inner sensuality and dance all night.

Places to Go

Arq

16 Flinders Street, Taylor Square, Darlinghurst; tel: 9380 8700; www.arqsydney.com.au; 24-hours; bus: 371, 392, 890; map p.137 E4

One of the current favourites, this funky club is

Below: Kings Cross characters.

Left: Oxford Street during the Mardi Gras parade, the annual highlight of the gay calendar.

With its prime location on the corner of Oxford and Crown, this retro bar and cocktail lounge is one of the most popular spots for gay crowds and their straight friends. Everyone is welcome. Always busy, so try to grab a spot on one of the stools at the front where you can watch the colourful world of Oxford Street skip past.

Palms on Oxford
124 Oxford Street, Darlinghurst; tel: 9357 4166; daily 10am–5am; bus: Oxford Street; map p.138 A3

Unlike the other well-polished, 'so cool it hurts' gay bars and clubs, Palms is the last stop shop for gay men and lesbians who just want to party with Kylie, Whitney and Britney. Everyone goes here. No one admits it. If your night is in need of a last-minute finale go to Palms and you will make enough friends to ensure your night out was a roaring success.

Below: suits you sir.

very straight-friendly, but dedicated to pleasing its camper than camp gay crowd. With weekly regular nights, such as the hugely popular Drag for Dollars show on Thursday – where the best and worst of drag performers battle it out for the $100 cash prize – and other special events throughout the year, the vibe is very modern.

Midnight Shift
85 Oxford Street, Darlinghurst; tel: 9360 4319; www. themidnightshift.com;

For current listings and info check out the monthly gay magazine *DNA* (www.dnamagazine.com.au) and Australia's lesbian magazine, *LOTL* (www.lotl.com). The International Gay and Lesbian Travel Association (tel: 9818 6669) is a professional body for people involved with gay tourism. Visitors can ring to be put in touch with providers of different travel services. For more on the Sydney Gay and Lesbian Mardi Gras, tel: 9568 8600, www.mardigras.org.au.

10pm–late; train: Museum Station, bus: Oxford Street; map p.137 E4

A cruisers' favourite, this split-level club with the Video and Locker Rooms downstairs and the upper level simply called 'upstairs', attracts a crowd which is almost all gay men. Incorporating the hardcore dance vibe upstairs, more laid-back schmoozing continues downstairs, where there are pool tables and popular DJs.

Deck Bar
91 Oxford Street, Darlinghurst; tel: 9365 9766; 24hrs; train: Museum Station, bus: Oxford Street; map p.137 E4

For an unknown reason Tuesday night is 'Lesbian' on Oxford Street, and Deck Bar is perhaps the best of what is available. Nowhere near as developed as Sydney's male gay scene, Deck is still a friendly bar for gay women to meet, greet and party.

The Colombian
117–23 Oxford Street, Darlinghurst; tel: 9360 2151; www.colombian.com.au; daily 10am–5am; bus: Oxford Street; map p.138 A3

History

*c.*45,000 BC	The first Aboriginal people arrive in the Sydney area; they live by hunting and fishing.
AD 1770	Captain James Cook lands at Botany Bay, claims the east coast of Australia for the British Crown.
1778	The First Fleet arrives from England under the command of Arthur Phillip, bringing 736 convicts. A prison camp is set up in Sydney Cove.
1789	The first convict is hanged for murdering a fellow-prisoner. Skirmishes with Aborigines.
1790	The ill-equipped Second Fleet arrives; the colony nearly succumbs to starvation.
1793	Free settlers arrive in the colony; ex-convict James Ruse begins the first farm in Parramatta.
1803	The *Sydney Gazette*, Australia's first broadsheet newspaper, is published.
1810	Governor Lachlan Macquarie begins to transform Sydney from a penal settlement to a colonial capital. Ex-forger and architect Francis Greenaway begins designing public buildings.
1815	Explorers Blaxland, Wentworth and Lawson find a way through the Blue Mountains, heralding Sydney's commercial expansion as a port.
1830s	Free settlers begin to arrive in large numbers.
1840	Transportation of convicts to Sydney is abolished.
1850	University of Sydney is founded.
1851	Gold discovered in the Blue Mountains, starting Australia's first Gold Rush.
1855	First railway between Sydney and Parramatta.
1880	Sydney hosts the southern hemisphere's first international exhibition.
1900	Bubonic plague results in large areas of Sydney's Rocks area being razed.
1901	The states join together to become the Commonwealth of Australia. Melbourne is the temporary capital, but Sydney insists that a new capital, Canberra, be built halfway between the two.

1770: Captain James Cook plants the British flag.

1778: Captain Arthur Phillip lands in Botany Bay.

1810: Lachlan Macquarie begins his term as Governor.

1895: busy Pitt Street, in the heart of the city.

1914	Sydneysiders enlist en masse for World War I. Australia suffers high casualties.
1919	Spanish influenza kills more people in Sydney than four years of war.
1932	Sydney Harbour Bridge opens.
1935	Luna Park, Sydney's harbourside entertainment centre, opens its gates.
1939	Sydneysiders enlist again to fight in Europe in World War II.
1942	Troops withdrawn from Europe as Japan threatens Australia. Three midget submarines cause havoc in Sydney Harbour.
1945	To celebrate the return to peace, the first Sydney to Hobart sailing race is held.
1956	Television comes to Sydney, bringing with it American influences.
1961	The last trams removed from Sydney's streets. First skyscrapers built in the city.
1970s	'Green bans' imposed by builders' union to save histrical districts from demolition.
1973	Sydney Opera House opens.
1978	The first Gay and Lesbian Mardi Gras parade.
1980	Sydney replaces Melbourne as the financial capital of Australia.
1988	Sydney is the focus of celebrations for Australia's bicentenary. Aborigines campaign for land rights.
1993	Sydney wins bid to hold the 2000 Olympics. Massive public building begins.
2000	Sydney hosts a successful Olympic Games.
2003	A $60-million City Gateways project begins, to upgrade and beautify the city's main entry points.
2005	Cross City Tunnel opens, linking Darling Harbour with Rushcutters Bay.
2006	Sydney is covered in smoke after raging fires in the Blue Mountains.
2007	Labor Party re-elected to NSW government for a historic fourth term.

1901: Lord Hopetoun, Governor-General of the new Federation.

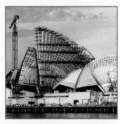

1958–73: building of the Sydney Opera House.

2000: Sydney hosts the Olympic Games.

2007: Bushfires threaten homes in North Sydney.

69

Hotels

Where to stay in Sydney? That depends on just what your heart desires: from cheap and cheerful dorm rooms to smart international hotels with glamorous private penthouses, Sydney comes up trumps. Stay in the bustle of the city, close to all the major attractions, or retreat to a quiet spot on the beach. There are even a few Sydney hotels that admit pets. Top-of-the-range accommodation does not come cheap in Sydney, but in this service-oriented city, you can be sure it will be worth every dollar. At the other end of the scale, backpackers can unload their rucksacks for as little as $20 a night.

Central Business District
Establishment
252 George Street; tel: 9240 3100; $$$$; train: Wynyard or Martin Place, bus: George Street; map p.139 D2
This is an intimate boutique hotel with just 31 luxurious rooms and even a private penthouse. There's also a gym. Voted Best Boutique Hotel in Australia in 2006. Its bar is the longest in Sydney and its Est restaurant one of the city's best.
SEE ALSO BARS, P.31; RESTAURANTS, P.98
Hyde Park Plaza
38 College Street; tel: 9331 6933; fax: 9331 6022; www. theoaksgroup.com.au; $$$;

train: Museum; map p.133 D1
Overlooking the park, this hotel offers a variety of self-contained apartments, ranging from studios to two- and three-bedroom suites. Rates include a light breakfast in bed. The Two Fat Ducks Bar is a pleasant lounge for coffee and drinks.
InterContinental Sydney
117 Macquarie Street; tel: 9253 9000; www.sydney. intercontinental.com; $$$$; train, bus, ferry: Circular Quay; map p.139 E1
Soaring out of the shell of the historic Treasury building in the business district, this 31-storey, 498-room hotel combines old-world style with

modern facilities. There are four restaurants and Pierpont's Bar stocks Australia's finest collection of Cuban cigars.
Menzies Hotel
14 Carrington Street; tel: 9299 1000; fax: 9290 3819; www. sydneymenzieshotel.com.au; $$$; train: Wynyard; map p.139 D2
One of Sydney's older hotels, the clubby Menzies has a traditional feel, but its spacious rooms, recently renovated, are fitted with all the latest amenities. In the heart of Sydney's downtown area.
Park Regis
27 Park Street; tel: 9267 6511; www.parkregissydney.com.au; $$; train: Town Hall; map p.133 C1

Below: the famous Marble Bar at the Hilton is a Sydney institution.

Left: the avant-garde bar at Blue, formerly a warehouse.

Sydney Marriott
36 College Street; tel: 9361 8400; www.marriott.com; $$$; train: Museum; map p.133 D1
Facing Hyde Park, this hotel enjoys a fine reputation for the quality of its rooms and service. Amenities include rooftop pool and spa, and modern-Australian cuisine in the hotel's restaurant.

HOSTELS
The Maze Backpackers/ CB Hotel
417 Pitt Street, CBD; tel: 9211 5115; www.mazebackpackers. com; $; metro: Capital Square; map p.131 C1
A 200-room hostel in the heart of the city, with TV lounges, juke box, games room etc. Dorms, doubles, twins and singles are available, but no ensuites. Cheap and cheerful.

Sydney Central YHA
Pitt Street and Rawson Place; tel: 9281 9111; fax: 9281 9199; www.yha.com.au; $; train, metro, bus: Central; map p.137 D4
Technically a youth hostel, it is also an excellent, centrally-located hotel in a heritage building opposite Central Station. A double room with private facilities costs from A$98 per night. The YHA also has a pool, sauna, laundry and self-catering kitchens.

The Rocks and Foreshore
Australian Hotel
100 Cumberland Street; tel: 9247 2229; fax: 9241 3262; www.australianheritagehotel.com; $$;

Occupies the top 15 floors of a 45-storey building, well placed in the central business district, near the Town Hall. Rooms have recently undergone refurbishment to offer a cool, contemporary look. There is also a rooftop pool, overall it is good value for the location.

Sheraton on the Park
161 Elizabeth Street; tel: 9286 6000; fax: 9286 6686; www. starwoodhotels.com; $$$$; train: St James; map p.133 C1
No harbour views, but you can gaze out on the verdant foliage of Hyde Park. The grand lobby and sweeping staircases are complimented by a modern health club and gym. Slick contemporary decor. Conveniently near Sydney's prime shopping venues and department stores.

Sofitel Wentworth
61–101 Phillip Street; tel: 9230 0700; fax: 9227 9133; www. accorhotels.com.au; $$$; train: Martin Place; map p.139 E2
The Wentworth has long been regarded as one of Sydney's grander establishments. Located in the heart of the CBD, it is close to the

Opera House, Circular Quay, The Rocks and the Royal Botanic Gardens. Its interior decor is warm and welcoming, though more suited to corporate pleated suits than relaxing holiday makers.

Swissôtel Sydney
68 Market Street; tel: 9238 8888; www.swissotel.com/ sydney; $$$; train: Town Hall; map p.133 C1
In the very centre of the city, atop the Sydney Central Plaza building. Rooms, furnished in Australian maple, with great views. In-house spa and sauna.

Sydney Hilton
488 George Street; tel: 9266 2000; fax: 9265 6065; www. hiltonsydney.com.au; $$$$; train: Town Hall, bus: George Street; map p.133 C1
This Hilton International-affiliated property has recently undergone extensive refurbishment and offers a luxurious level of amenities. The stylish lobby is far classier than the building's exterior would suggest. The ornate Marble Bar downstairs, built in 1893, is a Sydney institution.

SEE ALSO BARS, P.30

> Prices categories are for a standard double room without breakfast:
> $ = under A$100
> $$ = A$100–175
> $$$ = A$175–250
> $$$$ = over A$250

Above: boutique hotels now occupy many fine old buildings.

train, ferry, bus: Circular Quay; map p.139 D3
A lovely old pub built in 1913 with very comfortable rooms offering an inexpensive accommodation option in The Rocks. Bathrooms are shared. The roof terrace has views of the Harbour Bridge and Opera House. Price includes breakfast.
SEE ALSO BARS, P.32

Bed and Breakfast Sydney Harbour
140–142 Cumberland Street; tel: 9247 1130; fax: 9247 1148; www.bedandbreakfastsydney. com; $$; train, bus, ferry: Circular Quay; map p.139 D3
This restored early 20th-century mansion is located around the corner from the busiest part of The Rocks. The rooms, some of which have harbour views, are nicely fitted out with period furniture, and most have their own bathroom. The cooked breakfasts have been highly praised.

Four Seasons
199 George Street; tel: 9238 0000; www.fourseasons.com; $$$$; train, bus, ferry: Circular

Many Sydney hotels offer weekend discounts of up to 30 per cent. Be sure to enquire when making a reservation.

Quay; map p.139 D3
Formerly The Regent Sydney, this hotel has claims to be Australia's finest. It is in a wonderful location right on Circular Quay and has an impressive atrium foyer. There are suites on 34 floors and every possible facility, including a luxurious new spa.

Lord Nelson Brewery Hotel
19 Kent Street; tel: 9251 4044; www.lordnelson.com.au; $$; bus: 308, 431–434; map p.139 C3
The best value for money in Sydney, this historic pub provides cheap, comfortable rooms in the city's liveliest district.

Observatory
89–113 Kent Street, Millers Point; tel: 9256 2222; www.observatory hotel.com.au; $$$$; bus: 308, 431–434; map p.139 C3
Designed by prominent Sydney architect Phillip Cox, this opulent, yet intimate establishment offers absolute luxury in the heart of The Rocks precinct. There is also a 20-m indoor pool.

Park Hyatt
7 Hickson Road; tel: 9241 1234; www.sydney.park.hyatt.com; $$$$; map p.139 D4
Possibly Sydney's most luxurious hotel, the Park Hyatt opened in 1990 and was

completely renovated in 1998. It is still clinging to the best spot on the inner city's harbour shore, in a low, gracious building within a few minutes' walk of the city centre. There are great views from the restaurant and bar.

The Russell
143a George Street; tel: 9241 3543; www.therussell.com.au; $$$; train, ferry, bus: Circular Quay; map p.139 D3
A boutique hotel in The Rocks district. It has friendly, intimate surrounds, and is convenient. Some rooms have shared bathroom facilities.

Sebel Pier One
11 Hickson Road; tel: 8298 9999; toll-free: 1 800 780 485; www.sebelpierone.com.au; $$$; map p.139 D4
This 100-year-old wharf built on a pontoon over the water has been converted into a 161-room hotel with all-round views of the harbour and the Bridge. Its restaurant is, needless to say, right on the waterfront, with outside dining.

Shangri-La
176 Cumberland Street; tel: 9250 6000; www.shangri-la. com; $$$$; train, ferry, bus: Circular Quay; map p.139 D2

Opposite: Four Seasons Hotel rises above The Rocks.

Another huge Sydney hotel, but with a lot of style. The Blu Horizon bar is one of the city's best, and the Japanese restaurant is excellent too.
SEE ALSO BARS, P.32

The Opera House and The Domain

Blue

6 Cowper Wharf Road, Woolloomooloo; tel: 9331 9000; $$$$; bus: 311; map p.133 E2
Blue is a boutique hotel in the newly renovated warehouses of Woolloomooloo wharf, and is one of Sydney's most stylish places to stay. There are plenty of great restaurants within walking distance and one of Sydney's coolest bars, the Water Bar, is on the ground level.
SEE ALSO BARS, P.33

Quay Grand

61–9 Macquarie Street; tel: 9256 4000; fax: 9256 4040; www.mirvachotels.com; $$$$; train, ferry, bus: Circular Quay; map p.139 E3
This all-suite 'contemporary art-deco' hotel offers its guests uninterrupted views of Sydney Harbour, The Rocks, the Harbour Bridge, the city and the Royal Botanic Gardens. In the main bar you can sit and watch Sydney's ferries cross the bay.

Sir Stamford at Circular Quay

93 Macquarie Street; tel: 9252 4600; fax: 9252 4286; www.stamford.com.au; $$$$; train, bus, ferry: Circular Quay; map p.139 E2
Opposite the Royal Botanic Gardens and filled with oil paintings, Persian rugs and similar clubby trappings, the Sir Stamford offers a taste of old, colonial style.

Darling Harbour and Chinatown

Aarons Hotel

37 Ultimo Road, Haymarket; tel: 9281 5555; www.aaronshotel.com.au; $$; metro: Haymarket; map p.137 C4
This is a good motel-style place right in the middle of the city. The restaurant has cabaret Thur–Sun.

Capitol Square Hotel

Corner of Campbell, George and Day streets; tel: 9211 8633; $$; metro: Capitol Square, bus: Central; map p.137 D4
A newish boutique hotel adjacent to the Capitol Theatre and on the fringe of Chinatown. Korean BBQ, Thai and Japanese restaurants.

Crowne Plaza Darling Harbour

150 Day Street, Darling Harbour; tel: 9261 1188; www.darlingharbour.crowneplaza.co

Prices categories are for a standard double room without breakfast:
$ = under A$100
$$ = A$100–175
$$$ = A$175–250
$$$$ = over A$250

m; $$$; train: Town Hall; map p.132 C1
Formerly the Park Royal at Darling Harbour, this 12-storey hotel somehow keeps its boutique feel, while providing all the facilities expected of an international business hotel. Great location near the Darling Harbour waterside.

Four Points by Sheraton

161 Sussex Street, Darling Harbour; tel: 9290 4000; www.starwood.com/fourpoints; $$$; ferry: Darling Harbour, bus: 441, 442; map p.139 C1
One of Sydney's largest hotels (631 rooms on 15 floors), although its elegant, curved design facing Darling Harbour belies its size. The award-winning restaurant and pleasant pub are cosier than you would expect in a hotel of this size.

Grand Mercure Apartments

50 Murray Street, Pyrmont; tel: 9563 6666; $$$$; metro: Pyrmont Bay; map p.132 B1
Stylish two- and three-bedroom apartments with private

Above: the rooftop garden at Regents Court Hotel.

balconies, full kitchens and laundry, plus standard hotel services and facilities including a 50-m indoor rooftop pool, spa, gym and sauna.

Hotel Ibis Darling Harbour
70 Murray Street, Pyrmont; tel: 9563 0888; $$; metro: Pyrmont Bay; map p.132 B1
A modern (1995) three-star hotel on the west side of Darling Harbour. Standard rooms are not large, but comfortable enough. It is good value for its location. Fine views across the harbour, especially from the restaurant and bar, with an outdoor terrace.

Mercure Hotel Lawson
383 Bulwara Road, Ultimo; tel: 9211 1499; $$; map p.136 C4
Near Railway Square and within walking distance of Chinatown and Sydney's major entertainment venues, this hotel is well located. Sydney Football Stadium and Cricket Ground are also just minutes from the hotel. The hotel was recently refurbished with contemporary decor throughout.

Prices categories are for a standard double room without breakfast:
$ = under A$100
$$ = A$100–175
$$$ = A$175–250
$$$$ = over A$250

HOSTELS
Railway Square YHA
8–10 Lee Street; tel: 9281 9666; email: railway@yhansw.org.au; $; train, metro, bus: Central; map p.137 C3
This may be a youth hostel, but it is also a great centrally-located hotel in a heritage building that is walking distance from Sydney's major attractions. Try the Railway Carriage accommodation. Special rates for YHA members.

Kings Cross District
Boulevard
90 William Street; tel: 9383 7222; toll-free: 1800 671 222; www.boulevard.com.au: $$$; bus: 311; map p.133 E1
Situated between Kings Cross and Hyde Park on lively William Street, the Boulevard is a Sydney landmark, with luxurious facilities. It aims for the business market, but the views from its rooms and restaurant on the 25th floor make it popular with A-list guests as well.

De Vere Hotel
44–6 Macleay Street, Potts Point; tel: 9358 1211; fax: 9358 4685; www.devere.com.au; $$$; bus: 311; map p.134 A2
A good, comfortable choice

in the heart of the Potts Point/Kings Cross entertainment district, and close to city attractions. Some rooms on upper floors have harbour views.

Hotel 59
59 Bayswater Road, Kings Cross; tel: 9360 5900; www.hotel59.com.au; $$; train: Kings Cross; map p.134 A1
Located in a quiet section of Bayswater Road, this small hotel offers cheerful, fairly basic rooms that are kept spotlessly clean. Excellent cooked breakfasts.

Kirketon Hotel
229 Darlinghurst Road, Darlinghurst; tel: 9332 2011; www.kirketon.com.au; $$; train: Kings Cross, bus: 311; map p.134 A1
A well-run boutique hotel in a convenient location. Stylish enough to be voted one of 21 hip hotels for the 21st century. Remarkably good value, and in the thick of the café, restaurant and clubbing scene of Darlinghurst and Kings Cross.

Right: the boutique Kirketon Hotel.

L'Otel

114 Darlinghurst Road, Darlinghurst; tel: 9360 6868; $$; train: Kings Cross, bus: 311; map p.133 E1

This luxury European-style boutique hotel in the heart of Kings Cross has 16 all-white rooms described as 'a fusion of French chic and hi-tech'.

Medusa

267 Darlinghurst Road, Darlinghurst; tel: 9331 1000; fax: 9380 6901; www.medusa.com.au; $$$$; train: Kings Cross, bus: 311

A fine example of Sydney's boutique hotels, Medusa offers 18 individually designed studios complete with stereo equipment, TV, microwave and mini-kitchen. The decor uses bold light colours and huge beds. Staff are attentive and the reflection pool in the courtyard is delightful. They allow pets.

Oxford Koala Hotel and Apartments

55 Oxford Street, Darlinghurst; tel: 9269 0645; fax: 9283 2741; bus: Oxford Street; $$$; map p.137 E4

Close to Hyde Park and the city centre, this large hotel is on the route of Sydney's famous Gay and Lesbian Mardi Gras parade. Rooftop pool, parking and a restaurant.

Regents Court

18 Springfield Avenue, Potts Point; tel: 9358 1533; www. regentscourt.com.au; $$$$; train: Kings Cross; map p.134 A1

Converted in the early 1990s to become Sydney's first true designer hotel, it is located in a quiet cul-de-sac and has a rooftop garden with barbecue.

Right: two 1881 houses form Victoria Court in Potts Point.

Simpsons of Potts Point

8 Challis Avenue, Potts Point; tel: 9356 2199; www.simpsons hotel.com; $$$; map p.134 A2

Simpsons is an elegant boutique hotel located in a historic 1892 family home. It is within walking distance of the city, and only minutes from Macleay Street's restaurants.

Victoria Court Sydney

122 Victoria Street, Potts Point; tel: 9357 3200; fax: 9357 7606; www.victoriacourt.com.au; $$$; train: Kings Cross; map p.134 A1

Two neighbouring Victorian terraces have been joined and renovated to create this elegant bed and breakfast establishment. Rooms are comfortable and quiet and are decorated with period furniture. Nearby are good cafés and restaurants.

Y on the Park

5–11 Wentworth Avenue, Darlinghurst; tel: 9264 2451; $$; train: Museum; map p.137 D4

This terrific value-for-money hotel is one of Sydney's best budget places to stay. Backpacker dorms, singles and doubles. All rooms are clean and comfortable.

Paddington and Surry Hills

Alba Penthouse

437 Bourke Street, Surry Hills; tel: 9331 2881; $$$$; map p.137 E3

This ultra-hip three bedroom penthouse apartment is the perfect place to stay in complete privacy and glamour for two nights or more. Awe-inspiring views over the bridge and Opera House. There is a gym, sauna and swimming pool in the complex.

City Crown Motel

289 Crown Street, Surry Hills; tel: 9331 2433; fax: 9360 7760; www.citycrownmotel.com.au; $$;

bus: 301–303, 352; map p.137 E4

A trim, pleasant, family-run property in inner-city Surry Hills, a short stroll from Oxford Street and with plenty of cafés and restaurants around. All rooms have their own bathroom and balcony.

Mooghotel

413 Bourke Street, Surry Hills; tel: 8354 8200; $$$$; map p.137 E2

This hotel must be Sydney's most exclusive and luxurious: it has just one super-cool designer suite, and amazing facilities to go with it. There is a private plunge pool, a bar and restaurant, 24-hr butler service, a personal assistant, masseuse, personal trainer and chauffeured Jaguar. There is also a full recording studio: this is a place that's designed for rock stars.

Many of Sydney's fashionable boutique hotels, especially in the suburbs, are former homes, often of some historic or architectural interest, and provide intimate, personal accommodation. Their generally small size is both an advantage and a disadvantage: many offer only a few rooms, so need to be booked well in advance.

Left: Ravesi's on Bondi Beach.

minutes away. Each room is a suite and there is daily live entertainment in the lobby bar.

HOSTELS

Lamrock Hostel
7 Lamrock Avenue, Bondi Beach; tel: 9365 0221; $; map p.22
A 'boutique' hostel, this place deserves a special mention for its great location just up from the beach and its friendly, intimate atmosphere.

Bondi Backpackers
110 Campbell Parade; tel: 9130 4660; www.bondibackpackers. com.au; $; bus: 333, 380–382; map p.22
The only backpackers' hostel right on Bondi Beach has a bar/restaurant, TV room and 24-hour laundry. Breakfast included.

North Shore

Manly Pacific Parkroyal
55 North Steyne, Manly; tel: 9977 766; $$$; bus: 136, 139; map p.24
Situated right on the beach, this large hotel has a lively, resort-style atmosphere.

Periwinkle Guesthouse on Manly Cove
8–19 East Esplanade, Manly; tel: 9977 4668; www.periwinkle-manlycove.com.au; $$
Budget accommodation in a restored Victorian house close to the Manly ferry, harbour and shops. Rooms are plain, but clean and bright, and there is a communal kitchen and pleasant courtyard. Most rooms have a bathroom.

Inner West Suburbs

Glebe Point YHA
262 Glebe Point Road; tel: 9692 8418; $; p.18
A bright comfortable hostel with friendly staff who organise BBQs and backpackers activities. Great city views from roof-top recreation area.

Eastern Suburbs

Stamford Plaza Double Bay
33 Cross Street, Double Bay; tel: 9362 4455; fax: 9362 4744; www.stamford.com.au; $$$
Situated in leafy and pleasant Double Bay, a posh residential suburb, this inviting luxury property is just two blocks from the harbour. There are stunning views from the rooftop pool, and plenty of restaurants nearby. They also do good last-minute deals.

Eastern Beaches

Ravesi's on Bondi Beach
Corner of Campbell Parade and Hall Street, Bondi Beach; tel: 9365 4422; $$$$; bus: 333, 380–382; map p.22
This is a great place to combine a beachside holiday with a trip to a busy metropolis. Great beach views and an intimate atmosphere. Rooms are stylishly decorated and vary from compact rooms with no view to suites with a terrace overlooking the ocean. The hotel's restaurant is highly regarded.

Swiss-Grand Hotel Bondi Beach
Campbell Parade, Bondi Beach; tel: 9365 5666; fax: 9130 3545; www.swissgrand.com.au; $$$; bus: 333, 380–382; map p.22
Located right next to Bondi Beach, yet central Sydney and the airport are only 20

Prices categories are for a standard double room without breakfast:
$ = under A$100
$$ = A$100–175
$$$ = A$175–250
$$$$ = over A$250

Sebel Manly Beach
8–13 South Steyne Road, Manly; tel: 9977 8866; $$$; ferry: Manly Wharf, bus: 136, 139; p.24
This beachside hotel has 83 comfortable, recently refurbished rooms. **Will and Toby's** restaurant is excellent, and wide windows open out on to the beach so that sea breezes drift through.
SEE ALSO RESTAURANTS P.109

Vibe North Sydney
88 Alfred Street, Milsons Point; tel: 9955 1111; $$$; train: Milson's Point, bus: 269; map p.24
Long a favourite with corporate travellers, this hotel (formerly the Duxton) looks across the harbour from a North Shore perspective, with views of the Harbour Bridge and Opera House.

Blue Mountains

Echoes
3 Lilianfels Avenue, Katoomba; tel: 4782 1966; $$$$; map p.26
Modern luxury and old fashioned atmosphere.

The Mountain Heritage Hotel and Spa Retreat
Corner of Lovell and Apex streets, Katoomba; tel: 4782 2155; $$$; map p.26
Atmospheric old-world style

hotel with comfortable accommodation. Pamper yourself in the Day Spa after a day discovering the Blue Mountains on foot.

Peppers Fairmont Resort
Sublime Point Road, Leura; tel: 4784 4144; $$$$; map p.26
One of the luxury resorts built in the 1980s when the area was revived as a holiday escape. Lovely setting overlooking the Blue Mountains eucalypt forests.

Jemby Rinjah Lodge
336 Evan's Lookout Road, Blackheath; tel: 4787 7622; $$$; map p.26
A private bush retreat with cabin accommodation just outside one of the main mountain towns.

Kubba Roonga Guesthouse
9 Brentwood Ave, Blackheath; tel: 4787 5224; www.kubba roongaguesthouse.com; $$; map p.26
Operating as a guesthouse since the 1920s (Don Bradman honeymooned here), Kubba Roonga is set in attractive gardens, a short walk from Blackheath village. Rates include full English breakfast.

Above: Bondi Backpackers is the only hostel on the beach.

Lilianfels Blue Mountains
Lilianfels Avenue, Echo Point, Katoomba; tel: 4780 1200; $$$$; map p.26
A five-star resort in an English-style country house with two acres of gardens and a renowned restaurant.

Little Company Retreat
2 Eastview Road, Leura; tel: 4782 4023; $$; train: Leura; map p.26
Elegant guesthouse-style accommodation in this pretty Blue Mountains town.

Below: Kubba Roonga, an old-world guesthouse.

Literature

While painters such as Brett Whiteley have rendered their city in joyous Technicolour tones, Sydney's authors have a fetish for the city's darker side. From Ruth Park's tales of slum life onwards, many of the best books about the city dwell on its underside. Even Kenneth Slessor's *Five Bells*, considered by many to be the ultimate poem about Sydney Harbour, was inspired by a friend's drowning. Some of the best portrayals of the city have been by writers from abroad but, increasingly, native Sydneysiders have been using their home town as a character in their work. See our reading list below for examples.

Early Accounts

The very earliest account of the colony's early days by Marine captain Watkin Tench was first published in 1793, and is currently available under the title *1788*. Nineteenth-century works include Backhouse's *A Narrative of A Visit to the Australian Colonies* (1843) and Trollope's *Australia and New Zealand* (1876).

20th-Century Writers

Local novelists did not begin focusing on the city until the early 20th century. Louis Stone's *Jonah* (1909), telling

Many Sydney novelists have won international acclaim, but not always by writing about Sydney. Nobel Prize-winner Patrick White's *Riders in the Chariot* and *The Solid Mandala* are both set in the northwestern suburbs, and *The Vivisectionist* is about a Surry Hills painter. But Thomas Kenneally is best known for his Booker Prize-winning *Schindler's Ark* (set in Holocaust Europe) and Bryce Courtney for *The Power of One* (apartheid South Africa).

the story of a larrikin from the slums, was the first novel of any literary merit set in urban Sydney. Christina Stead's early novels (*Seven Poor Men of Sydney*, 1934; *For Love Alone*,1944) evoke Sydney during the 1920s and 1930s, while the novels of Kylie Tennant (*Foveaux*, 1939) and Ruth Park (*Harp in the South*, 1948; *Poor Man's Orange*, 1949) evoke life in Surry Hills, then Sydney's most notorious slum.

The city's seedy side is also the focus of contemporary authors such as Peter Corris and his fictional detective Cliff Hardy, and poet Dorothy Porter in her powerful verse novels, *The Monkey's Mask* and *What a Piece of Work*. Younger writers such as Christos Tsiolkas in *The Jesus Man* offer views of contemporary inner-city life.

Two of the most powerful portraits of the city have come from John Birmingham's 'shadow history' *Leviathan*; and Booker Prize-winner Peter Carey's *30 Days in Sydney*, which contains a far more vivid picture of the city than is captured in any of his novels.

Bookshops

Abbey's
131 York Street; tel: 9264 3111; Mon–Fri 8.30am–7pm (Thur until 9pm), Sat 8.30am–6pm, Sun 10am–5pm; train: Town Hall; map p.133 C1
Arguably Australia's biggest range of crime fiction, plus classics, text books, reference, fiction and audiobooks.

Ariel
42 Oxford Street, Paddington; tel: 9332 4581; daily 9am–midnight; bus: Oxford Street; map p.137 E4
Excellent range of cinema, travel, food, design, architecture and current fiction.

Berkelouw Books
19 Oxford Street, Paddington; tel: 9360 3200; daily 9am–midnight; bus: Oxford Street; map p.138 A4
New books downstairs, antiquarian and rare upstairs, secondhand further up again.

Dymocks Sydney
424–426 George Street; tel: 9235 0155; Mon–Fri 8.30am–6.30pm (Thur until 8.30pm), Sat 8.30am–6pm, Sun 10am–5.30pm; train: Town Hall, bus: George Street; map p.133 C1
Multi-storey book emporium with fiction and cookbooks

Left: Kinokuniya Bookstore.

ART & ARCHITECTURE
The Art of Australia, Robert Hughes
Sydney Architecture, Graham Jahn

BIOGRAPHY
A Fence Around the Cuckoo, Ruth Park
Unreliable Memoirs, Clive James

FICTION
For Love Alone, Christina Stead
A Harp in the South, Ruth Park
Oscar and Lucinda, Peter Carey
The Service of the Clouds, Delia Falconer

on the ground floor, history and philosophy upstairs.

Galaxy Bookshop
143 York Street; tel: 9267 7222; Mon–Fri 8.30am–7pm (Thur until 8.30pm), Sat 8.30am–6pm, Sun 10am–5pm; train: Town Hall; map p.133 C1
Best range of science fiction and fantasy books in town.

Gleebooks
49 Glebe Point Road, Glebe; tel: 9660 2333; daily 9am–9pm; bus: 434; map p.136 B3
Some 35,000 titles, including academic texts; strong on popular culture and sci-fi. A second shop at No. 191 sells children's and secondhand books, and there's a mini-outlet in Sydney Theatre.

Hordern House
77 Victoria Street, Potts Point; tel: 9356 4411; Tue–Fri 9am–5pm; train: Kings Cross; map p.134 A2
Rare books, manuscripts, prints, maps. Specialises in Australiana and Pacificana.

Kinokuniya Bookstore
The Galeries Victoria, 500 George Street; tel: 9262 7996; Mon–Sat 10am–7pm (Thur til 9pm), Sun 10am–6pm; train: Town Hall, bus: George Street; map p.133 C1

Cross-cultural store specialising in Japanese and Chinese books and magazines.

Lesley Mckay's
Queen's Court, 118 Queen Street, Woollahra; tel: 9328 2733; bus: 389; map p.138 C3; **14 Macleay Street,** Potts Point; tel: 9331 6642; Mon–Sat 9am–6pm, Sun 9am–5pm; bus: 311; map p.134 A2
Excellent range, including new fiction and strong non-fiction section. Separate children's shop connects with the Woollahra branch.

State Library of NSW
Macquarie Street; tel: 9320 1611; Mon–Fri 9am–5pm, Sat, Sun 11am–5pm; train, bus, ferry: Circular Quay; map p.139 E2
Great collection of Australian publications.

Reading List

ABORIGINAL AUSTRALIA
Dreamings: The Art of Aboriginal Australia edited by Peter Sutton
The Whispering in Our Hearts, Henry Reynolds

Right: State Library of NSW holds a copy of all books published in Australia.

FOOD & WINE
The Penguin Good Australian Wine Guide by Mark Shield and Huon Hooke
The Sydney Morning Herald Good Food Guide edited by Terry Durack and Jill Dupleix

HISTORY
A Secret Country, John Pilger
The Fatal Shore, Robert Hughes
The Future Eaters, Tim Flannery

TRAVEL COMPANIONS
Best Sydney Bushwalks, Neil Paton
Sydney, Jan Morris

Museums and Galleries

For a city with such a short history, Sydney has a surprising number of fascinating museums. Essentials include the Australian Museum, a great place to learn about the country's unique flora and fauna; the Maritime Museum, covering all things seafaring; and the Powerhouse Museum, full of interactive arts, science and social history. Art-lovers are also spoiled for choice, with the Art Gallery of NSW and the Museum of Contemporary Art supplemented by a thriving commercial gallery scene.

History

Cadman's Cottage
West Circular Quay; Mon–Fri 9.30am–4.30pm, Sat–Sun 10am–4.30pm; train, bus, ferry: Circular Quay; map p.139 D3

Cadman's Cottage, on the southern side of the Sailor's Home, is the oldest extant residence in Australia. Built in 1815 to house the crews of the governor's boats, it is named after John Cadman, a convict transported in 1798 for horse-stealing. Cadman was pardoned in 1821 and was appointed coxswain of government boats. He resided in this building with his family until 1846. The cottage was originally on the waterfront, but the 1840s reclamation of land left it high and dry. It later became part of the Sailor's Home, and today the small stone building houses the Sydney Harbour National Park Information Centre.

Discovery Centre
Botany Bay National Park, Kurnell; tel: 9668 9111; Mon–Fri 11am–3pm, Sat–Sun 10am–4.30pm; entrance charge; bus: 987

Commemorates the life and achievements of Captain James Cook. Shops and picnic facilities are nearby. Also contains National Parks and Wildlife Service pamphlets on recommended walking trails in the area and notes on the history of the site.

Elizabeth Bay House
7 Onslow Avenue, Elizabeth Bay; tel: 9356 3022; Tue–Sun 10am–4.30pm; entrance charge; bus: 311; map p.134 A2

This magnificent Georgian colonial mansion was built in 1839 to a design by John Verge for Alexander Macleay, who at the time was Colonial Secretary of New South Wales. The original land grant of 22 hectares comprised a good part of what is now Elizabeth Bay, and Macleay oversaw the development of the grounds, which included a magnificent garden of pools,

Below: a list of convicts and crimes at the Hyde Park Barracks museum.

	1825			...son John	36
Ploughman	1823		7 years	TURNER John	50
	1821			TURNER Robert	19
Brickmaker	1818		Life	TUTTON William	26
Shoemaker	1818		14 years	WADE Peter	19
Ploughman	1828	Stealing pig	Life	WAKELIN Joseph	23
Plaisterer	1823		7 years	WALKER John	25
Ploughman	1822		Life	WALL Charles	20
Servant	1824		7 years	WALPOLE George	27
Weaver & makes butter	1825		Life	WALSH Edward	19
Shoemaker	1826	Coining	7 years	WALSH Edward	25
				WALSH James	31
				WALSH John	19
				WALSH John	24

Left: Museum of Sydney's *Edge of Trees* sculpture remembers the area's original inhabitants.

Hambledon Cottage

63 Hassall Street, Parramatta; tel: 9635 6924; Wed–Thur and Sat–Sun 11am–4pm; entrance charge; train: Parramatta

Dating from 1822, Hambledon Cottage was the home of the Macarthurs' governess, and contains period interiors.

Harbour Bridge Pylon Lookout and Museum

Sydney Harbour Bridge; tel: 9240 1100; daily 10am–5pm; entrance charge; train, bus, ferry: Circular Quay; map p.139 D4

Located in the south-eastern pylon of the bridge, this museum contains a display documenting the building of the bridge. If you can make it up the 200 steps (there are places to rest along the way), you will be rewarded with a wonderful panoramic view of Sydney.

Hyde Park Barracks Museum

Queens Square, Macquarie Street; tel: 8239 2311; daily 9.30am–5pm; entrance charge; train: St James; map p.139 E1

These carefully-preserved barracks located at the northern curve of Hyde Park were commissioned by Governor Macquarie in 1819 to provide accommodation for convicts working in the city. They were designed by the colony's most prolific architect, Francis Greenway, himself an ex-convict. From the late 1840s,

walks and plantings stretching down to the harbour.

The house is fully furnished in period style and the internal staircase, sweeping upwards from an oval saloon beneath a domed ceiling, is regarded as one of the most beautiful in Australia. The interiors, generous spaces well-lit by huge north-facing windows, contrast with the more formal rooms which many associate with the Victorian period.

Elizabeth Farm

70 Alice Street, Rosehill; tel: 9635 9488; daily 10am–5pm; entrance charge; train: Harris Park

Built in 1793, just five years after the arrival of the First Fleet, Elizabeth Farm was the original abode of the Macarthurs and is arguably the oldest standing private European building in Australia.

Experiment Farm Cottage

9 Ruse Street, Harris Park; tel: 9635 5655; Tue–Thur 10.30am–4pm, Sun 11am–4pm; entrance charge; train: Parramatta

The cottage marks the site of the first grant of land in the colony, given to convicts James and Elizabeth Ruse, who were pardoned in 1789 as a reward for producing the first wheat crop in the colony. The land was eventually bought by a surgeon, John Harris, who built the cottage in 1834.

Government House

Macquarie Street; tel: 9931 5200; Fri–Sat 10.30am–3pm, grounds daily; train: St James Station; map p.139 E1

Designed by King William IV's architect, Edward Blore, and erected between 1837 and 1845, the building is in the form of a mock castle, complete with crenellated skyline and interiors of a baroque intensity. Its advanced blend of Gothic Revival and Regency styles set the architectural trend for the colony for decades after its completion. Until very recently, Government House was the residence for the State Governor of NSW; these days, the building and its collection of 19th-century furnishings and state rooms is open to the public.

As Australia's second-oldest white settlement, Parramatta has a particularly rich heritage of historic buildings. Maps for a self-guided walking tour are available from the Parramatta Heritage and Visitors' Centre (tel: 8839 3300).

Left: the Museum of
Sydney covers the area's
story, from Aboriginal
history to current affairs.

transportation of convicts
having ceased, the barracks
were used as a lodging house
for single women and
orphaned girls. Extensively
restored in the 1980s, today
the museum offers an insight
into the social history of the
state, including reconstructed
convict quarters and an exhibition detailing the work of
Greenway.

**Justice and
Police Museum**

Corner Phillip and Albert streets;
tel: 9252 1144; Sat–Sun
10am–5pm (daily during Jan
and school holidays); entrance
charge; train, bus, ferry: Circular
Quay; map p.139 E2

Housed in the former 19th-
century police buildings, the
museum covers everything to
do with the crimes and pun-
ishments of Sydneysiders
during the Victorian era. A
recreated courtroom, discipli-
nary instruments, prison uniforms and old photographs
and artefacts illustrate the
harsh justice that was meted

out at the time.

Lancer Museum

2 Smith Street, Parramatta; tel:
9365 7822; 2nd Sun of month,
10am–4pm; entrance charge;
train: Parramatta

The 1820 barracks building
was built for the British Garrison in 1820, and is the oldest
military establishment in Australia. The property also
includes a small museum
devoted to the Royal NSW
Lancers.

La Perouse Museum

Anzac Parade, La Perouse; tel:
9311 3379; Wed–Sun
10am–4pm; entrance charge;
bus: 393, 394; map p.22

La Perouse was the French-
man who arrived too late.
The explorer landed in
Botany Bay on January 26,
1788, just a few days after
the First Fleet. This museum,
located at the very end of
Anzac Parade, contains
expedition relics and provides an insight into the early
history of the area. The La
Perouse monument, dating

from 1828, was the brainchild
of another French explorer,
Baron de Bougainville, who
visited the site in 1825. The
French government con-
tributes towards its upkeep.
SEE ALSO PARKS AND
GARDENS P.96

The Mint

10 Macquarie Street; tel: 8239
2288; Mon–Fri 9am–5pm; train:
St James Station; map p.139 E1

Originally the Rum Hospital's
south wing, this building was
converted into a mint to
process gold-rush bullion
midway through the 19th
century. In the early days it
was used to produce 'holey
dollars', Spanish coins recycled to ease a desperate
shortage of cash. The new
colony used the equivalent of
both the doughnut and the
hole: the centres were
punched out and used as
15-pence coins, while the
remaining rings became
5-shilling coins, worth four
times as much. It ceased
operating as a mint in 1926,
and now houses a small display on the site's history.

Museum of Sydney

Corner Phillip and Bridge
streets; tel: 9251 5988; daily
9.30am–5pm; entrance charge;
train, bus, ferry: Circular Quay;
map p.139 E2

Situated on the site of the
city's first Government
House, the museum, which
opened in 1995, focuses on
the city's history from its
Aboriginal beginnings
through the colonial era and
up to today. Ancient hunting
tools detail the lives of Sydney's first inhabitants, the
Eora, while multimedia displays chronicle the 18th-
century European settlement

One of the star exhibits at the National Maritime Museum is a replica of the *Endeavour*, the ship in which Captain Cook discovered Australia. It was built using traditional techniques, and the interiors have also been faithfully recreated, right down to the smell of oakum, tar and canvas.

of Australia's east coast. The Edge of the Trees sculpture outside the museum is a moving memorial to the area's original inhabitants *(see picture p.80)*.

National Maritime Museum
2 Murray Street, Darling Harbour; tel: 9552 7777; daily 9.30am–5pm; free; metro: Pyrmont Bay; map p.132 B2
Beneath the thematic sail-like roofs are displays dealing with all facets of Australia's relationship with the sea. The museum covers everything from Aboriginal seafarers to early European explorers, from submarines to surfboards. Displays include a number of boats moored outside, including the destroyer *Vampire (see below)* and the submarine *Onslow,* and a wealth of nautical artefacts inside, including the figurehead from HMAS *Nelson*.

Old Government House
Parramatta Park, Parramatta; tel: 9635 8149; Mon–Fri 10am–4pm, Sat–Sun 10.30am–4pm; entrance charge; train: Parramatta, Westmead
Undoubtedly one of the most important historical buildings in Australia. Designed in neo-Gothic style by the London-based Edward Blore, Old Government House began as a relatively simple two-storey brick building in 1799. It was

remodelled and extended by Lieutenant John Watts in 1815. The ex-convict architect Francis Greenway is thought to have designed the front porch. Probably the oldest public building still standing in Australia, the house was used as a residence for governors and a meeting place for the social elite of the day. Also located in Parramatta Park is the shell of the river-fed Governor's Bath House, erected by Governor Brisbane in 1823, and the ruined Observatory, Australia's first, completed in 1822.

SEE ALSO PARKS AND GARDENS P.95

Susannah Place Museum
Gloucester Street; tel: 9241 1893; Sat–Sun 10am–5pm, daily during Jan; entrance charge; train, bus, ferry: Circular Quay; map p.139 D3
The museum is based in four adjoining terrace houses, built in 1844 for the free-settling couple Edward and Mary Riley, who arrived from Ireland in 1838 with their niece Susannah. Privately occupied until 1990; the buildings are particularly significant because they have preserved their original fire insulation, drainage, ventilation and sanitary systems. The terrace is now run as a period museum.

Sydney Jewish Museum
148 Darlinghurst Road, Darlinghurst; tel: 9360 7999; Sun–Thur 10am–4pm, Fri 10am–2pm; entrance charge; train: Kings Cross, bus: 311
Through a series of fascinating exhibits, this museum tells the story of Judaism and the story of Jewish settlement in Australia. A Holocaust display and memorial, spread across several floors, reveals the horrors of the 20th century's most tragic event.

Sydney Visitors' Centre
Corner Argyle and Playfair streets, The Rocks; tel: 9240 8788; daily 9.30am–5.30pm; train, bus, ferry: Circular Quay; map p.139 D3
There are many sites of interest in The Rocks, and a visit to its information centre is a good way to get an introductory overview. Among the brochures, maps and books you will find excellent displays on The Rocks, including artefacts from local archaeological digs. Pick up a self-guided historic walk brochure, or join a walking tour of the area. The centre is housed in the old Sailor's Home, which was built in 1864 as alternative accommodation for sailors to the brothels and dangerous inns. The Rocks by this stage had gained international notoriety as a location for 'leisure

Right: *Vampire* at the Maritime Museum.

that was even more perilous than the sea'.

Vaucluse House

Wentworth Road, Vaucluse; tel: 9388 7922; Tue–Sun 10am–4.30pm, grounds 10am–5pm; entrance charge; bus: 325; map p.20

One of Australia's most significant historic estates provides a glimpse into the lifestyles of Sydney's early rich and famous. The grand home, with its 7.5-hectare grounds, was the residence of William Wentworth (1790–1872), the son of a convict, an explorer, co-founder of the colony's first independent newspaper, *The Australian*, a founding member of the first Legislative Council and one of the authors of New South Wales' state constitution.

Vaucluse House is a mix of styles: Wentworth, who lived here between 1828 and 1862, continued to alter the structure whenever he found the time. A constantly changing population of between 24 and 37 servants were required to look after the complex and its inhabitants, which included the Wentworths' 10 children. From the grounds, it is easy to join a stunning foreshore walk that stretches from Rose Bay to Nielsen Park.

SEE ALSO PARKS AND GARDENS, P.94–5; WALKS AND VIEWS, P. 130

Victoria Barracks

Oxford Street, Paddington; tel: 9339 3330; Sun 10am–3pm;

Sydney's favourite art event is the Archibald Prize for Portraiture, which features controversial portraits of the great and the good. The winner generates headlines – and debate – when it is announced every March. The show is held at the Art Gallery of NSW.

entrance charge; bus: Oxford Street; map p.138 A3

Paddington begins – and began – with this historic convict-built sandstone complex still used by the Australian Army. The barracks was the main focus for the infant village of Paddington, and it stands today as one of the finest examples of British imperial military architecture. The old jailhouse is no longer used for its original purpose, but houses a museum on the nation's military history. Across the road on Shadforth Street and many nearby lanes, you can see the original tiny cottages that were built to house the skilled artisans who worked on the construction of the attractive barracks buildings.

Nature

Australian Museum

6 College Street; tel: 9320 6000; daily 9.30am–5pm, entrance charge; train: Museum; map p.133 D1

On the eastern edge of Hyde Park, housed in a Georgian sandstone building, is

Australia's country's oldest museum. It contains the country's largest collection of natural history exhibits, from prehistoric times to the modern-day environment.

The museum has an international reputation in the fields of natural history and indigenous studies, and its user-friendly displays make it a favourite with Sydney families.

Permanent displays include Indigenous Australia, with artefacts that illuminate Aboriginal cultures and lifestyles; the Living Harbour and the Wildlife of Sydney; a huge collection of birds, mammals and insects; and Australia's Lost Kingdoms, a gripping journey through evolution, featuring genuine fossils and life-size models of dinosaurs and some of Australia's extinct megafauna. Plenty for children to enjoy.

SEE ALSO CHILDREN, P.46

Sydney Observatory

Watson Road, Observatory Hill; tel: 9217 0485; daily 10am–5pm; free; night tours: booking essential, entrance charge; bus: 339, 343; map p.139 C3/D3

Observatory Hill is the highest point in the city, and for this reason was chosen as the site for this Observatory, established in 1858. (The colony's first grain-grinding windmills also stood here.)

The Observatory contains an interactive museum of

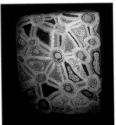

Right: Art Gallery of New South Wales.

astronomy, with educational programmes and evening viewings through the telescope. The first ever photographs of the southern skies were taken from here in the 1880s. Observatory Hill also offers some pretty nice terrestrial views: looking north, visitors are treated to a close-up view of the Bradfield Highway as it leads onto the Harbour Bridge; to the left, below the Bridge, is tree-lined Lower Fort Street, noted for its stately, multi-storey terrace houses.

Science

Powerhouse Museum
500 Harris Street, Ultimo; tel: 9217 0111; daily 10am–5pm; entrance charge; train, metro: Central, bus: 501; map p.137 C4
One of Sydney's most celebrated museums, it covers the topics of Australian arts, science and social history via dynamic hands-on displays, including interactive and multimedia presentations.

The building, as the name suggests, once housed the power station that serviced Sydney's tram system, and the museum still incorporates the boiler, switch and turbine houses. The new wings, with an acclaimed design by architects Denton Corker Marshall, recall the grandeur of classic European railway stations. Display areas include technology: transport, from planes, boats and trains to bicycles and wheelbarrows; engineering achievements, from crossbows to clocks, and from Samurai armour to

Opposite: multicoloured minerals, Aboriginal art and native perils at the Australian Museum.

printing presses; high-tech exhibits including computers, robots and early televisions. Decorative arts and design include fashion, ceramics, furniture, musical instruments and coins; and scientific displays cover astronomy, timekeeping, navigation, medicine and much more.
SEE ALSO CHILDREN, P.46

Art

Art Gallery of New South Wales
Art Gallery Road, The Domain; tel: 9225 1744; daily 10am–5pm (Wed until 9pm); free; train: Museum; map p.139 D2/E2
The gallery, established in 1874, has been housed in the present classical building since 1885. Various alterations, extensions and additions were made between 1897 and 1909, with another extension in 1971 almost doubling the available exhibition space. The Cook Bicentenary Wing, added in 1988, uses natural light and magnificent exterior views to help combat exhibition fatigue.

The gallery holds a number of major collections of Australia's finest works, European works from the 19th century, the largest permanent exhibition of Aboriginal and Torres Strait islander art in the world, a rich field of Pacific and Asian work, and an international collection of contemporary paintings. There is also a dedicated photography gallery.
SEE ALSO CHILDREN, P.46

Australian Centre for Photography
257 Oxford Street, Paddington; tel: 9332 1455; Tue–Sat 11am–6pm; bus: Oxford Street; map p.137 E4
Sydney's longest-running contemporary art space features Australian and international photography in its galleries, and also runs specialist workshops.

Brett Whiteley Studio
2 Raper Street, Surry Hills; tel: 9225 1880; Sat–Sun 10am–4pm; entrance charge; bus: Central; map p.137 E2
Brett Whiteley's Studio is a Surry Hills landmark and

Above: Martin Browne Fine Art Gallery.

important site for art pilgrims. Whiteley died in 1992 at the age of 53, at which time he was Sydney's most famous living artist. His paintings are large, sensuous and full of the light and colour of the city; one of his favourite subjects was the harbour, and probably no one has captured it quite so vividly. Many of his paintings are on display at what was his original studio, as well as work by friends and Whiteley's mementos and personal effects.

Museum of Contemporary Art (MCA)
140 George Street, West Circular Quay; tel: 9245 2396; daily 10am–5pm; bus, train, ferry: Circular Quay; map p.139 D3
This museum is housed in the old Maritime Services Board building, which was begun in 1939 but not completed until 1952 due to the outbreak of World War II. Its art deco style and building materials were designed to complement the functionalist style of Circular Quay Railway Station. The MCA has occupied the building since 1991, and has a reputation

for wide-ranging exhibitions that cover the latest works and trends in international contemporary art. Its own collection includes works by luminaries such as Warhol, Hockney and Christo, as well as contemporary Australian artists. The highly regarded MCA Café looks across the water to the Opera House.

Norman Lindsay Gallery and Museum
14 Norman Lindsay Crescent, Faulconbridge, Blue Mountains; tel: 4751 1067; daily 10am–4pm; entrance charge; taxi: 4.5-km from Springwood
One of Australia's most accomplished writers, artists and sculptors, Lindsay lived in this stone cottage for 57 years until his death in 1969. The house contains an important collection of his paintings, drawings, etchings (he specialised in scenes of voluptuous Bacchanalia), novels and ship models. A whole room in the house is devoted to *The Magic Pudding*, Lindsay's most famous children's book, an Australian classic, and there is an authentic re-creation of his original artist's

studio. The peaceful landscaped gardens, set amid surrounding bushland, include several of his larger statues and fountains.

SH Ervin Gallery
National Trust Centre, Watson Road, Millers Point; tel: 9258 0123; Tue–Fri 10am–2pm, Sat–Sun noon–5pm; entrance charge; bus: 339, 343; map p.139 C3/D3
While the gallery's main focus is the study of Australian art and architecture, it houses several high-profile exhibitions throughout the year, including the Portia Geach Portraiture Award for female artists, and the Salon des Refusés, an alternative selection of works entered in the Archibald, Wynn and Sulman Awards.

Commercial Galleries

Sydney has a lively gallery scene. Pick up a copy of the *Sydney Morning Herald* on Friday or Saturday for an overview of high-profile exhibitions, or simply spend a day trawling through a neighbourhood such as Paddington. Here are some of the best commercial galleries:

Every April, Sydney hosts Discovery After Dark, in which dozens of museums open their doors between 6pm and midnight. A single ticket gets you into all the venues, and special buses travel between the various museums.

2 Danks Street
2 Danks Street, Waterloo; Tue–Sat 11am–6am; bus: 301–304, 339, 343

This art space houses a number of different galleries, such as The Depot, and Utopia Art. Most are open Tuesday to Saturday, and display a range of indigenous and non-indigenous artists.

Annandale Galleries
110 Trafalgar Street, Annandale; tel: 9552 1699; Tue–Sat 11am–5pm

Housed in a former Methodist church, this beautiful exhibition space exhibits a wide range of artists including Korean star Yong Ha-Pak.

Australian Galleries
15 Roylston Street, Paddington (painting and sculpture); tel: 9360 5177; Mon–Sat 10am–6pm; train: Edgecliff
25 Glenmore Road, Paddington (works on paper); tel: 9380 8744; Mon–Sat 10am–6pm, Sun 11am–5pm; bus: 339, 343; map p.138 A4

Australian Galleries are famous for helping to launch the careers of artists such as Sydney Nolan and Albert Tucker. They also represent greats of today, including Jeffrey Smart and George Gittoes.

Coo-ee Aboriginal Art Gallery
31 Lamrock Avenue, Bondi; tel: 9332 1544; Tue–Sat 10am–5pm; bus 380; map p.22

Art, sculptures and artefacts from throughout Australia, particularly the Northern Territory and Western Australia.

Eva Breuer
83 Moncur Street, Woollahra; tel: 9362 0297; Tue–Fri 9.30am–6pm, Sat 10am–5pm, Sun 1–5pm; bus: 389; map p.138 C3

Features works on paper from Australia's best-known artists, including Brett Whitely, Donald Friend, Robert Dickerson and Margaret Olley.

Hogarth Galleries
Aboriginal Art Centre, 7 Walker Lane, Paddington; tel: 9360 6839; Tue–Sat 10am–5pm; map p.138 A4

Australia's oldest established Aboriginal fine art gallery, presenting works by established and emerging artists from around Australia.

Martin Browne Fine Art
22 Macleay Street, Potts Point; tel: 9331 0100; Tue–Sun 11am–6pm; train: Kings Cross, bus: 311; map p.134 A2

Features an interesting selection of Australian and New Zealand artists.

Mori Gallery
168 Day Street; tel: 9283 2903; Wed–Sat 11am–6pm; train: Town Hall; map p.132 C1

Showing both established and new contemporary artists.

Object Gallery
St Margarets, 417 Bourke Street, Surry Hills; tel: 9361 4511; Tue–Sat 11am–6pm; map p.137 E3

Sydney's premier applied arts gallery displays jewellery, textiles, homeware and glassware, but is worth visiting for the architecture alone.

Ray Hughes Gallery
270 Devonshire Street, Surry Hills; tel: 9698 3200; Tue–Sat 10am–6pm; train: Central; map p.137 E2

Founded by one of the characters of the Sydney art scene, the gallery has an emphasis on vibrant Australian art and more unusual overseas works.

Roslyn Oxley 9 Gallery
8 Soudan Lane Paddington; tel: 9331 1919; Tue–Fri 10am–6pm, Sat 11am–6pm; train: Edgecliff

Features new work in a range of media, including painting, sculpture, photography, performance, installation, video and other electronic media.

Sherman Galleries Goodhope
16–20 Goodhope Street, Paddington; tel: 9331 1112 Tue–Fri 10am–6pm, Sat 11am–6pm; map p.138 B4

Exhibits contemporary painters and sculptors from Australia and the Pacific Rim.

Utopia Art
2 Danks Street, Waterloo; tel: 9699 2900; Wed–Fri 10am–5pm, Sat noon–5pm

Specialises in work from the celebrated Papunya Tula settlement, as well as Utopia artists Emily Kame Kngawarreye and Gloria Petyarre.

Watters Gallery
109 Riley Street, East Sydney; tel: 9331 2556; Tue–Sat 10am–5pm (Wed and Fri until 7pm); train: Museum Station; map p.133 D1

One of Sydney's oldest and most respected galleries. Represents artists including James Gleeson, Chris O'Doherty (Reg Mombassa) and the late Tony Tuckson.

Below: a Norman Lindsay statue outside his former home.

Music and Dance

A performance at the Opera House is a ritual every visitor should experience. With a large range of quality local music and dance ensembles, there is always something worth catching. The Australian Opera and the Sydney Symphony Orchestra are both based at the Opera House, but plenty of other groups also perform there. Otherwise, try to catch a show from such cutting-edge performers as the Sydney Dance Company or the indigenous Bangarra Dance Theatre.

Classical

A number of quality musical groups perform regularly at the city's main concert venues, the Sydney Opera House, and the City Recital Hall in Angel Place in the CBD.

Australian Chamber Orchestra
Tel: 8274 3888;
www.aco.com.au
The ACO is known for its varied programme of classics and new commissions, and for the $10-million antique violin played by orchestra leader Richard Tognetti.

Brandenburg Orchestra
Tel: 9328 7581;
www.brandenburg.com.au
Baroque programmes performed on period instruments from original-edition scores.

Musica Viva
Tel: 8394 6666;
www.mva.org.au
Prolific chamber music group presenting hundreds of concerts nationwide every year.

Opera Australia
Sydney Opera House; tel: 9250 1777; www.opera-australia.org. au; train, bus, ferry: Circular Quay; map p.139 E4
The summer and winter seasons of this flagship company both take place in the Opera House.

Sydney Conservatorium of Music
Macquarie Street; tel: 8256 2222; www.music.usyd.edu.au; train, bus, ferry: Circular Quay; map p.139 E4
Sydney's premier music school hosts regular concerts by staff and students. The historic building in the Royal Botanic Gardens is worth a visit in its own right.

Sydney Symphony Orchestra
Tel: 8215 4600; www. sydneysymphony.com
The largest orchestra in the southern hemisphere presents an extensive programme each year.

Dance

The **Australian Ballet**, the main classical dance company, is based in Melbourne, but has two seasons every year in the Opera House.

The main contemporary dance ensemble, **Sydney Dance Company**, was founded in the 1970s by choreographer Graeme Murphy, and has since become famous around the world.

The highly-regarded **Bangarra Dance Theatre**, under the direction of Stephen Page, is an indigenous company performing works that draw on both traditional forms and contemporary styles.

Australian Ballet
Tel: 9250 7777;
www.australianballet.com.au
The national company performs two annual seasons at the Opera House, featuring classics and new works by Australian composers and choreographers.

Bangarra Dance Theatre
Tel: 9251 5333;
www.bangarra.com.au
Based at The Wharf theatre in Miller's Point (see p.125), this indigenous company combines Aboriginal, Western and other dance traditions.

Sydney Dance Company
Tel: 9211 4811; www.sydney-dancecompany.com
Graeme Murphy, founder and choreography of this acclaimed contemporary dance company, recently resigned. What comes next for the SDC is still to be seen.

Left: the Opera House at night, Sydney's cultural cornerstone.

9810 7931; www.thecatand
fiddle.net; live music Wed–Sat
evening, Sun afternoon; bus:
432, 433, 434, 445
Live acoustic, folk and blues.

Enmore Theatre
130 Enmore Road, Newtown;
tel: 9550 3666; www.enmore
theatre.com.au; train: Newtown,
bus: 355, 423, 426, 428
Hosts a range of big-name
international and local acts.

Excelsior Hotel
64 Foveaux Street, Surry Hills;
tel: 9211 4945; www.excelsior
hotel.com.au; train, metro, bus:
Central; map p.137 D3
A venue for R&B and indie
rock enthusiasts.

Hopetoun Hotel
416 Bourke Street, Surry Hills;
tel: 9361 5257; map p.137 E3
Intimate venue for rock, hard
blues and ska.

Metro Theatre
624 George Street; tel: 9550
3666; www.metrotheatre.
com.au; train: Town Hall, bus:
George Street; map p.133 C1
International and local acts at
the city's main rock venue.

Sandringham Hotel
387 King Street, Newtown; tel:
9557 1254; train: Newtown, bus:
King Street
DJs nightly and live music
upstairs three nights a week.
Stand-up comedy on Monday.

Sound Lounge
Seymour Centre, Cleveland
Street, Chippendale; tel: 9351
7940; opening Tue–Sat eve; bus:
352; map p.136 B2
Located downstairs at the
Seymour Centre, it hosts a
weekend world music venue.

The Vanguard
42 King Street, Newtown; tel:
9557 7992; www.thevanguard.
com.au; Tue–Sat evening; bus:
King Street; map p.136 A2
Great venue for local and
international acts of all kinds.

Sydney's Town Hall is home to
a 19th-century Romantic organ
that is considered to be the
finest in the world. Shipped
over from England and installed
in 1890, it is still used for
regular concerts. Check
newspapers for details.

Jazz

The Basement
29 Reiby Place, Circular Quay;
tel: 9251 2797; train, bus, ferry:
Circular Quay; map p.139 D2
One of Sydney's best jazz
venues hosts a mix of international and local acts.

Wine Banq
Basement, 53 Martin Place; tel:
9222 1919; daily noon–3pm,
5pm–late; train: Martin Place;

map p.139 E1
Sophisticated wine bar has
live jazz at weekends.
SEE ALSO BARS, P.31

Woollahra Hotel
Corner Queen and Moncur
streets, Woollahra; tel: 9363
2782; www.woollahrahotel.com.
au; bus: 389; map p.138 C3
Classy jazz (Sun from
6.30pm) and world music
(Thur from 7.45).

Rock and Pop

Annandale Hotel
17 Parramatta Road, Annandale;
tel: 9550 1078; www.annandale
hotel.com; nightly; bus: 413,
435–3, 440, 461, 480, 483
The place for indie rock fans.

Cat & Fiddle Hotel
456 Darling Street, Balmain; tel:

Left: rocking at the Anandale Hotel.

Nightlife

If the top DJ acts at one of the big dance clubs do not take your fancy, you are not just limited to a dinner-and-drinks evening. You can choose between comedy clubs, open-air cinemas, bars with bands, or the huge Star City, the only casino in New South Wales. For the most comprehensive guide to what's on in Sydney, buy the *Sydney Morning Herald* on Friday for its lift-out *Metro* section. The paper's website (www.sydney.citysearch.com.au) also has extensive culture and entertainment listings. The free mags *Drum Media* and *3D World*, available in shops and bars, also list upcoming club nights and concerts.

Comedy

The Laugh Garage

Corner Church and Phillip streets, Parramatta; tel: 8883 1111; www.thelaughgarage.com; Fri, Sat 9pm (doors 8pm); bus: 412

If you are looking for hardcore, down and dirty comedy, this is the place for you. The ruthless New York-style comics will rip into every PC ethic known to man, and then go on to you. Definitely not a night out for the kids.

Sydney Comedy Store

The Entertainment Quarter, 207/122 Lang Road, Moore Park; tel: 9357 1419; www.comedystore.com.au; Tue–Sat 8.30pm (doors 8.15pm); bus: 355; map p.138 A1/B2

As well as helping to establish some of the country's top comics, this venue also hosts international acts, including the likes of Robin Williams. Ask about their dinner deals.

Fringe Bar

Unicorn Hotel, 106 Oxford Street, Paddington; tel: 9360 5443; www.thefringe.com.au; Mon evening; bus: Oxford Street; map p.138 A4

A recent refurb has transformed this bar into one of the more popular drinking establishments on Oxford Street. The regular Monday comedy night can happily compete with what else is on offer in town, and their comedy and dinner deal (pre-book only) is an absolute bargain. Get there early to sit close to the stage.
SEE ALSO BARS P.35

Gambling

Star City Casino

Pyrmont Wharf; tel: 9777 9000 or 1 800 700 700 (toll-free); www.starcity.com.au; 24 hours; metro: casino, bus: 443, 449 ferry: Pyrmont Bay Wharf; map p.132 B2

Taking up an enormous amount of space in Darling Harbour, Sydney's only legal venue for gambling offers much more than just poker and roulette. There are

For more suggestions on what to do after dark, *see Bars, p.30; Cafes, p.42; Film, p.60; Music and Dance, p.88; Restaurants, p.98 and Theatre, p.124.*

shops, cafés, bars, live shows, and a 352-room hotel. One of the recent additions is the stage show of the popular movie *The Adventures of Priscilla, Queen of the Desert*.

Outdoor Cinemas

St George Open Air Cinema

Botanical Garden at Mrs Macquarie's Chair; www.stgeorgeopenair.com.au; nightly Jan–Feb; map p.133 E4

With a mix of new, old and premiere screenings, there is no better way to see a summer movie in Sydney. The season only lasts for a month, and tickets go on sale at 9.30am on Boxing Day, so get in quick! This event is popular and the view of the bridge and Opera House behind the screen is worth the ticket price on its own.

Moonlight Cinema

Centennial Park, Oxford Street entrances; www.moonlight.com.au; nightly Dec–Mar, gates 6.30pm; bus: Oxford Street; map p.138 B2/C2

A popular way to get the most out of the summer

Left: a girls' night out.

nights; there is no seating here so invest in one of the beanbags or take a rug. Then simply set up a picnic, open a bottle of wine and relax until the movie starts at sunset. Pre-booking is still advised, but luckily these screenings continue from Dec–Mar.

Clubs

Spectrum
34 Oxford Street, Darlinghurst; tel: 9360 1375; www. pashpresents.com; nightly; bus: Oxford Street; map p.138 B3
Famous for its Indie nights and live bands, this is a rare departure from Sydney's typical dance scene.

Tank
3 Bridge Lane (off George Street), CBD; tel: 9240 3007; www.tankclub.com.au; Fri, Sat 10pm–6am; train, bus, ferry: Circular Quay; map p.139 D2
Tank is one of very few clubs in the CBD and despite the endless queue that tails around the block at weekends, is a popular choice among the young trendy dance set in Sydney.

Right: Oxford Street at night.

Ruby Rabbit and De Nom
231 Oxford Street, Darlinghurst; tel: 9326 0044; www.rubyrabbit. com.au; De Nom Tue–Sun, Ruby Rabbit Thu–Sat 10pm–late; bus: Oxford Street; map p.137 E4
Check the mirror before you leave on your way to either of these venues (housed in the same building) because if you are not beautiful enough you will not get past the bouncers. De Nom is the newest elite club in Sydney (and Australia) and an annual $10,000 membership ensures you a limo pick-up. Ruby Rabbit is slightly less exclusive, but someone forgot to tell the door staff.
SEE ALSO BARS P.34

Home
Cockle Bay Wharf, Darling Harbour; tel: 9266 0600; www.homesydney.com; nightly 11pm–late; metro: Darling; map p.132 C1
The biggest club in Sydney, this venue hosts some of the world's best DJs and has a good mix of music types weekly. No matter how packed, because of the size of the club there is always somewhere to sit and take a time out from the dance floor.

Moulin Rouge
39 Darlinghurst Road, Kings Cross; tel: 8354 1711; nightly 8pm–late; train: Kings Cross, bus: Oxford Street; map p.133 E1
Tucked in the heart of the red light district, this cavernous little club hosts mostly heavy dance DJs and attracts an after-hours clubber who just will not go home.

34b Burlesque
34b Oxford Street, Darlinghurst; nightly; bus: Oxford Street; map p.138 B3
An offbeat venue which includes an old fashioned black-and-white photo booth and pool tables, 34b also hosts regular burlesque nights. A great excuse to dress up and express your cheeky side.

Pampering

Where better to indulge yourself than in the city that is regarded by other Australians as the most 'polished' (ie self-absorbed) in the country? For many female Sydneysiders, a weekly massage, facial or nail treatment is as high on their list of priorities as paying their store-card bills. A few hours in a luxury spa is not just something that is indulged in only on holiday, which means there is lots of choice in the city, from the exclusive and expensive to more affordable options. Spas are also starting to cash in on the metrosexual trend and there are often tailored treatments for men.

Spas

As well as the dedicated spas listed here, you will find many walk-in clinics and massage centres in shopping malls and shopping streets such as Oxford Street. But if you are looking for something a bit special it is worth seeking out a specialist and booking ahead.

Ginseng Bathhouse
Crest Hotel, 111 Darlinghurst Road; tel: 9356 6680; www.ginsengbathhouse.com.au; Mon–Fri 9.30am–9.30pm, Sat and Sun 9am–9.30pm; train: Kings Cross, bus: 311; map p.133 E1
Although you can have private treatments at this hotel-housed spa, their pièce de résistance is the more traditional share room. Not for the shy, it is a rule that from the moment you walk out of the dressing room, where you are given your own locker, you remain naked, both in and out of the different temperature pools and when you are having one of the most vigorous massages you will ever get. A favourite among hen parties,

you will come out laughing and with fewer inhibitions than when you went in.

Spa Chakra
6 Cowper Wharf Road, Woolloomooloo; tel: 9368 0888; www.chakra.net; Mon–Sat 9am–9pm, Sun 10am–6pm; bus: 311; map p.133 E2
Tucked away on the exclusive Woolloomooloo Wharf, behind the plush Blue hotel, this is the definition of what a spa should be if you are looking for classic luxury. Do not be put off by the almost clinical reception: the treatment rooms are much more relaxed, and the range of services, although expensive, are carried out by highly qualified, international staff. A word of warning: they have both male and female masseurs, so if you have a preference, make sure you say when booking.
SEE ALSO HOTELS P.73

Zen Day Spa
116–118 Darlinghurst Road; tel: 9361 4200; www. zendayspa.com.au; Mon–Fri 9am–9pm, Sat 8am–8pm, Sun 10am–7pm; train: Kings Cross, bus: 311; map p.133 E1

Well known for its waxing treatments – often hailed as the best in town – Zen asks you to turn off your mobile and talk quietly so as not to disturb patrons looking for a relaxing bolthole in the middle of the busy city. As well as the traditional massage and facial treatments, Zen also offers acupuncture and Chinese herbal medicine consultations.

Beauty Treatments and Cosmetics

Ella Baché
www.ellabache.com.au
City-wide, this well-known and well-respected chain of beauty salons is very much a middle-market option. They are not a place to linger: your treatments will be performed quickly and well, but do not expect any of the herbal tea and candlelit luxury you will get at pricier spas. Ideal if you need a quick treatment, as they will often have room to take walk-ins, especially if you go midweek. They also stock their own range of skin care products and provide tanning services.

Left: doing lengths in luxury.

this. Think feather boas, burlesque nights and chandeliers. The treatment rooms are ornate and beautifully decorated, but the staff are open, friendly and very down to earth, so there is no need to feel that you have to go dressed in your best. Not cheap, but worth every cent. You will come out feeling like royalty.

Perfect Potion
Shop 62, lower ground level, Queen Victoria Building, CBD; tel: 1800 988 999; www. perfectpotion.com.au; Mon–Sat 9am–6pm (Thur until 9pm), Sun 11am–5pm; train: Town Hall, bus: George Street; map p.133 C1
With inexpensive treatments and a lovely atmosphere, this sweet-smelling spot is best known for its own range of products, also stocked in David Jones. With a dedication to natural ingredients, it is a favourite for those looking for a totally organic skin-care experience. There is also a branch at the airport, where you can treat yourself to a pre-flight pamper.

Kit
140 Oxford Street, Paddington; tel: 9360 7711; www. kitcosmetics.com.au; Mon–Sat 10am–6pm (Thur until 9pm), Sun 11am–5pm; bus: Oxford Street; map p.138 A3
Like Mecca (see below) in that it stocks the most popular, high-performing products from around the globe, this young brand is for the highly-polished girl who wants to look low-maintenance. The in-store atmosphere is so relaxed you will be best friends with the salesgirls by the time you leave. It might cost a month's wages, but you will be feeling 100 per cent more beautiful.

Mecca Cosmetica
126 Oxford Street, Paddington; tel: 1800 007 844; www. meccacosmetica.com.au; Mon–Sat 10am–6pm (Thur until 8pm), Sun 11am–5pm; bus: Oxford Street; map p.137 E4
Ten years ago Mecca was a new breed of boutique skin care. Stocking only the best international ranges, they also offer skin consultations for individuals and in-store events hosted by worldwide

make-up artists and skin care specialists. The stores have a sparse, open-plan layout, so you get the opportunity to touch, smell and sample all the products before you buy.

Miss Frou Frou Beauty Parlour
10 William Street, Paddington; tel: 9357 6063; bus: Oxford Street; map p.138 B3
You will not find another beauty parlour that is more indicative of Sydney style-conscious residents than

Below: hot stone treatments are very popular and help to relieve stress and increase circlation.

Parks and Gardens

D on't worry about keeping off the grass. Sydney's parks are egalitarian playgrounds where picnics on the lawn are encouraged. They range from vast parklands such as Centennial Park to smaller harbourside pockets such as the charming Nielsen Park. As a general rule, Sydney's parks are open during daylight hours, and rarely charge an entrance fee. If you have time, a visit to one of the many national parks surrounding Sydney is recommended, for a glimpse of the real Australian bush.

City Parks

Blues Point Reserve
Blues Point Road, McMahons Point; 24 hours; bus: 269, ferry McMahons Point; map p.24
A great spot for a harbourside picnic, with a superb view of the Harbour Bridge.

Centennial Parklands
tel: 9339 6699; www.cp.nsw.gov.au; daily summer: 6am–8am, winter: 6am–6pm; bus: Oxford Street, Moore Park; map p.138
Three major parks in the city's east give the area green lungs. The most visitor-friendly is Centennial Park, created to mark Australia's centenary in 1888. It has over 200 rolling hectares of lawns, trees, bridle paths and duck ponds. Feed the ducks and eels in the ponds, hire a horse or bike, and eat in style at the park's restaurant.

Chinese Garden of Friendship
Corner Pier and Harbour streets, Darling Harbour; tel: 9281 6863; www.darlingharbour.com.au; daily 9.30am–5pm; entrance charge; metro: Haymarket; map p.137 C4

Built in 1988 as a bicentennial gift by the government of China's Guangdong Province, this walled garden offers a peaceful refuge in the CBD, with its lakes covered with lotus flowers, waterfalls and perfect Chinese landscaping.

Hyde Park
Elizabeth Street; 24 hours; train: St James or Museum; map p.133 D1/D2
Created in 1810, this green oasis in the heart of the city contains a number of interesting monuments, including the art deco Anzac War Memorial, built in 1934, and the Archibald Fountain (see p.6). At the northern curve of the park are the carefully preserved Hyde Park Barracks. On its eastern edge is the country's oldest museum, the Australian Museum.
SEE ALSO MUSEUMS AND GALLERIES P.81–2, 84

Nielsen Park
Greycliffe Avenue, Vaucluse; 24 hours; bus: 325; map p.20
This perfect little harbour cove, fronted by a sandy beach and flanked by bush-

Below: Blues Point Reserve, on the north side of the harbour.

Left: the Chinese landscaping of the Garden of Friendship.

colony's first farm, established by Governor Phillip in 1788 at Farm Cove. Highlights include the Herbarium (containing about one million specimens, including some of those collected in 1770 by Captain Cook's botanist, Joseph Banks); Palm Grove, which has over 140 types of palm; and the Tropical Centre (entrance charge), a complex contained in two glasshouses, shaped as a pyramid and an arc. The pyramid holds Australian tropical plants, including living specimens from the monsoonal woodlands of the tropical north, and the arc provides a botanic tour through lowland rainforests and high-altitude tropical zones from around the world.

The Botanic Gardens is also home to a wide array of native Australian wildlife, including white cockatoos, blue wrens, tawny frogmouths, brush-tailed possums and fruit bats, to name but a few. A 'trackless train' runs through the gardens on regular guided tours, leaving from the entrance near the Opera House.

clad cliffs on either side, is a favourite with locals. Stretches of national park lie on either side of the beach, and a magnificent foreshore walk winds back towards Rose Bay.

SEE WALKS AND VIEWS, P.129–30

Parramatta Park
Corner Pitt and Macquarie streets, Parramatta; tel: 8833 5000; daily summer: 6am–8pm, winter: 6am–6pm; train: Westmead
Home to Old Government House, the oldest public building in Australia, as well as the shell of the river-fed Governor's Bath House, erected by Governor Bris-

bane in 1823, and the ruined Observatory, completed in 1822.

SEE ALSO MUSEUMS AND GALLERIES P.83

Royal Botanic Gardens
Mrs Macquarie's Road, Sydney; tel: 9231 8111; www.rbgsyd. nsw.gov.au; daily Nov–Feb: 7am–8pm, Mar and Oct: 7am–6.30pm, Apr and Sept: 7am–6pm, May and Aug: 7am–5.30pm, Jun and Jul: 7am–5pm; train, bus and ferry: Circular Quay; map p.133 E3
Thirty hectares of green space on the site of the

If you're visiting the Olympic Stadium, take a wander through the nearby **Bicentennial Park** (Showground Road, Homebush Bay; tel: 9714 7888; www.sydneyolympicpark. com.au). There are 60 hectares of parkland covered by walking and cycling tracks, playgrounds and picnic areas, as well as 40 hectares of conservation wetlands. Tours can be arranged through the Visitor Centre.

Below: the Royal Botanic Gardens, a place of natural beauty.

Right: a lizard at Garigal National Park.

National Parks

More details on all NSW national parks can be found at the website www.national-parks.nsw.gov.au

Botany Bay National Park
Captain Cook Drive, Kurnell; tel: 9668 9111; and Anzac Parade, La Perouse; tel: 9311 3379; entrance charge for cars; Kurnell daily summer: 8am–8pm, winter: 8am–6pm; La Perouse daily summer: 8am–8.30pm, winter: 8am–7.30pm; bus: 987, 394; map p.22

This 324-hectare national park stretches along both sides of the bay where Captain Cook landed in 1770 and made the first European contact with the Aboriginal people. It is also where the French explorer Jean François de Galaup, Comte de La Pérouse *(see p.82)*, arrived within a week of the British First Fleet in 1788.

Beneath the park's gouged sandstone cliffs, there are rich marine environments. Above them, you will find remnants of the heathland plants that were studied by Banks and Solander, Cook's botanists. The Banks-Solander Track provides fascinating insights into this once-widespread vegetation, while the Cape Baily Coast Walk offers windswept heaths, historic sites and spectacular coastal views.

Garigal National Park
End of Ferguson Street (off Warringah Road), Forestville NSW; tel: 9451 3479; daily summer: 6am–8pm, winter: 6am–6.30pm; entrance charge for cars

Only 12km north of Sydney's CBD is the 22sq. km Garigal National Park, an impressive expanse of bush and sandstone country with great water views. Davidson picnic area on Middle Harbour is a popular spot for boating and fishing and has accessible toilet facilities. Bushwalkers can enjoy the scenery from an extensive walking track system. Camping is not permitted in the park.

Ku-ring-gai Chase National Park
Bobbin Head Road, Mount Colah, NSW; tel: 9472 9300; daily summer: 6am–8pm, winter: 6am–6pm; entrance charge for cars; train: Berowra, Cowan, bus: 185, 190

Ku-ring-gai, 30km north of the city, is where the Hawkesbury meets the sea. Named after the area's Aboriginal inhabitants, the Guringai, Australia's second national park was dedicated in 1894 with the aim of preserving a sample of Sydney's original landscape.

The park's 147sq. km contains some the prettiest

Although the state's national parks are home to a large range of wildlife, shy native mammals can be difficult to spot. Birdwatchers will have better luck: sightings may include iridescent rosellas, shrieking sulphur-crested cockatoos, glossy satin bower birds and whip birds (whose call sounds like the crack of a stockwhip).

scenery in Sydney, including heathlands, dense forests, mangroves, hidden coves and trickling creeks. Highlights include the stunning views across Lion Island from West Head lookout, the tranquil waters of the Basin (catch the Palm Beach ferry) and the Aboriginal carvings, best seen on the Red Hand Trail, the Ekidna Track and especially the Basin Track.

Road access into the park is from the Pacific Highway to Bobbin Head or from Mona Vale Road. Other entry points are off Mona Vale Road at Terrey Hills into Cottage Point, Akuna Bay and West Head or along the shoreline from Church Point. The Kalkari Visitors' Centre, off Ku-ring-gai Chase Road has maps and advice for those wanting to head out along one of the many walking tracks in the area.

Lane Cove National Park
Lady Game Drive, Chatswood NSW; tel: 9412 1811; daily summer: 9am–7pm, winter: 9am–6pm; entrance charge for cars; bus: 292, 545 from Chatswood railway station

The picturesque Lane Cove River winds through a peaceful bushland valley within easy reach of the city centre, extending from East Ryde to Wahroonga/ Pennant Hills.

The river is the focus of most activities, and you can visit the Kukundi Wildlife Shelter, take a stroll along the bank, or hire a rowing boat. Swimming is not advisable, however. There are dozens of picnic spots and you can stay overnight in cabins or powered/unpowered camping sites at the nearby caravan park.

Royal National Park
Audley NSW (main entry points along the Princes Highway); tel: 9542 0648; daily 8am–8.30pm; train: Royal National Park or others (see below), ferry: Bundeena (from Cronulla)
This 16,000-hectare national park in Sydney's south is the second oldest national park in the world after Yellowstone in the USA. As the original plans called for a pleasure ground for city-dwellers, to be modelled after London's Hampstead Heath, native Australian bush was cleared to be replaced by more 'attractive' imported plants and manicured lawns. Despite those early depredations, it remains an area of sweeping beauty, with heath-covered sandstone plateaux punctuated by forest-filled valleys that range from rainforest to woodlands.

Park highlights include Lady Carrington Drive, a walking and cycling track that passes through dense forests along the Hacking River; the causeway, picnic area and row boats for hire at Audley; and the 26-km Coastal Track, taking in beaches such as Wattamolla. Just below the southern border of the park, the foreshore road leading down to Wollongong has some of the best coastal views in Australia.

The park is accessible by train, ferry or road. The ferry service runs between Cronulla Wharf, directly behind Cronulla railway station, and Bundeena, a small coastal village completely surrounded by the park. You can also enter the park by train. Royal National Park Station lies near the park headquarters on Farnell Avenue at Audley. There are also walking trails that stretch from the railway stations at Engadine, Heathcote, Otford, Loftus and Waterfall.

Sydney Harbour National Park
Tel: 9247 5033; daily
The Sydney Harbour National Park covers the various scattered reserves and islands that fringe the harbour shore. It is truly remarkable that this collection of sandstone cliffs, rocky coves and crescent-shaped beaches, open woodland and pockets of rainforest still exists in the heart of a major city, and its survival is due mostly to the fact that the military traditionally held large areas of the foreshore. When the army finally abandoned the area, Sydneysiders refused to relinquish their bush-clad harbour to modern development.

In the city's east, the park covers sections of Vaucluse and Watsons Bay, as well as five harbour islands: Fort Denison, Goat, Shark, Clark and Rodd. Goat Island and Fort Denison can only be visited on a tour. To visit Shark, Clark or Rodd islands, you will need to book and pay landing fees beforehand.

On the north side of the harbour, the park covers the verdant foreshore of Kurraba and Cremorne Points and Bradley's Head, much of which is covered by a spectacular scenic walk. Much of the foreshore between the Spit Bridge and Manly is also included, as is North Head.

Below: Royal National Park includes a 26-km coastal walk.

Restaurants

In range, quality and value, Sydney offers some of the best dining in the world. Successive waves of immigrants have introduced many different national styles of cooking, putting to good use the incredible diversity and quality of Australia's natural produce, particularly seafood. Although Sydney likes to pride itself on its sophistication – and certainly the city has a variety of excellent 'exclusive' dining options – good food at cheap prices is relatively easy to find. Add to this the unrivalled settings and views that the harbour and beaches offer, and you have a combination that is hard to beat.

Central Business District

MODERN AUSTRALIAN

Est
Establishment, 252 George Street; tel: 9240 3010; Mon–Fri L, Mon–Sat D; $$$; train: Martin Place, Wynyard, bus: George Street; map p.139 D2
Chef Peter Doyle's elegant food, showcasing the best local produce, is perfectly matched by the sophisticated decor of this stylish dining room.

Forty One
Chifley Tower, Chifley Square; tel: 9221 2500; Tue–Fri L,

Below: fine wines and fine dining at Est.

Mon–Sat D; $$$$; train: Martin Place; map p.139 E2
Confusingly located on level 42 of one of Sydney's tallest towers, this restaurant offers serious food and serious views for those with serious money.

The Summit
Level 47, Australia Square, 264 George Street; tel: 9247 9777; Sun–Fri L, Mon–Fri D; $$$; train: Wynyard, bus: George Street; map p.139 D2
Revolving restaurants are not traditionally associated with good food or stylish decor, but this little beauty, which gives a stylistic nod to Stanley Kubrick, has both.

Tetsuya's
529 Kent Street; tel: 9267 2900; Tue–Sat D; Sat L; $$$; train: Town Hall; map p.133 C1
Tetsuya Wakada is not just one of Australia's top chefs, but one of the top chefs in the world. His degustation menu is an essential Sydney experience for foodies. Reservations essential.

EUROPEAN

Capitan Torres
73 Liverpool Street; tel: 9264

5574; daily L and D; $$; train: Town Hall; map p.133 C1
Seafood is a speciality of this long-established Spanish restaurant in the heart of Sydney's Spanish strip.

Encasa
423 Pitt Street; tel: 9211 4257; daily L and D; $; metro: Capital Square; map p.137 D4
Encasa has great tapas if you are in a hurry, and wonderful paella if you are not (there is a 45-minute wait).

FRENCH

Becasse
204 Clarence Street; tel: 9283 3440; Tue–Fri L, Tue–Sat D; $$$; train: Town Hall; map p.133 C1
Exquisite French cuisine makes this one of Sydney's most acclaimed restaurants.

GREEK

Omega
161 King Street; tel: 9223 0242; Mon–Fri L, Mon–Sat D; $$$; train: Martin Place; map p.139 E1
Melbourne may have more Greek eateries per square kilometre, but Sydney has Omega, the latest high-end eatery from celebrated chef

Left: Sydney's restaurants make the most of local ingredients and maintain a casual atmosphere even in the most chic surroundings.

Price indications are for a three-course meal for one, including half a bottle of house wine, coffee and service:
$ = under A$50
$$ = A$50–75
$$$ = A$75–115
$$$$ = over A$115

Peter Conistis. Every dish on the modern Greek menu is a classic, from anchovy baklava to the legendary rabbit and black olive pie.

The Rocks

MODERN AUSTRALIAN
Cruise
Overseas Passenger Terminal, Circular Quay West; tel: 9251 1188; Mon–Fri L, Mon–Sat D; $$$; train, bus, ferry: Circular Quay; map p.139 D3
Soak up the magnificent harbour views through the full-length windows, or watch the seven chefs in the open kitchen whip up signature dishes such as the rabbit terrine and the superlative seafoods.
MCA Café
140 George Street; tel: 9241 4253; daily L; $$; train, bus, ferry: Circular Quay; map p.139 D3
Do not be fooled by the name: this is definitely a restaurant, with proper tablecloths and an upmarket menu. With ringside seats to the ever-changing panorama of Circular Quay, it is the perfect place to spend your afternoon.

Quay
Overseas Passenger Terminal, Circular Quay West; tel: 9251 5600; Tue–Fri L, daily D; $$$; train, bus, ferry: Circular Quay; map p.139 D3
It is one thing to have the best location in town; it is another to create food that almost exceeds the setting. One of Sydney's landmark restaurants, where head chef Peter Gilmore creates an exotic menu that ranges from suckling pig belly to silken tofu. Lunch menu is for two to three courses, while dinner is chosen from a four course, à la carte menu.

Rockpool
107 George Street; tel: 9252 1888; Tue–Sat D; $$$; train, bus, ferry: Circular Quay; map p.139 D3
Neil Perry was one of Australia's first star chefs. Other restaurants have come and gone, but after almost 20 years, this flagship restaurant keeps on keeping on. Its tasting menu, with up to 12 courses, is a popular way to sample the wide variety of seafood available.
The Wharf
Pier 4, Hickson Road, Walsh Bay; tel: 9250 1761; Mon–Sat L and D; $$; map p.139 C4
Is there a better place for a pre-theatre meal than this? The old wooden wharf is atmospheric, the harbour view is exquisite, and the food's not bad either. And it

Below: the award-winning Rockpool at The Rocks.

Left: Wildfire on West Circular Quay.

Perhaps the only place in town where you can eat quality Italian food in surroundings reminiscent of an Outback shearing shed. The wine list is extensive and exotic.

SOUTHEAST ASIAN
Sailor's Thai
106 George Street, The Rocks; tel: 9251 2466; Mon–Fri L, Mon–Sat D; $–$$; train, bus, ferry: Circular Quay; map p.139 D3

Two restaurants in one: the more expensive downstairs dining, and the casual canteen upstairs. The food is exquisite in both.

Opera House and The Domain
MODERN AUSTRALIAN
Aria
1 Macquarie Street, East Circular Quay; tel: 9252 2555; Mon–Fri L, daily D; $$$; train, bus, ferry: Circular Quay; map p.139 E3

A dress-circle setting near the Opera House, sleek decor, a knock-out wine list, and a seasonal menu that never fails to impress. Fine dining for grown-ups.

is only a few steps to your theatre seats, too.
Wildfire
Overseas Passenger Terminal, West Circular Quay; tel: 8273 1222; Mon–Fri L, Mon–Sun L and D; $$$; train, bus, ferry: Circular Quay; map p.139 D3

Wildfire is over-the-top in all the good ways, from the giant chandeliers and the wine wall to the dizzying range of menu options. These include sensational seafood, wood-fired meats, steak and thin-crust pizza.

ITALIAN
Bel Mondo
Gloucester Walk, The Rocks; tel: 9241 3700; Mon–Sat D; $$; train, bus, ferry: Circular Quay; map p.139 D3

Price indications are for a three-course meal for one, including half a bottle of house wine, coffee and service:
$ = under A$50
$$ = A$50–75
$$$ = A$75–115
$$$$ = over A$115

FRENCH
Guillaume at Bennelong
Sydney Opera House, Bennelong Point; tel: 9241 1999; Mon–Sat D, Thur–Fri L; $$$; train, bus, ferry: Circular Quay; map p.139 E4

Plenty of restaurants have a harbour view, but if you want a gourmet experience inside the Opera House, there is only one place to go. The superb food lives up to the stunning setting.
SEE ALSO BARS P.33

INDIAN
Aki's
Shop 1, The Wharf, 6 Cowper Wharf Road, Woolloomooloo; tel: 9332 4600; daily L and D; $$; bus: 311; map p.133 E2

If you have a hankering for tandoori lamb and butter chicken, this is not the place to come. However, if you are after something completely different, treats such as whole braised aubergine with peanuts and cashews will hit the spot.

Below: octopus at Bel Mondo and the best in Asian cuisine.

ITALIAN
Manta
6 Cowper Wharf Road, Woolloomooloo; tel: 9332 3822; daily
L and D; $$$; bus: 311; map
p.133 E2
Sensational seafood served
with Mediterranean flavours
and that lovely view. Where
Manta stands out is that
there is enough distance
between tables to offer you a
bit of privacy.
Otto Ristorante
6 Cowper Wharf Road, Wool-
loomooloo; tel: 9368 7488; daily
L and D; $$$; bus: 311; map
p.133 E2

Above: the Asian Food Halls.

Still a favoured haunt of Sydney powerbrokers, this is Italian comfort food elevated to
a fine art. From pea soup to
duck livers, all nonna's
favourites are here.

SOUTHEAST ASIAN
China Doll
6 Cowper Wharf Road, Woolloomooloo; tel: 9380 6744; daily
L and D; $$$; bus: 311; map
p.133 E2
You will pay serious prices
for this seriously good Viet-
namese food, from tea-
smoked ocean trout with
green herb salad to twice
cooked duck with plum and
tamarind sauce.

Darling Harbour
and Chinatown
MODERN AUSTRALIAN
Flying Fish
Jones Bay Wharf, 19–21
Pirrama Road, Pyrmont; tel:
9518 6677; Tue–Fri and Sun L,
Tue–Sun D; $$$; metro:
casino, bus 443, 449; map
p.132 B3
A converted timber wharf
offering divine seafood, not
to mention some of the best
hand-cut chips in town.
Sugaroom
Shop 2, 1 Harris Street, Pyrmont; tel: 9571 5055; Tue–Sat L,
Mon–Sat D; $$; metro: John

Street Square, bus: 443, 449;
map p.132 A2
Pyrmont is the latest har-
bourside area to be devel-
oped, and perhaps the one
place where you can still
enjoy harbour views without
a hefty price tag.

EAST ASIAN
Asian Food Halls
Dixon Street, Haymarket; daily L
and D; $; metro: Haymarket
Captal Square; map p.137 C4
Whether they are office work-
ers on a lunch break or uni
students here for dinner, bar-
gain hunters of all kinds head
here for cheap and filling
meals. A variety of stalls
serve Chinese, Malaysian,
Vietnamese, Indonesian and
Japanese dishes, either pre-
prepared or cooked in front
of you. Expect to pay around
$20 for two courses, with rice
and vegetables.
BBQ King
18–20 Goulburn Street, Haymar-
ket; tel: 9267 2586; daily L and
D; $$; metro: Capital Square;
map p.137 D4
The decor is basic but the
food is authentic, the servings are big, and it is open
until 2am. No wonder it has
become a Sydney classic.
Peking duck and Chinese
barbecue pork are house
specialties.

Dragon Star Seafood
Level 3, Market City, 9 Hay
Street, Haymarket; tel: 9211
8988; daily L and D; $$; metro:
Haymarket; map p.137 C4
Sydney's biggest Chinese
restaurant and yum cha
(dumplings) venue. Go for
brunch on Sunday and
watch the waiters communi-
cate by walkie-talkie as
they serve some 800 patrons
with a traditional Chinese
breakfast.
East Ocean
Level 1, 421–429 Sussex Street,
Chinatown; tel: 9212 4198; daily
L and D; $$; metro: Capital
Square; map p.137 D4
Great yum cha and meat
dishes. In the evening, insist
on sitting in the front room:
the back room is karaoke
central.
Golden Century Seafood
Restaurant
393–399 Sussex Street, Haymarket; tel: 9212 3901; daily L
and D; $$; metro: Capital
Square; map p.137 C4/D4
Chinese-style seafood at its
best, with all the hustle and
bustle of Hong Kong. Kitchen
stays open until 4am.
Kam Fook
Level 3, Market City, 9 Hay
Street, Haymarket; tel: 9211
8988; daily L, Thur–Sun D;
$$; metro: Haymarket; map
p.137 C4

101

Above: service (and preperation) with a smile.

Sydney's biggest *yum cha* venue. Go for brunch on Sunday and watch the waiter-and-trolley spectacle that is the traditional Chinese breakfast for 800 people.

INDIAN
Zaaffran
Shop 345, Level 2, Harbourside Shopping Centre, Darling Harbour; tel: 9211 8900; daily L and D; $$; metro: Convention,

Price indications are for a three-course meal for one, including half a bottle of house wine, coffee and service:
$ = under A$50
$$ = A$50–75
$$$ = A$75–115
$$$$ = over A$115

Pyrmont; map p.132 B1
Not your average Indian. This upmarket restaurant takes traditional Indian cusine to the next level. The biryani is magnificent.

ITALIAN
Coast
Cockle Bay Wharf, 201 Sussex Street; tel: 9267 6700; Mon–Fri L, Mon–Sat D; $$$; bus: 441, 442; map p.132 C1
Delicious seafood with lovely views over Cockle Bay.

SOUTHEAST ASIAN
Chinta Ria
Temple of Love
Roof Terrace, Level 2, Cockle Bay Wharf; tel: 9264 3211; daily L and D; $$; train, bus: Wynyard, 10-minute walk,

monorail: Darling Park; map p.132 C1
The cheery Buddha, the pagoda-like roof, and the pleasant deck area would be enough to make this an after-work favourite. The excellent menu (think fish cooked in tamarind sauce with tomatoes and pineapple) is a bonus.
The Malaya
King Street Wharf, 39 Lime Street; tel: 9279 1170; daily L and D; $$; ferry: Darling Harbour; map p.132 C2
The location is new, but the restaurant has been around for ever. Regulars just can't get enough of the Singapore noodles and the famous laksa.

Kings Cross District

MODERN AUSTRALIAN
Bayswater Brasserie
32 Bayswater Road, Kings Cross; tel: 9357 2177; Mon–Sat D; $$; train: Kings Cross; map p.134 A1
In the heady 1980s, the Bayswater specialised in lunches that kicked on into the next morning. These days, it is still a great brasserie, with a bar in the back, a pleasant garden, and a conservatory in the front.
Bill's
433 Liverpool Street, Darlinghurst; tel: 9360 9631; daily B, L and D; $$; map p.138 A4
While owner Bill Granger works the international celebrity chef circuit, his sunny corner café-restaurant still serves up perfect pastas and plated dishes. The real attraction here, however, is breakfast. The ricotta hot-cakes are a winner.
Yellow Bistro
57 Macleay Street, Potts Point; tel: 9357 3400; daily L, Tue–Sat D; $$; bus: 311; map p.134 A2
Classic bistro food in an elegant dining room that shares the premises with a food

store, which means you can pick up tomorrow's dinner while you are there.

EAST ASIAN
Fu Manchu
249 Victoria Street, Darlinghurst; tel: 9360 9424; daily D; $$; train: Kings Cross, bus: Oxford Street; map p.138 A4

Not the place to loiter – the stools are not that comfortable – but this old faithful diner offers tempting Chinese treats, from Spanish mackerel dumplings to sensational chilli cuttlefish.

EUROPEAN
Balkan Seafood
215 Oxford Street, Darlinghurst; tel: 9331 7670; Tue–Sun D; $$; bus: Oxford Street; map p.137 E4

Most of the delicacies grilling in the window are from the sea, but there are also meat specialities like *pola pola* at this long-standing Sydney favourite.

Onde
346 Liverpool Street, Darlinghurst; tel: 9331 8749; daily D; $$; map p.138 A4

Trattoria-style bistro with a casual atmosphere and some of the best-value meals around. Favourites include duck confit with apple and garlic-studded pork sausages.

Una's
338–340 Victoria Street, Darlinghurst; tel: 9360 6885; daily L and D; $; train: Kings Cross, bus: Oxford Street

An old, economical Kings Cross favourite serving hearty portions of German and Austrian food from breakfast to supper. Another outlet has recently opened in Double Bay.

FRENCH
Café Sel et Poivre
263 Victoria Street, Darlinghurst; tel: 9361 6530; daily B, L and D; $$; train: Kings Cross, bus: 311; map p.138 A4

Good-value and authentic French cuisine, served with gusto. The cosy interior recalls a typical Parisian café and there is a good selection of French wines.

INDIAN
Oh, Calcutta!
251 Victoria Street, Darlinghurst; tel: 9360 3650; Mon–Sat D; $$; train: Kings Cross; map p.138 A4

Despite having two storeys, this award-winning contemporary Indian restaurant is often packed, which tells you something about the delicious food. The innovative menu changes frequently.

Below: a colourful Kings Cross menu

ITALIAN
Bill and Toni
74 Stanley Street, East Sydney; tel: 9360 4702; daily B, L and D; $; train: Museum Station; map p.133 D1

For good-value, no-frills Italian, this cheap and cheerful neighbourhood favourite is the place to go. It serves a range of pasta and meat dishes, with free fruit drinks for the kids.

Fratelli Paradiso
12 Challis Avenue, Potts Point; tel: 9357 1744; daily L and D; $$; map p.134 A2

Unpretentious neighbourhood Italian restaurant serving simply stunning food. The gnocchi with prawns, and the wonderfully tender calamari are unbeatable.

Hugo's Bar Pizza
33 Bayswater Road, Kings Cross; tel: 9332 1227; daily D; $$; train: Kings Cross; map p.134 A1

Fantastic pizzas and more. Quality Italian food, killer cocktails, and one of the grooviest crowds in town. No bookings, but it is worth the wait.

SEE ALSO BARS P.34

SOUTHEAST ASIAN
Libertine
1 Kellett Street, Kings Cross; tel: 9368 7507; daily D; $$; train: Kings Cross; map p.134 A1

Kellett Street is packed with places to savour a couple of courses. This dimly-lit and exotically-furnished Vietnamese is one of our favourites.

Phamish
354 Liverpool Street, Darlinghurst; tel: 9357 2688; Tue–Sun D; $; map p.138 A4

With no reservations, you may have to wait for a table at this buzzing local Vietnamese, but it is worth the wait. Daily specials are on the board. The salt and pepper calamari are the best in town.

Pink Peppercorn
122 Oxford Street, Darlinghurst; tel: 9360 9922; daily D; $; bus: Oxford Street; map p.137 E4

Thai and Vietnamese restaurants are a dime a dozen in Sydney, but this simple yet stylish diner, tucked away from Oxford Street's main restaurant strip, is the place to discover the delights of Laotian cuisine.

Paddington and Surry Hills

MODERN AUSTRALIAN

Marque
355 Crown Street, Surry Hills; tel: 9332 2225; Mon–Sat D; $$$; bus: Crown Street; map p.137 E4

The subtle decor is a reminder that you are here for

> **Top tip: Thai**
> Longrain, 85 Commonwealth Street, Surry Hills; tel: 9280 2888; Mon–Fri L, Mon–Sat D; $$$; train, bus: Central Station; map p.137 E4
> It does not take bookings, it is not cheap and the tables are communal, but this glamorous converted warehouse serves some of the best Thai food you will ever eat. The cocktails in the bar are pretty special too.

the food. And what food it is! Try roast Kangaroo Island chicken with foie gras sauce, a millefeuille of potato, mackerel, truffles and hazelnut. It is all exquisite.

Mohr Fish
202 Devonshire Street, Surry Hills; tel: 9318 1326; daily L and D; $; map p.137 D3

This little seafood diner has been enchanting locals since long before Crown Street became a hip dining strip. The neighbouring offshoot, Mohr and Mohr, offers well-priced bistro food.

EAST ASIAN

Billy Kwong
355 Crown Street, Surry Hills; tel: 9332 3300; daily D; $$; bus 301, 303, 303, 352; map p.137 E3

Sharpen your elbows before

dining at Billy Kwong: it gets decidedly cramped in here. Her highly-flavoured modern take on Chinese favourites has made chef Kylie Kwong a culinary star.

Mahjong Room
312 Crown Street, Surry Hills; tel: 9361 3985; daily D; $$; bus: 301, 310, 343, 393; map p.137 E4

The old-faithful neighbourhood Chinese gets a revamp at this funky modern diner.

ITALIAN

Arthur's Pizza
260 Oxford Street, Paddington; tel: 9332 2220; daily D; $; bus: Oxford Street buses; map p.138 A3

Cheap and cheerful eatery serving simple yet sensational pizzas.

La Sala
23 Foster Street, Surry Hills; tel: 9281 3352; Thur–Fri L, Tue–Sat D; $$

Exquisite Italian, ranging from superior versions of old favourites (handmade spaghetti alle vongole) to more unusual dishes such as rabbit stuffed with dried apricots, pine nuts, bread and herbs.

Lo Studio
53–5 Brisbane Street, Surry Hills; tel: 9212 4118; Mon–Fri L, Mon–Sat D; $$; train: Central Station; map p.137 D4

Below: stylish service and the house wine at Longrain's.

Above: the Boathouse on Blackwattle Bay, for seasonal fish and seafood.

A gorgeous dining room with an art deco feel and a wide-ranging menu that delights the palate.

MIDDLE EAST
Erciyes
409 Cleveland Street, Surry Hills; tel: 9319 1300; daily L and D; $; bus: Cleveland Street; map p.137 E2
Cheap, cheerful, and well-patronised Turkish restaurant specialising in *pide* (Turkish pizza). Bellydancers perform Friday and Saturday nights.
The Prophet
274 Cleveland Street, Surry Hills; tel: 9698 7025; Mon–Sat L, daily D; $; bus: Cleveland Street; map p.137 D2
Great flavour and friendly service at a stalwart of the Lebanese restaurant scene. BYO.

SOUTHEAST ASIAN
Red Lantern
545 Crown Street, Surry Hills; tel: 9698 4355; Tue–Sun L and D; $; bus: Crown Street; map p.137 E2
A sleek and stylish diner serving richly-flavoured South Vietnamese favourites.

Spice I Am
88 Wentworth Avenue, Surry Hills; tel: 9280 0928; Tue–Sun L and D; $$; train: Museum; map p.137 D4
If you are after real homestyle Thai cooking, from northern pork sausages to fermented rice dishes, this is the place for you.

Inner-West Suburbs
MODERN AUSTRALIAN
The Boathouse on Blackwattle Bay
End of Ferry Road, Glebe; tel: 9518 9011; Tue–Sun L and D; $$$; metro: Glebe; map p.18
Some of Sydney's best seafood, on the edge of the harbour in a converted boathouse with floor-to-ceiling windows. The menu changes with the season, but consistently features oysters from around Australia.

Price indications are for a three-course meal for one, including half a bottle of house wine, coffee and service:
$ = under A$50
$$ = A$50–75
$$$ = A$75–115
$$$$ = over A$115

Three Clicks West
127 Booth Street, Annandale; tel: 9660 6652; Mon–Sat D; $$; map p.18
Leafy Annandale is not a suburb that attracts a lot of visitors, but Three Clicks West is worth the trip. The small but inventive menu might include quail, rabbit rillettes and smoked salmon tart; desserts are a speciality.

SOUTHEAST ASIAN
Sumalee Thai
Bank Hotel, 324 King Street, Newtown; tel: 9557 1692; daily L and D; $$; bus: King Street; map p.
The highlight of the elaborately revamped Bank Hotel is this mouthwatering Thai restaurant with a menu designed for sharing dishes among friends and featuring curry, stir-frys and hotpots.
Thanh Binh
111 King Street, Newtown; tel: 9957 1175; daily D, Sat–Sun L; $; bus: King Street; map p.18
King Street has no shortage of good Vietnamese restaurants; this unpretentious place is one of the best.

105

R

Left: home to Sydney's finest Italian cuisine.

INDIAN
Darbar
134 Glebe Point Road; tel: 9660 5666; Tue–Sun L, daily D; $; bus: 370; map p.136 A4
Excellent southern Indian food served in an atmospheric old sandstone building on Glebe's main dining and shopping street.

MIDDLE EAST
Al Mustafa
23 Glebe Point Road, Glebe; tel: 9660 9006; daily D; $; bus: 370; map p.136 B3
Traditional Lebanese cuisine with belly-dancing on Friday and Saturday.

ITALIAN
Elio
159 Norton Street; Leichhardt; tel: 9560 9129; daily D; $$; bus: 370, 445, 440; map p.18
Possibly the best restaurant on Norton Street, the heart of Sydney's Italian quarter, with an unpredictable, sophisticated menu.

> Price indications are for a three-course meal for one, including half a bottle of house wine, coffee and service:
> $ = under A$50
> $$ = A$50–75
> $$$ = A$75–115
> $$$$ = over A$115

Mixing Pot
178 St John's Road, Glebe; tel: 9660 7449; Mon–Fri L, Mon–Sat D; $$; map p.136 3A
Italian seafood cuisine and outdoor dining amid the relaxed chic of inner-city Glebe.

EUROPEAN
Steki Taverna
2 O'Connell Street, Newtown; tel: 9516 2191; Wed–Sun D; $$; bus: King Street; map p.136 A1
One of Sydney's best Greek restaurants, serving traditional cuisine with live entertainment at weekends.

Eastern Suburbs
MODERN AUSTRALIAN
Catalina Rose Bay
1 Sunderland Avenue, Lyne Park, Rose Bay; tel: 9371 0555; daily L, Mon–Sat D; $$$; bus: 323, 324, 325, ferry: Rose Bay; map p.20
The decor has been kept deliberately simple, so nothing detracts from the magnificent panorama of Rose Bay in front of you. The seafood in particular is superb. Watch for the friendly pelicans that like to pay a visit.
Doyle's on the Beach
11 Marine Parade, Watson's Bay; tel: 9337 2007; daily L and D; $$;

ferry: Watson's Bay; map p.20
Australia's first seafood restaurant (opened 1885) remains one of Sydney's favourite places for Sunday lunch on a sunny day. The seafood is simple, but fresh, the beachfront views are dazzling, so bring your sunglasses.
Pier
594 New South Head Road, Rose Bay; tel: 9327 6561; daily L and D; $$$; bus: 323, 324, 325, ferry: Rose Bay; map p.20
Consistently voted Sydney's best seafood restaurant, this beautifully sleek outfit hovers over the harbour waters. The more casual Tasting Room next door offers less pricey portions from the same kitchen.
Two Rooms
40 St Pauls Street, Randwick; tel: 9398 1011; Tue–Sat D; $$; bus: 373, 374; map p.20
The wonderfully flexible menu lets you order almost every dish as either entrée or main, and most are perfect for sharing. The Mediterranean fare ranges from air-dried wagyu beef to calzone.

FRENCH
Bistro Moncur
Woollahra Hotel, 116 Queen Street, Woollahra; tel: 9363

Right: Doyle's pins its ethical colours to the mast.

Above: Singapore-born Chui Lee Luk, chef at Claude's.

2519; Tue–Sun L and D; $$$; bus: 389; map p.138 C3
Classic French bistro cuisine served in a stylish restaurant. They do not take reservations, so arrive early and have an aperitif in the bar.

Claude's
10 Oxford Street, Woollahra; tel: 9331 2325; Tue–Sat D; $$$; bus: Oxford Street; map p.138 B3
One of the permanent stars of the local dining scene, Claude's is small, discreet and BYO. Chef Chui Lee Luk *(see above)* puts a modern spin on classic French cuisine. One tip: leave room for dessert.

Restaurant Balzac
141 Belmore Road, Randwick; tel: 9399 9660; Tue–Sun D; $$; map p.20

The thick sandstone walls set a special-occasion tone; the food lives up to it, especially the exquisite risottos (think southern rock lobster, confit rabbit, chorizo and saffron). With eminently-reasonable prices, no wonder this is a foodies' favourite.

ITALIAN
Beppi's
21 Yurong Street, East Sydney; tel: 9360 4558; Mon–Fri L, Mon–Sat D; $$; train: Museum Station; map p.
Some of the Italian ground-breakers who introduced fine dining to Sydney decades ago refuse to hang up their chef's hats. Beppi's restaurant is one of the champions, 50 years old and still going strong.

Buzo
3 Jersey Road, Woollahra; tel: 9328 1600; Mon–Sat D; $$; map p.138 B3
Italian food that is a cut above average, offering such treats as Sicilian roast lamb leg, and lasagne of porcini, prosciutto and truffle. *Molto bene.*

SOUTHEAST ASIAN
Spice Market
340 New South Head Road, Double Bay; tel: 9328 7499;

Wed–Mon D; $; buses 323, 324, 325, 326; map p.20
There are no bookings, and the communal table does not offer too much elbow room, but with Thai fare this tasty, no-one is complaining.

Eastern Beaches

MODERN AUSTRALIAN
Sean's Panorama
270 Campbell Parade, Bondi Beach; tel: 9365 4924; Mon–Sat D, Sat–Sun B and L; $$; bus 333, 380, 381, 382 or Bondi Explorer; map p.22
A place of pilgrimage for those who love a serious weekend breakfast, but just as popular for its dinners. It may look like a neighbour-hood noshery, but this is food for serious diners, using the best local produce.

EAST ASIAN
Oceanic Thai
309 Clovelly Road, Clovelly; tel: 9665 8942; Tue–Sat D; $$; bus 339; map p.22
Clovelly is not exactly one of Sydney's fine-dining districts, but this extraordinary Thai restaurant is one of the best in town. The room is small, and bookings are essential.

Raw Bar
35 Ramsgate Avenue, Bondi Beach; tel: 9365 7200; daily L and D; $; map p.22
Hip sushi bar popular with locals and visitors. Do not let the name fool you: it is not all raw.

ITALIAN
Icebergs Dining Room and Bar
1 Notts Avenue, Bondi Beach; tel: 9365 9000; Tue–Sun L and D; $$$; map p.22
It does not get more Bondi than this, with hip young things in sleek surroundings enjoying sensational food and views to match. Classic Sydney.

107

North Bondi Italian Food

North Bondi RSL, 118 Ramsgate Avenue, Bondi Beach; tel: 9300 4400; daily D, Wed–Sun L; $$; map p.22

At the other end of the beach from Icebergs, this venue is less super-styled and less expensive, but the seafront ambience is just as sensational, as is the food.

Pompei's Gelateria and Pizzeria

126 Roscoe Street, Bondi Beach; tel: 9365 1233; Tue–Sun D, Fri-Sun L; $; map p.22

Neighbourhood Italian offering quality pizza and outstanding *gelato*.

North Shore

MODERN AUSTRALIAN

Aqua Dining

Corner Paul and Northcliff streets, Milsons Point; tel: 9964 9998; daily L and D; $$$; train, ferry: Milsons Point; map p.24

Swimming pools are not necessarily associated with sophisticated dining but Aqua Dining, overlooking North Sydney Olympic Pool, is the exception. Mouthwatering meals are accompanied by knockout views of the Harbour Bridge, Opera House and CBD.

Below: a laid-back lunch menu, Bondi-style.

Bathers Pavilion

4 The Esplanade, Balmoral Beach; tel: 9969 5050; daily L and D; $$$; bus: 233, 238, 247, 257; map p.24

Inside this 1930s art deco building *(see above)* on the North Shore's prettiest beach, you will find Serge Dansereau at work, the chef who helped re-shape Sydney dining in the 1980s with his passion for local ingredients and classical technique. The building also houses a cheaper café.

Pacific Grill

352 Barrenjoey Road, Newport; tel: 9999 2398; Tue–Sun D; $$; bus: Barrenjoey Road; map p.24

Laid-back and casual place for steaks, seafood and salads, with all meals available in a small or large size. Also a classy bar offering snacks such as oysters and calamari.

AFRICAN

Out of Africa

43–45 East Esplanade, Manly; tel: 9977 0055; Tue–Sun L, Mon–Sat D; $$; bus, ferry: Manly Wharf; map p.24

The decor at this Moroccan restaurant is decidedly kitsch – plenty of zebra skin – but

the food is exquisite. *Tagine* is the speciality of the house.

EAST ASIAN

Ying's

270 Pacific Highway, Crows Nest; tel: 9966 9181; daily L and D; $$; bus 200, 140, 143, 144; map p.24

The no-frills decor offers no hints that this is one of Sydney's most acclaimed Chinese restaurants. Load up on *yum cha* during the day, or treat yourself to a multi-course banquet at night.

FRENCH

La Grillade

118 Alexander Street, Crows Nest; tel: 9439 3707; Mon–Fri L, Mon–Sat D; $$$; map p.24

An elegant dining room, a menu stuffed with beautifully-executed classics, and a reputation for serving up

Price indications are for a three-course meal for one, including half a bottle of house wine, coffee and service:
$ = under A$50
$$ = A$50–75
$$$ = A$75–115
$$$$ = over A$115

Left: the Art Deco Bathers Pavilion on Balmoral Beach.

2534; daily L and D; $$; train: Leura Station; map p.26
Classy surroundings and classy food, crafted with top-notch produce and strong, simple flavours.
Solitary
90 Cliff Drive; Leura Falls; tel: 4782 1164; Sat–Sun L, Wed–Sun D; $$; train: Leura Station; map p.26
The setting is stunning, with its glorious views over the Jamison Valley, and the food is just as enticing. Save room for a soufflé, the speciality of the house.
Vulcan's
33 Govett's Leap Road, Blackheath; tel: 4787 6899; Fri–Sun L and D; $$; train: Blackheath; map p.26
Ordering here is simple: have anything from the wood-fired oven, plus one of Philip Searle's classic desserts, and you will be in heaven.

FRENCH
Mes Amis
The Old Church, corner Waratah and Lurline streets, Katoomba; tel: 4782 1558; Wed–Sun D; $$; train: Katoomba station; map p.26
Classic French food in an atmospheric former church.

some of the best steaks in town.

INDIAN
Nilgiri's
81–3 Christie Street, St Leonards; tel: 9969 0636; Sun–Fri L, daily D; $$; train: St Leonards; map p.24
One of Sydney's most acclaimed Indian restaurants is determinedly eclectic, focusing on a different region of the Subcontinent each month.

ITALIAN
Will and Toby's
8–13 South Steyne, Manly; tel: 9977 5944; daily B, L and D; $$; ferry: Manly Wharf; map p.24
Inner-city's favourites Will and Toby have opened a relaxed seaside outlet, combining quality food with a stylish fit-out and friendly service.

SOUTHEAST ASIAN
Prasit's Northside Thai
77 Mount Street, North Sydney; tel: 9957 2271; Mon–Fri L, Tue–Sat D; $$; train: North Sydney; map p.24
Something of an institution, this first-floor restaurant

offers reliable Thai standards and a more exciting specials menu. Lunch on the leaf-fringed balcony is always a treat.

Blue Mountains
MODERN AUSTRALIAN
Dry Dock
54 Waratah Street, Katoomba; tel: 4782 7902; Mon–Sat D, Fri L; $$; train: Katoomba; map p.26
Ocean-fresh seafood in the heart of the mountains? Absolutely, and perfectly prepared to boot.
Silk's Brasserie
128 The Mall; Leura; tel: 4784

Below: Bondi Beach cuisine: quick, tasty and healthy.

Shopping

Sydney has some of the classiest malls any-where in the world, at least as regards their architecture. The ornate Victorian shopping arcades that have been restored to their 19th-century glory are worth a visit even if you do not plan to buy anything. If you do, they are even more enticing, with their galleries of upmarket shops. There are large modern shopping centres, too, and a number of highly popular department stores, not to mention the intriguing boutiques and specialist shops that stretch into the suburbs. Sydney's thriving markets, selling anything from fashion to fish, should not be overlooked.

What to Buy

ANTIQUES

The Paddington and Wool-lahra districts are full of antiques shops. Treasures worthy of hunting down include clocks, jewellery, porcelain, silverware, glass-ware, books and maps. Start your search in Queen Street, off Oxford Street.

GEMSTONES

Australia is the source of about 95 per cent of the world's opals. 'White' opals are mined from the fields of Andamooka and Coober Pedy in South Australia. 'Boulder' opals – bright and vibrant – come from Quilpie in Queensland, while the pre-cious 'black' opal (actually more blue than black) is mined at Lightning Ridge and White Cliffs in New South Wales.

After opals, sapphires are Australia's most-mined gem-stones, and creative Aus-tralian jewellery designers work wonders with them.

Australia has one of the world's richest deposits of

Above: gemstones in all colours at Flame Opals

diamonds. The gems are mined by Argyle Diamond Mines in the rugged Kimber-ley region in the west. Kimberley is famed for its 'pink' diamonds, sometimes marketed under the descrip-tion 'champagne'. Hues range from lightly flushed to deep red.

Many jewellery shops in the central shopping district, particularly in Pitt and Castlereagh streets and around The Rocks, sell Aus-tralian opals and sapphires, either set or loose.

Shopping Centres and Areas

Argyle Stores

12 Argyle Street, The Rocks; tel: 9251 4800; 9am–8pm; train, bus, ferry: Circular Quay; map p.139 D3

Filled with boutiques, gour-met restaurants and cafés, Argyle Stores are currently closed for renovation and expected to re-open at the end of 2007.

Broadway Shopping Centre

1 Bay Street and Broadway; tel: 9213 3333; Mon–Fri 10am–7pm (Thur until 9pm), Sat 9am–6pm, Sun 10am–6pm; bus: 431–8; map p.136 B3

This landmark department store, with its distinctive clock towers and globes, was built in 1923. Since renovated as a top-notch shopping cen-tre, it is one of the focal

Some Sydney department stores, like David Jones, offer a home (or hotel) delivery serv-ice. Check with the information counter if you are planning on a major bout of retail therapy.

Left: the magnificent clock in the Queen Victoria Building.

A trendy shopping centre with slick metal and glass architecture. Have lunch at the Art House Hotel, attached to the shopping centre, or browse Sydney's largest international bookstore, Books Kinokinuya, which also has a fabulous selection of art and design books.
SEE ALSO LITERATURE P.79

Harbourside Shopping Centre
Darling Harbour; tel: 9281 3999; daily 10am–9pm; train: Pyrmont Bay or Convention Square; map p.132 B1
If it can be said that there was a model for today's Darling Harbour development, it would be Fisherman's Wharf in San Francisco. In keeping with this, the Harbourside Shopping Centre is an enormous speciality shopping centre with more than 200 shops and many food outlets, offering a range of cuisines reflecting the diversity of Australia's cultural base.

Imperial Arcade
168 Pitt Street; tel: 9233 5662; Mon–Fri 9am–6pm (Thur until 8pm), Sat 9am–5pm, Sun 11am–4pm; train: Wynard; map p.139 D1

points for shopping in this part of Sydney, with many of the major chains and lots of interesting boutiques plus a 12-screen cinema, showing the latest releases.

Chatswood Chase
345 Victoria Avenue, Chatswood; tel: 9419 6255; Mon–Fri 9.30am–5.30am (Thur until 9pm), Sat 9am–5pm, Sun 10am–5pm; bus: 136, 137, 275, 272, 273, 275; map p.24
Located on the North Shore, this popular centre, with over 100 retailers (including many local names), manages to be practical and elegant at the same time.

Chifley Plaza
2 Chifley Square, corner Hunter and Phillip streets, CBD; tel: 9221 4500; Mon–Fri 9.30am–5.30am (Thur until 9pm), Sat 9am–5pm, Sun 10am–5pm; train: Martin Place; map p.139 E1
Modern shopping plaza with luxury specialist shops including Max and Co., Kikki K and Bristol and Brooks. Buy your RM Williams gear here.

Direct Factory Outlets (DFO)
Corner Underwood Road and Homebush Bay Drive; tel: 9748 9800; daily 10am–6pm; bus: 525
A vast shopping complex, and a favourite with brand-name junkies. The site acts as the Sydney clearance centre for over 100 upmarket retailers and fashion labels, with prices below those that even the most hardened duty-free shopper would expect.

Galeries Victoria
500 George Street; tel: 9265 6888; Mon–Fri 9am–6pm (Thur until 9pm), Sat 9am–5pm, Sun 11am–5pm; train: Town Hall; map p.133 C1

Below: some of the trendiest designers started their careers at Paddington Bazaar (see p.117).

Over 60 stores offering a mix of fashion, footwear and accessories, and jewellery.

Market City
Corner Hay and Thomas Street; tel: 9212 1388; daily 10am–7pm (Thur until 8pm); metro: Haymarket; map p.137 C4
In the middle in Sydney's Chinatown, and located above Paddy's Markets, this is where East meets West. As well as an array of retail outlets, there is great food, including some of Sydney's best *yum cha*.

MLC Centre
Corner King and Castlereagh streets, City; tel: 9224 8333; Mon–Fri 8.30am–5.30pm (Thur until 6.30pm), some retailers open Sat–Sun; train: Martin Place; map p.139 D1
Close to Martin Place Station. You will find all the famous brands here, spread throughout the 80 or so shops; also boutiques, bars and restaurants.

Moore Park SupaCenta
2a Todman Street, Kensington;

…and for the dog who has everything: **Dogue** is Sydney's house of 'canine couture', selling designer 'outfits' and all sorts of accessories. There is even a 'deli' section, and a doggie day spa here. Dogue is at 134 Edgecliff Rd, Woollahra, tel: 9388 9969.

tel: 9313 8340; Mon–Fri 9am–5.30pm (Thur until 7pm), Sat 9am–5pm, Sun 10am–5pm
Located in one of the southern suburbs, this centre has many of the big names in homewares including Ikea and Freedom.

Paddington
bus: Oxford Street; map p.138
Past Juniper Hall on Oxford Street, Paddington's main shopping strip begins, with fashion for the young and trendy, excellent book, print and music shops, and corner pubs that do a roaring trade. If browsing this strip makes you hungry, there are plenty of upmarket restaurants and

cafés where it is fashionable to see and be seen while dining on 'Modern Australian' cuisine.

The Oxford Street shopping stretch comes to an end at the junction with Queen and Park streets. To your left, around the corner in Queen Street, Woollahra, there is more excellent shopping if your tastes run to very expensive antiques.

Pitt Street Mall
train: Town Hall; map p.139 D1
A pedestrian mall on Pitt Street between Market and King Streets, this is a busy shopping precinct leading to a number of shopping arcades. Major outlets include Myer and there are 600 other stores.

Queen Victoria Building
455 George Street, City; tel: 9264 9209; Mon–Sat 9am–6pm (Thur until 9pm), Sun 11am–5pm; train: Town Hall, bus: George Street; map p.133 C1
One of the least expected and therefore all the more

Below: the Queen Victoria Building.

enchanting aspects of Sydney's abundant retail industry is the survival of its ornate Victorian shopping arcades, reminiscent of wealthy 19th-century Europe. The most important of these are the Strand Arcade *(see below)* and the Queen Victoria Building (QVB).

The Queen Victoria Building is the Cinderella story of all Sydney architecture. Occupying a complete city block beside the town hall on George Street, the QVB opened in 1898 as a produce market, designed by City Architect George McRae. Yet for much of the mid-20th century it was regarded as a white elephant and was due for demolition until Sydney started to get smart about its own heritage (although it was purchased for restoration by a Malaysian firm).

By the time the QVB closed for restoration in 1980 it consisted of offices and low-rent shops running perpetual 'closing down' sales. Six years and A$75 million later, after one of the finest refurbishing programmes ever seen in the city, the Queen Victoria Building re-emerged as it is today: tiered galleries of high-quality shops in a building worth a visit if only for its beautiful stained-glass windows, wrought-iron details and Romanesque-style arches.

The attention to detail, both old and new, is evident everywhere in this fine building – not only in its stained glass, but also the elegant shopfronts, polished timbers and patterned floor tiles. The standard of the setting is echoed in the nearly 200 shops and boutiques it houses, with retail stock covering the spectrum of fashion, footwear, jewellery,

Above: hat, complete with flotation devices.

leather goods, antiques and crafts. French fashion designer Pierre Cardin has referred to the QVB as the 'most beautiful shopping centre in the world'.

On the lowest level are the 'Eat Street' restaurants and cafés, which cater for rushed food-on-the-go or leisurely sit-down meals. There is also an over-rated, kitsch-encrusted 'Royal Clock' cluttering the ceiling that many stop to admire.

Skygarden
77 Castlereagh Street, CBD; tel: 9231 1811; Mon–Fri 9.30am–5.30pm (Thur until 8pm), Sat 9.30am–5pm, Sun 11am–4pm; bus: 303; map p.139 D1
Many high-quality local and international designer boutiques.

Strand Arcade
412–4 George Street, CBD; tel: 9232 4199; Mon–Fri 9am–5.30pm (Thur until 9pm), Sat 9am–4pm, Sun 11am–4pm; bus: George Street; map p.139 D1
When it was built in 1891–92, the Strand Arcade was described as the very latest in shopping centre design. A century on, after two Depressions and two World Wars, it is still a vital and unique part of Sydney life. Almost destroyed in a catastrophic

fire in 1976, the tiered mezzanines of this iron-and-glass damsel were completely restored, while carefully preserving the individual character of English architect John Spencer's 1890s design. Attention to detail was of paramount importance; even the patterns on the shop windows match those of the floor tiles.

Today jewellers, watchmakers, leading fashion designers and craftsmen ply their trade side-by-side with purveyors of speciality chocolates and nuts, old-style coffee houses and gift and souvenir shops. Many of the shops are Sydney landmarks, and one of the most popular is the Strand Hatters, which sells traditional Australian Outback Akubra hats (without the corks). For light refreshments, visit Harris Coffee & Tea, on the ground floor near the Pitt Street entrance, where they have been since 1892.

You do not need to shop at the airport to buy goods without paying duty. Thanks to the Tourist Refund Scheme (TRS), you can reclaim the goods and services tax (GST) on purchases worth $300 or more that you buy within 30 days of your departure date. To claim a refund, you will need to get a tax invoice from the store, and present it with your passport and boarding card to the Customs TRS facility at the airport. For more information, see www.customs.gov.au. And check out Downtown Duty Free in the Strand Arcade (tel: 9233 3166). It is a city branch of the airport's duty free store, where you can pre-order your duty free goods and collect them at the airport when you leave Australia.

113

The Strip, Chatswood

Victoria Street; train: Chatswood, bus: 272; map p.24

A close contender for the Australian suburb with the largest shopping centre is to be found along the North Shore railway line, just to the right off the Pacific Highway.

When the city department store of Grace Bros (recently renamed Myer) made the conspicuously successful decision to decentralise to Chatswood (and elsewhere) in the early 1970s, it started a shift to the suburbs which forever changed the face of Australian retailing.

Today, Victoria Street leading east from the railway station is 'The Strip' and several large shopping complexes lead off it: Westfield, Lemon Grove, Chatswood Chase and the Myer arcade. The extensive range of shops ensures that people of the area rarely need to travel into the city centre to shop.

Sydney Central Plaza

Corner Hay and Thomas streets, City; tel: 9212 1388; Mon–Sat 9am–6pm (Thur until 9pm), Sun 11am–5pm; metro: Haymarket; map p.137 C4

Home to Myer's flagship department store, plus all the leading Australian fashion stores and one of the largest food courts in the city.

Sydney Tower

Centrepoint Westfield, Level One, 100 Market Street, City; tel: 9231 9300; daily 9am–10.30pm (Sat until 11.30pm); individual stores vary; train: Town Hall station; map p.133 C1

A large retail area located at the base of Sydney Tower, featuring over 150 shops.

Westfield Shopping Centre

500 Oxford Street, Bondi Junction; tel: 9947 8000; Mon–Fri 9.30am–7pm (Thur until 9pm), Sat 9.30am–6pm, Sun 10am–6pm; train: Bondi Junction, bus: Oxford Street; map p.20

One of nine big Westfield Malls, this one is conveniently close to the city and offers parking and all the major stores under cover.

World Square

Corner George, Liverpool, Pitt and Goulburn streets; tel: 8669 6900; open Mon–Sat 10am–7pm (Thur until 9pm), Sun 11am–5pm; metro: World Square, bus: George Street; map p.137 D4

This open-air square surrounded by shops, cafés and restaurants is the newest shopping centre in the CBD. As well as the shopping, this is a bit of an entertainment hub. The Equilibrium Hotel is one of the hotspots with music and dancing, food and drinks over four levels.

Department Stores

David Jones

65–77 Market Street; tel: 9266 5544; Mon–Wed 9.30am–6pm, Thur 9.30am–9pm, Fri 9.30am–7pm, Sat 9am–6pm, Sun 10am–6pm; train: Town Hall; map p.133 C1

Sydney's favourite department store, David Jones (known as DJs), is billed as 'the most beautiful store in the world'. There are two DJs in Sydney, one on Elizabeth Street and one on Market Street, the former the more elegant of the two but the latter well worth visiting for its basement food hall filled with scrumptious offerings.
SEE ALSO FASHION P.57; FOOD AND DRINK P.65

Myer

436 George Street, tel: 9238 9111; Mon–Wed 9am–6pm, Thur 9am–9pm, Fri 9am–7pm, Sat 9am–6pm, Sun 10am–6pm; train: Town Hall, bus: George

Below: the grandeur of the 19th-century Strand Arcade.

Above: Aboriginal art.

Street; map p.139 D1
Sidney Myer arrived in Australia in 1899 as a penniless Russian immigrant, and began his shopping empire with a drapery store in Melbourne. This has expanded to become one of the largest – and most loved – Australian department store chains. It is perhaps one step down from David Jones, but just as ubiquitous.

Australiana

Australiana covers a multitude of sins (and skins). Americans (who have enough beef at home) tend to stock up on Akubra felt hats and Driza Bone oilskin coats for the *Man from Snowy River* look.

Australian Geographic Shop
Shop C5A Centrepoint, Castlereagh Street, City; tel: 9231 5505; Mon–Fri 9am–6pm (Thur until 8pm), Sat 9am–5pm, Sun 11am–4pm; train: St James, bus: George Street; map p.139 D1
Many excellent Australian products to do with the great outdoors.

Flame Opals
119 George Street, The Rocks; tel: 9247 3446; Mon–Fri 9am–6.30pm, Sat 10am–5pm, Sun 11.30am–5pm; train, bus,

ferry: Circular Quay; map p.139 D3
One of Sydney's many opal jewellers.

R.M. Williams
389 George Street, CBD; tel: 9262 2228; Mon–Fri 10am–6pm, Sat 9am–6pm, Sun 10am–5pm; train: Town Hall, bus: George Street; map p.139 D1
Many stores stock Australian rural gear, but the most famous one is the bushman's outfitter R.M. Williams, because the old living legend, 'R.M.' himself designed, wears and still manufactures much of it. Gear includes riding boots, Akubras and oilskin bushmen's coats.

Independent Shops

Planet
419 Crown Street; tel: 9698 0680; Mon–Sat 10am–5.30pm, Sun noon–4pm; bus: Crown Street; map p.137 E3
Custom designed furniture from Australian timbers, handcrafted fabrics by Australian designers and an emphasis on organic and recycled materials. Planet is Sydney's treasure trove of environmentally aware design.

Space Furniture
84 O'Riordan Street, Alexandria; tel: 8339 7588; Mon–Fri 10am–

6pm, Sat–Sun 10am–5pm; train: Green Square, bus: 434
There is Italian and European contemporary furniture over six levels here: all the accoutrements of funky designer living, both large and small. Space are exclusive Australian distributors of many imported brands, and have a huge and eclectic product list. Go with plenty of energy if you intend to browse round the entire store.

Salvage
2 Danks Street, Waterloo; tel: 9699 1005; Tue–Sat 10am–6pm; map p.137 D1
This antiques shop sells all sorts of aged treasures. There are chandeliers, statues and period furniture as well as wonderful salvaged architectural pieces. Well worth a browse after a Sunday morning coffee.

Rococo Flowers
303a Liverpool Street, East Sydney; tel: 9357 6688; Tue–Sat 10am–6pm; map p.137 E4
Rococo Flowers receives its wares fresh from the gardens of small growers every morning. There is nothing mass produced here. Romantic, old-world breeds are the mainstay here: think peonies, roses and gardenias.

115

Dinosaur Designs
339 Oxford Street, Paddington;
tel: 9361 3776; Mon–Sat
10am–6pm, Sun noon–5pm;
bus: Oxford Street; map
p.138 B3
Organic, nature-inspired
designs of jewellery, accessories and functional homewares. Dinosaur Designs'
hand-modelled products all
look like jewels in glowing,
bright coloured resin. This
design team's products have
iconic status among those in
the know.

Opus
344 Oxford Street, Paddington;
tel: 9360 4803; Mon–Sat
10am–6pm; bus: Oxford Street
buses; map p.138 B3
This is the place to pick up
gifts for all the Sydney friends
you will be visiting. Opus
sells all sorts of novelties and
giftware for children and
adults, as well as homeware
for the most discerning Sydney households. All manner
of cards and wrapping too.

Markets
Sydney's enticing markets
offer a myriad buying opportunities. Sharp-eyed bargain
hunters will usually be
rewarded if they browse for
long enough among the huge
variety of merchandise.

Balmain Markets
St Andrews Church, corner Darling Street and Curtis Road, Balmain; Sat 8.30am–4pm; bus:
433, 434, 441, 442, 445;
map p.18
This 'alternative' market
offers a wide range of ethnic
foodstuffs, clothing, locally
made ceramics and wood-
work. Food stalls indoors
and lots of restaurants and
pubs nearby.

Bondi Beach Market
Campbell Parade, Bondi; Sun
10am–5pm; bus: 333, 380, 381,
382, 389; map p.22
These markets are held
each Sunday in the grounds
of Bondi Beach Public
School, just across the road
from the famous beach.
They are the place to hunt
for offbeat clothing by up-
and-coming designers, hand
made jewellery, vintage
clothes and retro furniture.
You can hardly beat the
beach-front location.

Flemington Markets
Parramatta Road, Flemington;
daily 10am–4.30pm; train:
Flemington station, then
10 minutes' walk
A half-hour drive from the
city. Wide range of goods
and fresh produce. Every-
thing from flowers to fruit to
fashion.

Glebe Markets
Glebe Public School, 193 Glebe
Point Road, Glebe; Sat
10am–5pm; bus: 370, 431, 434;
map p.136 A4
A laid-back market offerng a
wide selection of arts and
crafts, foodstuffs and
clothes. Popular with alternative types and the fashionable inner city set. There
are around 200 outdoor
stalls.

Below: Dinosaur Designs.

Right: The Rocks Market, busy every weekend.

North Sydney Market
Miller Street; 2nd Sat of the month; train: Fish Market; map p.24
A little more upmarket than most. Nearly 200 stalls selling artworks, foodstuffs, jewellery, antiques; also fortune-telling, massage and reflexology. Live music 11am–1pm.

Opera House Market
Sydney Opera House forecourt; Sun 9am–7pm; train, bus, ferry: Circular Quay; map p.139 E4
Lots of tourist-oriented wares, local artists' works, sepia-toned historic Sydney photographs and Sydney-themed souvenirs.

Paddy's Market
9 Hay Street, Haymarket; Thur–Sun 9am–4.30pm; metro: Haymarket; map p.137 C4
Sydney's oldest market, with 1,000 stalls. Huge range, from fresh produce to appliances, toys and clothing.

Paddington Bazaar
Uniting Church, corner Oxford and Newcombe streets, Paddington; Sat 9am–4pm; bus: Oxford Street; map p.138 B3
This extravaganza takes place every Saturday in the grounds of the Uniting Church, and the crowds are as kaleidoscopic as the goods on sale. Always on parade are the young and fashionable, wearing the look of the moment, children and dogs scrambling in all directions at knee level, and visitors from all corners of

While some produce markets are open throughout the week, other 'community' markets open only at weekends. Most stallholders handle cash only, and be prepared to bargain over the cost of your purchase.

the world speaking a babel of languages.
   Stallholders sell every conceivable variety of new and used clothing, plants, jewellery, pottery, leather goods, stationery and imported exotica. This is also the place to pick up a seemingly outrageous piece of clothing from a design student, who may well be a big name in five years' time: many talented students attempt to launch their careers here.

The Rocks Market
George Street, The Rocks; Sat and Sun 10am–5pm; train, bus, ferry: Circular Quay; map p.139 D3
A colourful, lively market in the shadow of the Harbour Bridge. Lots of tourist-oriented and arty goods on sale. Vast umbrellas protect shoppers from wet weather. Hundreds of stalls sell antiques, paintings and homeware. Also offers street performances featuring the best Australian buskers.

Surry Hills Markets
Corner Crown and Collins streets, Surry Hills; first Sat of every month 10am–5pm; bus: Crown Street; map p.137 E3
These markets began life as a trading spot for recycled and secondhand goods. Nowadays a focus for community life in the area, they are a great spot to experience the diversity of inner-city Sydney, and to pick up a bargain.

117

Sport

Like the rest of Australia, Sydney is addicted to sport. Sydneysiders loved the idea of staging the Olympics (although they complained about the logistics), they love their homegrown rugby, and they love a summer's day at a cricket match. But most of all they love the social possibilities that sport brings: the chance for a big event, preferably with fireworks, a good time and a bit of an argument. They recognise that sport is, by nature, a diversion, particularly in a city as beautiful and energetic as this one. And there are plenty of opportunities for the visitor to share the experience, as a spectator or a participant.

The Home Code – Rugby League

Rugby League, 'the toughest game on earth', is what people generally mean when they talk about football in Sydney. It is a large-scale physical game, a war between teams comprising 13 muscular players apiece.

Rugby League began here in 1907, 12 years after the new code was established in England. The game took off immediately in Sydney, and the South Sydney Club won the first premiership in 1908.

For many years the competition was strictly local, but in the 1980s Rugby League became a national affair, drawing in clubs from Queensland, regional NSW and Canberra, as well as losing local favourites such as Newtown Jets, the oldest club in the League. In the 1990s, under pressure from media baron Rupert Murdoch, the League split into two. But the fans were not happy, and displayed deep apathy towards both the Australian Rugby League and the new Murdoch-sponsored Super League. To salvage the situation, the two sides came together in 1998, putting an unwieldy 20 teams into competition under the banner of the National Rugby League; the number of teams was changed to 14 in 2000, then to 15 the following year.

The rough and tumble of rugby makes it a terrific spectator sport. Games are played from March to September. There are a number of venues around town, but the home ground of the Sydney Roosters – New South Wales' most successful team in recent years – and the South Sydney Rabbitohs is the **Telstra Stadium** at Sydney Olympic Park. Tickets to most of the season's games are inexpensive and easily procured.

Some of the most fierce and exciting matches are played in the State of Origin series, where players discard club allegiances to play for their home state. Look out for games at the Telstra Stadium in Olympic Park from May to July each year.
Telstra Stadium
Olympic Park; tel: 8765 2000; www.telstrastadium.com.au; train: Olympic Stadium; map p.18

Below: early morning rugby training for the Wallabies.

Left: Australian cricket captain, Ricky Ponting, signs shirts for fans in Sydney after Australia won the Cricket World Cup... again.

www.austadiums.com; bus:355, shuttle buses operate from Central Station on match days; map p.138 A3

Hosts all major rugby league and union games (bar the finals, which are at Telstra Stadium, see opposite).

Cricket

Like many former outposts of the British Empire, Australia looks on cricket as one of the compensations for years of colonial rule.

The first official match was played in Sydney in 1804 (it is hard to imagine why it took so long), on a site that would later become Hyde Park. Sydney Cricket Ground saw its first action in 1854, with a match between locals and Victorians. Cricket today is played at state level in the Pura Cup, and at international level in Test Match series (where the players sensibly wear traditional and cooling white) and World Series one-day matches (brightly coloured nylon uniforms for the benefit of the cameras).

Sydney's largest stadium, hosting all the most important rugby league and union, Australian Rules and soccer matches.

Rugby Union

Rugby Union takes a fairly quiet course through the Sydney football scene. Born of the English public school rugby code, it was first played in the colony in 1829, and remained strictly an amateur sport until 1996, when the game was commercialised at the top level.

The Wallabies are Australia's international team, playing around six home games a year, but a lot more than that in 2003, when Australia hosted the Rugby World Cup. The Wallabies were beaten 20–17 by England in the final, played at **Aussie Stadium**.

The New South Wales Waratahs play in the Super 14, an international provincial series that consists of five teams from New Zealand, five from South Africa and four from Australia. The Waratahs play

their home games at Aussie Stadium.

Aussie Rules

Australian Rules Football is Melbourne's version of rugby, the one that paralyses the southern city for the final few weeks of the season in September. When there was talk in 1998 of scheduling a Federal Election one week after the Grand Final, great minds went to work on the question of whether or not football fever might prove too much of a distraction to the voters.

Aussie Rules went national in the 1980s, and Sydney, somewhat spellbound by this strange code, agreed to take on the old South Melbourne team as their official home team. The result is the Sydney Swans, a fairly successful side. They play their home games at the Sydney Cricket Ground, and occasionally at the Telstra Stadium, from March through to August or September. Watch a game if you can; there is no other code like it in the world.

Aussie Stadium

Moore Park; tel: 9360 6601;

> Though it has nothing like the profile of the other footbal codes, soccer enjoys the highest participation rate in Australia, with some 100,000 players in Sydney alone taking to the field each weekend. The Ericsson Cup, the national league competition, is played from October to May. Several Sydney clubs are involved and games are played at venues across town, with finals at Sydney Football Stadium in Centennial Park.

119

Above: a competitor at the Southside Eliminators surfing competition.

For a decade or more, Australia has been the dominant team in both the one-day and five-day versions of the game. Outstanding New South Wales players who have represented their country in recent years include Mark and Steve Waugh, Brett Lee, Glenn McGrath, Michael Bevan, Michael Slater and Stuart MacGill.

Tickets are readily available for most of the local matches, but book ahead for the World Series matches, which are by far the most popular. A traditional way to watch a match is on the 'outer', where the tickets are cheapest.

Sydney Cricket Ground
Moore Park; tel: 9360 6601; www.sydneycricketground.com.au; bus: 355, shuttle buses operate from Central Station on match days; map p.138 A2
Hosts all the major cricket matches and most Australian Rules Football.

Basketball

Basketball dominates the winter indoor activity in the country, with Sydney being handsomely represented in the National Basketball League by the Sydney Kings. To borrow a cliché, the game has gone ahead in leaps and bounds in Australia since the national league was launched in the late 1970s.

The Kings and their arch rivals West Sydney Razorbacks both play at the Sydney Entertainment Centre and the State Sports Centre in Olympic Park, where they do battle with sides from all other major cities, as well as each other.

Although Australia's semi-professional league is still dominated by imported American players, the national team has enjoyed a strong standing within the world's top 10 since its creation.

Horse Racing

No aspect of Sydney life has more intrigue, drama or colourful characters than the world of horse racing. Australians, they say, will bet on two flies crawling up a wall;

Sydney has turned that passion into a way of life.

The action takes place on tracks in the suburbs of Canterbury (King Street), Royal Randwick (Alison Road), Rosehill (James Ruse Drive) and the suburban Warwick Farm (Hume Highway). They all rate among the best racecourses in the world in terms of the comforts they afford to the average racegoer: there are ample parking facilities, but the tracks are also accessible by public transport.

Sydney races all year round, with major midweek and Saturday afternoon meetings. The biggest dates on the calendar feature in March and April when the Autumn Carnival draws Australasia's finest horseflesh to the Sydney Turf Club's Rosehill course and Royal Randwick, headquarters of the Australian Jockey Club (AJC). Not to be missed during the Carnival is the Golden Slipper at Rosehill. It may only be a 1,200-m sprint for two-year-old colts and fillies but

The big sailing event of the year is the Sydney to Hobart Yacht Race, which starts in the harbour on Boxing Day. This is one of the city's favourite celebrations, attracting hoards of Christmas-fatigued residents carrying picnics of left-overs to whatever bit of the craggy foreshore offers a view of the billowing sails of the million-dollar boats as they head out to the Tasman Sea.

with prize money of A$3.5million on offer, it stops the nation during its 70-second run. At Randwick at Easter, catch the 3.2-km Sydney Cup and the 2.4-km AJC Derby.

Of course, you do not have to make it to the track to watch the action. Satellite TV, available in pubs and clubs, covers metropolitan and provincial race meetings. You can bet in almost any number of combinations at a branch of the Totalizator Agency Board (TAB).

Canterbury Park Racecourse
King Street, Canterbury; tel: 9930 4000; bus: 471, 472; map p.18

Rosehill Gardens Racecourse
Unwin Street, Rosehill; tel: 9930 4000; map p.18

Royal Randwick Racecourse
Alison Street, Randwick; tel: 9663 8400; bus: 370, 400, 410

The Sydney Turf Club
Canterbury Park Racecourse, King Street, Canterbury; tel: 9930 4000; www.stc.com.au
Can handle most information inquiries.

Warwick Farm Racecourse
Hume Highway, Warwick Farm; tel: 9602 6199; train: Warwick Farm

Sailing

Sydney Harbour provides superb sailing for all levels, from professional racers to amateur weekend sailors. Racing takes place right through the summer, and the best way to take a look is to hop aboard a Manly Ferry in the early evening. By far the most impressive of these races are those held for the 18-ft-class yachts, which skim, scud and scurry their way across the foam-tipped harbour waters with amazing speed. The Sydney Flying Squadron (tel: 9955 8350), which organises some of the races, offers tag-along ferry trips for spectators, leaving from the clubhouse in Milson's Point.

Surf Carnivals

Between October and March, so-called surf carnivals are held almost every weekend up and down Sydney's beautiful coastline.

As well as providing the chance to watch professional surfers ride the waves with apparent ease, these are great family days out, with daredevil life-saving displays,

Iron Man competitions and boat races all part of the fun.

Since the carnivals obviously depend on the wave conditions, many locations are not finalised until the day of the event. If you want to catch a local carnival, tune in to local radio stations on a Saturday morning to get the latest venue information.

Swimming

It is actually quite hard not to swim in a city like Sydney, surrounded as it is by water and basking in a climate that can be called Mediterranean one week, subtropical the next. Lap swimmers head for the Andrew 'Boy' Charlton Pool in the Domain or the North Sydney Pool, both with salt water and harbour frontage. During Sydney's brief winter, the North Sydney Pool shelters under a huge balloon, to protect swimmers from the occasional cold nip in the air.

The Sydney International Aquatic Centre at Olympic Park has raised the stakes considerably in terms of what Sydneysiders may expect from an indoor pool. This sleek glass-encased facility has two Olympic-sized pools,

Below: pleasures on the harbourside.

121

a tropical-inspired leisure pool complete with rapids, and temperature and hygiene controls to rival those on a NASA spaceship.

A quintessentially Sydney experience is sea-bath swimming. Although these pools were once out of favour, the chlorine-fatigued are returning to have another look at these naturally filled marvels, perched along the edges of the suburban coastlines. The Bondi Icebergs is a Sydney institution as well as a pool, the place where the grand old citizens of the city strip down to their bathers in the middle of winter and jump into an ice-filled pool to mark the start of the winter swimming season. Around the corner, Bronte offers another possibility. Down the coast at Coogee, female swimmers can visit a pleasing anachronism, the Women's Baths, while those of both sexes can lap it up at Wiley's Sea Baths.

Andrew 'Boy' Charlton Pool
Mrs Macquaries Road, Domain; tel: 9358 6686; www.abcpool. org; open summer: 6am–8pm, winter: 6am–7pm; bus: 441; map p.133 E3

Bondi Icebergs
Notts Avenue, Bondi; tel: 9130 3120; www.icebergs.com.au; map p.22

The Sydney Marathon, run every September, is one of the world's most scenic. The route begins by crossing the Harbour Bridge, winds through the City and up Oxford Street, and then through Centennial Park. The finish is at the steps of the Opera House.

Coogee Women's Baths
Neptune Street, Coogee; map p.22

North Sydney Olympic Pool
Alfred Street, Milsons Point; tel 9955 2309; Mon–Fri 5.30am–9pm, Sat–Sun 7am–7pm; train, ferry: Milsons Point; map p.24

Sydney International Aquatic Centre
Olympic Park, Homebush; tel: 9752 3666; www. aquatic centre.com.au; train: Olympic Stadium; map p.18

Wiley's Baths
Neptune Street, Southern end of Coogee Beach; tel: 9665 2838; map p.22

SEE ALSO BEACHES, P.38–41

Jogging, Walking and Cycling
The ultimate jog in Sydney is the course of the City to Surf fun run, a 14-km route along which more than 40,000 mad and merry men and women set out each August for the ultimate prize of having their

name printed in the *Sydney Morning Herald*, provided, of course, that they finish the race. Those who feel tired at the mere thought of such a run can select a choice spot from which to watch what is an amazing spectacle.

Less ambitious joggers, and cyclists as well, should head for Centennial Park for a gentle plod or pedal around this superb inner-city parkland, which was the site of the marathon and various road-cycling events at the 2000 Olympics. Bicycles can be hired at Centennial Park, as well as horses for equestrians in need of a gallop.

The Domain is a spectacularly beautiful jogging location, as are Bondi Beach and the parkland around the lower North Shore, where you might just spot the prime minister, John Howard, stepping out from Kirribilli House for his regular morning constitutional.

Golf
Australia has the most golf courses in the world per head of population; there are around 100 in Sydney alone. Many of the private clubs have reciprocal membership arrangements with overseas clubs, so enquire at home before you leave.

If you have no club membership but fancy a round, the public courses are plentiful, cheap and very good. Suggestions include Moore Park, for its proximity to the city, and Long Reef, for the fact that it sits out on a finger of land with ocean on three sides. The ocean gales cause no end of problems but with those views, anything is tolerable. The cost of 18

Left: Wiley's Sea Baths at Coogee.

Right: marathon runners cross the Harbour Bridge.

holes ranges from around $10 to $80.

The top championship golf courses hosting major tournaments are the Royal Sydney Golf Course (the city's most exclusive), the Lakes, the Australian and the New South Wales Golf Course, on the cliffs of La Perouse. According to golfing legend Greg Norman, this last could easily become – perhaps with a little work – one of the top 10 golf courses in the world. The New South Wales Golf Association is the place for golfers in need of advice (tel: 9505 9105; www.nswga.com.au) and is a good starting point for golfers from abroad looking for a round in Sydney.

The Australian
53 Bannerman Crescent, Rosebery; tel: 9663 2273; www.australiangolfclub.com

The Lakes
Corner of King Street and Vernon Avenue, East Lakes; tel: 9669 1311 www.thelakesgolfclub.com.au

Long Reef Golf Course
Anzac Avenue, Collaroy; tel: 9971 8188; www.lrgc.com.au

Moore Park Golf Club
Corner of Cleveland Street and Anzac Parade, Moore Park; tel: 9663 1064; www.moorepark golf.com.au

NSW Golf Course
Botany Bay National Park, off Anzac Parade, La Perouse; tel: 9661 4455; www.nswgolfclub. com.au; map p.22

Royal Sydney Golf Club
Kent Road, Rose Bay; tel: 9371 4333; www.rsgc.com.au

Tennis

Australia's main tennis tournament, the Australian Open, is staged in Melbourne, but visitors to Sydney might be able to catch some warm-up games at the Adidas International Tennis Tournament, held in mid-January at the NSW Tennis Centre in Olympic Park.

Those who want a set of their own should try the picturesque courts at Rushcutters Bay or the synthetic grass surfaces at Primrose Park Terrace in Cremorne on the lower North Shore. Tennis is cheap in Sydney compared to courts in Europe or the US; expect to pay between A$10 and A$15 for a game. Many courts are also floodlit for those wishing to play after dark. Contact Tennis New South Wales with court or event queries.

A good stop for information is Tennis NSW. See www.tennisnsw.com.au

Millers Point
Tennis Courts
Kent Street, Millers Point; tel: 9256 2222; bus: 431, 432, 433, 434; map p.139 C3

Rushcutters Bay
Tennis Centre
Waratah Street, Rushcutters Bay; tel: 9357 1675; bus: 200, 323, 324; map p.134 B1

White City
30 Alma Street, Paddington; tel: 9360 4113; map p.138 B4

Watching Sport

All you have to do to keep up with spectator sports in Sydney is open any newspaper or flick channels on the TV, where, at weekends, you can find broadcasts of everything from lawn bowls to netball.

If you are keen to see one of the big football or cricket games, you would be well advised to ask your travel agent to find out about tickets prior to arrival. The ticket agency, Ticketek (tel: 13 28 49), handles ticketing for most of the big spectator games in Sydney.

123

Theatre

Sydney's theatre scene recently got an extra dose of glamour when it was announced that Oscar-winner Cate Blanchett and her playwright husband Andrew Upton were taking up the reigns as joint artistic directors of the Sydney Theatre Company, commencing in 2008. But the city also has plenty of other companies offering a diverse array of productions, including acclaimed Company B and the cutting-edge Griffin Theatre Company. The blockbuster musicals imported from Broadway and London's West End can usually be seen at the Theatre Royal, the Capitol or her Majesty's Theatre.

Big Budgets and New Talent

Sydney theatre comes in many flavours. The high-end of town favours performances at the **Sydney Theatre Company** (STC), with its big budgets, its glamorous harbourside venues, and its imported crowd-pleasers. The STC also has a talented company in residence, the Actors Company, and a development arm featuring work from emerging writers.

The city's most acclaimed theatre is **Belvoir Street**

Below: the Capitol Theatre.

Theatre, home to Company B. It is headed by director Neil Armfield, a favourite with actors such as Geoffrey Rush. The **Bell Shakespeare Company**, not surprisingly, specialises in Shakespeare.

Up-and-coming talent is featured at the respected Griffin Theatre Company (housed in the tiny **Stables Theatre**, an old horse stable in the back blocks of Kings Cross) and at fringe venues such as the **Darlinghurst Theatre** and the **Old Fitzroy Theatre**. Also keep an eye out for the Sydney Fringe Festival (see p.59) each summer.

Bell Shakespeare Company
Tel: 9241 2722; www.bellshakespeare.com.au
A touring company that stages unusual productions of Shakespeare. In Sydney, the company appears at the Playhouse Theatre in the Opera House.

Belvoir Street Theatre
25 Belvoir Street, Surry Hills; tel: 9699 3444; www.belvoir.com.au; map p.137 D2
An old tomato sauce factory is now home to the acclaimed

Company B, under the artistic direction of Neil Armfield. This is the place to see alternative, well-crafted work.

Capitol Theatre
13 Campbell Street, Haymarket; tel: 9320 5000; www.capitoltheatre.com.au; metro: Capital Square; map p.137 D4
Built in the 1920s to a design inspired by the grand palaces of Italy, this 2,000-seat theatre hosts major musicals and large concerts.

The Carriageworks
245 Wilson Street, Eveleigh; tel: 8571 9000; www.carriageworks.com.au; train: Macdonald Town; map p.136 A1
Sydney's newest venue is beautifully-converted old train repair yard, which will host theatre, music and dance performances.

Darlinghurst Theatre
19 Greenknowe Avenue, Potts Point; tel: 8356 9987; www.darlinghursttheatre.com; bus: 311; map p.134 A1
One of the venues to watch for its eclectic array of up-and-coming productions.

Ensemble Theatre
78 McDougall Street, Kirribilli; tel: 9929 0644; www.ensemble.

Left: an Ensemble Theatre 2007 production.

you: there is more than just opera on offer at the Opera House. The Drama Theatre and the Playhouse focus on more mainstream theatre, while the intimate Studio offers a range of cutting-edge dramatic and musical productions.

Sydney Theatre Company
The Wharf Theatre, Pier 4, Hickson Road, Millers Point; tel: 9250 1777; Sydney Theatre, 22 Hickson Road, Millers Point; tel: 9250 1900; www.sydney theatre.com.au; map p.139 D4
Sydney's flagship company has not one but two stunning venues: its traditional home at the Wharf and, across the road, another, more recent sleek industrial conversion. Both venues have quality restaurants and are worth a visit in themselves.

Theatre Royal
MLC Centre, King Street, CBD; tel: 9224 8444; www.mlccentre.com.au; train: Martin Place; map p.139 E1
Central venue frequently plays host to large-scale musicals.

Buying Tickets

Performance venues often sell tickets through ticket agencies such as Ticketek and Ticketmaster. Names and numbers of venues are published in all listings of what's on.

Ticketek
17 outlets in Sydney; tel: 13 28 49; www.ticketek.com.au

Ticketmaster
1st floor, 66 Hunter Street; tel: 13 61 00; www.ticketmaster.com.au

> The STC and Company B feature the work of local playwrights. Look for Michael Gow *(Away)*, Stephen Sewell *(The Blind Giant is Dancing)*, Louis Nowra *(Cosi, Radiance)* and Alanna Valentine *(Savage Grace)*.

com.au; ferry: Kirribilli Wharf; map p.24
This nice little harbourside theatre hosts plays appealing to the middle-class locals.

Old Fitzroy Theatre
129 Dowling Street, Woolloomooloo; tel: 9294 4296; www.oldfitzroy.com.au; map p.133 E1
This sprawling old pub is a home-from-home for Sydney's young acting community, who come here to cheer on each other's plays and performances. The laksa-and-show package is great value.

Seymour Theatre Centre
Cleveland Street, Chippendale; tel: 9351 7940; www.seymour.usyd.edu.au; bus: 352; map p.136 B2
A varied range of local and international productions take place at this performance centre associated with the University of Sydney. The

larger Everest and York Theatres feature touring productions; independent productions take place in the Downstairs Theatre, and there is live music in the Sound Lounge.

Stables Theatre
10 Nimrod Street, Kings Cross; tel: 1300 306 776; www.griffintheatre.com.au; train: Kings Cross; map p.134 A1
Home to the innovative Griffin Theatre Company, which performs new Australian works in this intimate venue.

State Theatre
49 Market Street, CBD; tel: 13 16 00 (tickets); www.statetheatre.com.au; train: Town Hall; map p.133 C1
A 2,000-seat theatre built in 1929 in Cinema baroque style. Better known these days as a venue for concerts and as the home of the Sydney Film Festival than for stage performances.
SEE ALSO FILM P.61

Sydney Opera House
Bennelong Point; tel: 9250 7111; www.sydneyoperahouse.com; train, bus, ferry: Circular Quay; map p.139 E4
Do not let the name fool

> Balmoral Beach's Shakespeare by the Sea is the city's longest-running Shakespeare fixture, but keep an eye out for similar events in other suburbs, such as Coogee and Waverton.

Transport

Sydney is one of the more difficult places to reach in an eco-friendly way, but once you have landed, you will find a city that is surprisingly easy to navigate on foot, with the reference point of the harbour to look out for. Traffic problems are increasing, but with multiple links to the outer suburbs and beaches provided by the many forms of public transport – including buses all through the night – a car is generally not necessary anyway. In this section, you will find an overview of the ways of reaching Sydney and getting around the city and its suburbs during your stay.

Getting to Sydney

BY AIR

Around 50 international airlines land in Sydney. Fares vary widely, but can be expensive, particularly in December, so it is worth seeking advice from a knowledgeable travel agent before booking a ticket. Some of the major airlines include:

British Airways
tel: 1300 767 177; www.ba.com
Qantas
tel: 13 13 13;
www.qantas.com.au
United Airlines
tel: 13 17 77; www.united.com
Air Canada
tel: 1300 655 767;
www.aircanada.com
Singapore Airlines
tel: 13 10 11;
www.singaporeair.com

It is highly likely that you will be flying a great distance travelling to Sydney. To minimise your carbon footprint and measure your travel usage visit one of the following websites to see how you could gain carbon emission credits: www.climatecare.org; www.carbonresponsible.com

BY SEA

If time and money permit, there is no better introduction to this harbour city than arriving by boat. Ocean liners berth at the Overseas Passenger Terminal in Circular Quay and at the Darling Harbour Terminal. Passengers pass through customs on arrival.

These companies include Sydney as a destination or stopover on their routes:
Cunard Line
tel: 9250 6666; www.cunard.com
P&O
tel: 9364 8400;
www.pocruises.com.au

Getting From the Airport

Sydney Airport is situated approximately 8km from the city centre. AirportLink trains run to and from Central Station up to eight times an hour on weekdays, and four times an hour at weekends; journey times take 12 min from the terminal to the station. A single adult journey costs A$12.60.

The only bus to the city is No. 400, which takes 40 min and runs from Bondi Junction. For exact times and information, tel: 13 15 00 or visit: www.airportlink.com.au.

Many hotels run shuttle buses to the airport. A taxi to Sydney city centre will cost from A$25 and take about 20 min in light traffic. Each terminal has its own sheltered taxi rank.

If you intend to hire a car, all the major companies have offices at the airport terminals.

Getting Around Sydney

BUSES

Sydney's extensive bus service has its main termini at Circular Quay, Wynyard and Central Station. At Circular Quay, there is an information kiosk.

The red Sydney Explorer and blue Bondi Explorer hop-on hop-off buses leave regularly from Circular Quay and run a continuous loop around the city's main attractions.
Transport Infoline
tel: 131 500:
http://131500.com.au.

TRAINS

The efficient and frequent CityRail services provide excellent transport coverage

as will toll roads. Companies include:

Premier Cabs
tel: 131 017

Taxis Combined
tel: 133 300

Legion Cabs
tel: 131 451

For more information:
www.nswtaxi.org.au

Water taxis are good for getting to waterfront attractions or taking cruises, but are quite expensive.

Water Taxis Combined
tel: 9555 8888

DRIVING

By international standards, hiring a car in Australia is expensive. If you do choose to drive, the main hire companies are Avis, Hertz and Budget, who offer near-identical deals. Smaller outfits offer cheaper rates, but may not provide the same coverage as the major companies.

Overseas drivers only need to be in possession of an up-to-date driving licence from their home country. For information about road rules and conditions, tel: 13 11 11.

Below: the monorail.

The Sydney Pass is good value if you intend to use public transport extensively. It provides unlimited travel on all buses, trains and ferries for 3, 5 or 7 days, as well as discounts on some major attractions. For more information, see:
www.sydneypass.info

---

for Sydney's inner-city and suburbs. Trains run until midnight, when they are replaced by a Nightrider bus service.

All suburban lines can be caught at Town Hall and Central Station, which is also Sydney's main terminal for other parts of the country. For more information: www.cityrail.com

METRO LIGHTRAIL
AND MONORAIL

The monorail provides an elevated journey around Darling Harbour, Chinatown and the CBD. Lightrail connects the CBD with the inner-west suburbs.

FERRIES

Ferries provide an efficient and picturesque commuter service to many of the harbourside areas, with most services beginning and ending at Circular Quay. There is also a high-speed catamaran service, the JetCat, which travels to Manly. Tickets and timetables can be found at the Circular Quay ferries office, or at: www.sydneyferries.info

CYCLING

Thoughtfully designed systems of bicycle paths stretch across Sydney, providing good views and access to tourist sites. For free maps and a complete list of Sydney's cycling tracks, contact the Roads and Traffic Authority: tel: 13 22 13,
www.rta.nsw.gov.au

Several companies provide hire services, including **Centennial Park Cycle Hire**
tel: 9398 5027

TAXIS

Taxis can be hailed in the street and all should run on a meter. There is an initial A$2.90 'flag fall' charge, then A$1.68 per km thereafter. This rises by 20 per cent between 10pm and 6am. Booking a taxi by phone will incur surcharges,

Walks and Views

Few cities offer as many spectacular walks as Sydney does. With miles of bush-fringed harbour foreshore and a coastline of rugged sandstone cliffs alternating with beautiful beaches, the most difficult decision is which scenic route to explore first. If it is warm, remember to take your swimsuit and a towel because there is bound to be somewhere to have a dip along the way. If your walk includes bushland, you are almost certain to see some local wildlife: colourful and noisy birds or creatures such as the impressive goanna, the large native lizard (they do not bite).

Sydney Centre

Dawes Point to Woolloomooloo (1hr)

This walk along the foreshore is rich in both nature and history. If you are pressed for time, start at Circular Quay and either head west to Dawes Point (short option) or east to Woolloomooloo (long option).

Dawes Point was the site of the first fort ever built in Australia, the Dawes Point Battery. These days, with the Harbour Bridge soaring above it, and

Below: refreshments by the water in Woolloomoolo.

the palm trees lining the foreshore, it is a popular spot for wedding photos. Following the foreshore towards Circular Quay, you pass in turn the sandstone **Park Hyatt Hotel**; the elegant warehouse row at Campbells Cove, now converted to restaurants; the Overseas Passenger Terminal; and the **Museum of Contemporary Art**.

Continue past the ferry wharves and the East Circular Quay development towards the Opera House. Look for the old flight of sandstone steps hidden amid the restaurants and shops of East Circular Quay, and for the walkway plaques commemorating Australia's most famous authors.

If you have not yet visited the **Opera House**, stroll along the pedestrian promenade that skirts its perimeter, before continuing east into the **Royal Botanic Gardens**. This foreshore walk features some of Sydney's most scenic views. Rounding the point of Mrs Macquarie's Chair, you reach the spectacularly-located **Andrew 'Boy' Charlton Swimming Pool**, and then the

The Sydney Visitors Centre (see p.55) has brochures featuring self-guided heritage walks through The Rocks and Parramatta. You can also download a number of interesting walks from the City of Sydney's website. See the Visitor Guides section at www.cityofsydney. nsw.gov.au/AboutSydney

Art Gallery of NSW. Beside the art gallery, a flight of steps runs down to Woolloomooloo, where you can recover from your exertions with a drink and a bite to eat in one of the Finger Wharf's great eateries. For a shortcut back to town, head back to the art gallery, then cut across the Domain to come out onto Macquarie Street near Hyde Park.
SEE ALSO HOTELS P.72; MUSEUMS AND GALLERIES P.85–6; PARKS AND GARDENS P.95–6; SPORT P.122

Sydney Harbour Bridge (1hr)

The essential Sydney walk starts at Cumberland Street in The Rocks, a 10-minute

Opposite: get an aerial view of the harbour from the bridge.

Left: the cliff walk south of Bondi leads to Tamarama, Bronte and other beaches.

ing the day or at night. Book ahead as far as possible, as this attraction is justly popular. For more information, tel: 8274 7777 or visit www.bridge climb.com (entrance charge).

Eastern Suburbs

Rose Bay to Nielsen Park and back (2hrs)

See how the other half lives on this walk that offers a glimpse of Sydney's most exclusive suburbs. For a shorter version, catch the bus back to town from Nielsen Park.

The walk starts at the Sacred Heart Convent School, one of the many private schools in the Rose Bay area blessed with superb harbour views. The 324, 325 and L24 buses all stop here; alight and walk down to the end of Bayview Hill Road, where a clearly marked footpath takes you onto the coastal walk heading east.

The walk, which winds through coastal scrub and bamboo thickets, offers picturesque views across the harbour, the same views shared by the grand mansions perched on the hillside

walk from Circular Quay. From here, four flight of stairs lead up to the bridge's walkway, which offers spectacular views east across the Opera House and harbour. The energetically-inclined can climb to the lookout at the top of the **Harbour Bridge Pylon** (entrance charge), where the panorama is even more spectacular.

The walkway ends at Kirribilli, where a flight of steps deposits you at Milson's Point station. Take the underpass to Alfred Street, and walk down to the harbour,

where you will find **North Sydney Olympic Pool** and the **Luna Park** funfair. From here, you can catch a ferry back into town, or walk back up to the station for a train.

SEE ALSO CHILDREN P.46–7; SPORT P.122

Sydney Harbour Bridge Climb (3½hrs)

For a more dramatic Harbour Bridge experience, Bridge Climb offers two separate routes across the arch of the Harbour Bridge. Both involve walking along catwalks and ladders, and can be experienced at dawn or dusk, dur-

Above: the cliff path from Bondi to Bronte.

above. If you get hot, take a dip at one of the tiny crescent beaches at Hermit Bay (great for picnics), Tingara Beach and Milk Beach. The grassy area above Milk Beach is part of the grounds of Strickland House a grand old 1856 stone mansion built for Sydney's first Lord Mayor, John Hoskin, that can be inspected from the outside.

From Strickland House, the track continues towards **Nielsen Park**, a favourite spot with families. The landscaped park has plenty of picnic facilities, a café, and a beach protected by a shark-proof net. At the rear of the park is Greycliffe House, an ornate sandstone house built by William Charles Wentworth, one of the colony's most famous statesmen.

From here, you can either catch a bus to the city, or walk up Coolong Road to the intersection with Wentworth Road, where you will find the elegant estate of **Vaucluse House**, Wentworth's home and one of Sydney's most impressive Victorian buildings.

Behind the house, take the path through the open area leading to a steep flight of steps up Hopetoun

Avenue. Turn right at the top and you will find yourself back on New South Head Road, near your starting point. From here, catch a bus back to the city.

SEE ALSO MUSEUMS AND GALLERIES, P.84; PARKS AND GARDENS, P.94–5

Southern Beaches
Bondi to Clovelly Cliff Walk (1½hrs)

The Bondi to Bronte walk is a favourite with eastern suburbs types, but it is just the first stretch of a longer walk. How far you go is up to you: the views are spectacular the whole way along. Bear in mind public transport is problematic and if you want to return to Bondi, you will end up walking back the way you came.

The walk starts at the south end of **Bondi Beach**, near the **Icebergs** restaurant, and continues along the sheer sandstone cliffs, taking in several flights of stairs on the way. The first beaches you reach are the rocky Mackenzies Bay, where dog owners bring their pooches for a dip, and **Tamarama**, known as 'Glamarama' for the body-beautiful types who hang out here. Bronte Marine Drive winds around from here to **Bronte Beach**, where many people choose to finish the walk, either by relaxing in the pretty park that extends back to Bronte House, a landmark dating back to 1846, or in one of the cosy cafés that line the street.

Those with extra energy can take the steps at the far end of the beach and continue along the cliff face. At the top, leaving behind the road that swings to the right, continue into the open space of Calga Reserve and you will

come to Waverley Cemetery, a clifftop sanctuary where the tombstones have a spectacular view. Following the service road that winds through the lower end of the cemetery, continue along the cliff top past the Clovelly Bowling Club, and you will come to **Clovelly Bay**. Thanks to the concrete ledges on either side of the bay, it feels like an open-water swimming pool, while a shallow reef at the far end separates it from the open ocean. This is a great place for snorkelling: you may see families of squid, or the massive blue grouper that haunts this territory. From Clovelly Bay, buses go back to the city.

SEE ALSO BEACHES, P.38–41; RESTAURANTS P.107

North Shore
Spit Bridge to Manly Walk (2½hrs)

Right: Clontarf Point.

Catch a Manly or Northern Beaches bus from Wynyard, and ask to be let off just before Spit Bridge. This is the start of one of Sydney's best walks, through pristine bushland with breathtaking harbour views all the way to the seaside suburb of Manly.

From the bus stop, cross the road and walk across the Spit Bridge. Take the service road immediately on your right as you leave the bridge, and you will reach a small park. On the far side of the park, a clearly marked path takes you along the foreshore, through bush and past overhanging rocks, to Sandy Bay.

Walk along the beach and into Clontarf Beach Reserve. Its netted pool and picnic facilities make it a popular spot with families, few of whom realise that in 1868, this was the scene for

Sydney Architecture Walks has a weekly programme of four separate walks, each focusing on a different aspect of the city's built landscape, including the harbour foreshore; Opera House designer Jørn Utzon; and public art. Tickets cost $25. For more information, visit www.sydneyarchitecture.org, or tel: 8239 2211 for bookings.

one of the most violent moments in Australian politics, an assassination attempt on the visiting Duke of Edinburgh.

Continue along the beach on the far side of the reserve and you come to the start of the well-signposted track. This is an energetic walk, with plenty of uphill and downhill climbs. Most of the way is dirt track, although there are boardwalks in places. You can refresh your-

self at one of the tiny, tranquil beaches scalloping the coastline, though getting there can be a bit of scramble. Highlights of this stretch include Grotto Point, where an old lighthouse is visible. Nearby are Aboriginal rock carvings, protected by weathered boards.

Once you reach Forty Baskets Beach, you will start seeing signs of civilization again. After North Harbour Park, the walk follows the streets of King Avenue and Lauderdale Avenue before rejoining the foreshore. From here it is not far to **Manly**. The track ends at **Oceanworld**, near Manly Wharf. If you have not yet visited Manly, take some time to explore the suburb before catching a ferry back to town.

SEE ALSO BEACHES, P.40; CHILDREN P.47

THE ROCKS

Sydney Harbour Bridge
Sydney Harbour Tunnel
Darling St Wharf

Park Hyatt Hotel
Campbells Cove
Sydney Visitors' Centre
Overseas Passenger Terminal
Cadman's Cottage
Museum of Contemporary Art
Ferry Wharves
FIRST FLEET Rd

Cahill Expressway

Customs House
Justice & Police Museum
Museum of Sydney
BMA House
Rose Garden

Endeavour Fountain
State Library of NSW
Parliament House
Sydney Hospital
The Mint
Hyde Park Barracks
Land Titles Office

St Stephens Church

MLC Centre
Theatre Royal
St James Ch
The Skygarden
Sydney (AMP) Tower

State Theatre
Wesley Chapel
Pitt Cinema
GALERIES VICTORIA
Great Synagogue

HYDE PARK
Archibald Memorial Fountain
St Marys Cathedral
SANDRINGHAM MEMORIAL GARDENS
PHILLIP PARK
COOK PARK
Pool of Reflection
Anzac War Memorial
St Pauls Ch

St Georges Church
Australian Museum
St Peters Anglican Ch
Telstra Plaza

DAWES PT PARK
Bennelong Point

Sydney Harbour

Kirribilli Wharf — Cremorne Wharf
Taronga Zoo Wharf
Jet Cat to Manly
Ferry Wharves - Watsons Bay
Fort Denison

Sydney Opera House
Man O'War Jetty

Mrs Macquarie's Chair
Mrs Macquarie's Point

Government House

Farm Cove

Fleet Steps

Conservatorium of Music
ROYAL BOTANIC GARDENS
Restaurant and Kiosk

Pioneer Garden
Shakespeare Place
Tropical Centre
Herbarium Bldgs
Visitors Centre

The Andrew (Boy) Charlton Pool

Potts Point
Fitting Out Wharf

Woolloomooloo Bay

Finger Wharf

Cahill Expressway
THE DOMAIN
Art Gallery of NSW
Art Gallery Rd

Lincoln Cr
Cowper St
Blanc St
Nicholson St
Wilson St
Plunkett St
Griffiths St
Harmer Stephen St
Best St

POTTS POINT
St Stephens
Wayside Chapel
Manning St
Hughes St
Rockwall Cr
Orwell St
Macleay St

Wylde St
Roadway
Grantham Ln
Grantham Oak
St Neot Ave
McDonald Ln.
Challis Ave

FITZROY GDNS.

WOOLLOOMOOLOO

Sir John Young Cr
Palmer St
Dowling St
Victoria St
Brougham St
McElhone St

KINGS CROSS

St Peters St
Bourke St
Forbes St
Clapton Pl
Farrell Ave
Kings Cross Rd
Darlinghurst Rd
Kellett St
Ward Ave
St Lukes Hospital

D E

0 100 200 300 400 500m
0 100 200 300 400 500yds

4

3

2

1

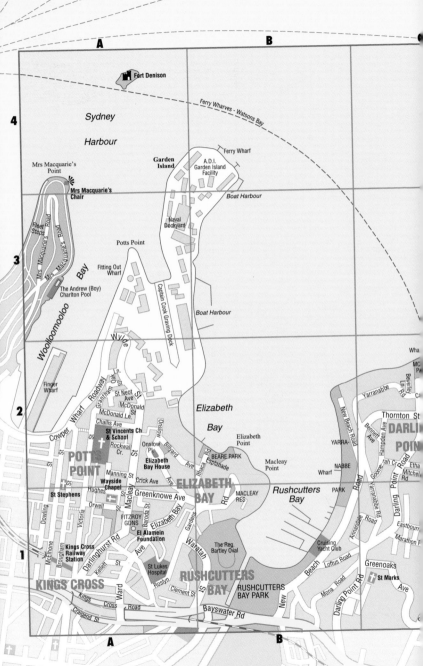

A

B

4

Fort Denison

Sydney

Harbour

Ferry Wharves - Watsons Bay

Garden
Island

A.D.I.
Garden Island
Facility

Ferry Wharf

Mrs Macquarie's
Point

Mrs Macquarie's
Chair

Boat Harbour

Naval
Dockyard

3

Fleet
Steps

Potts Point

Fitting Out
Wharf

The Andrew (Boy)
Charlton Pool

Boat Harbour

Woolloomooloo

Bay

Wylde

2

Finger
Wharf

Cowper

Wharf

Grantham

Challis Ave

St Neot
Ave

Oak

St

McDonald

McDonald La

St Vincents Ch
& School

Rockwall Cr.

Elizabeth
Bay House

Onslow

Pl

Elizabeth

Bay

Billyard

Ave

Ithaca

Rd

BEARE PARK

Elizabeth
Point

Esplanade

Macleay
Point

Elizabeth
Bay

Rd

MACLEAY
RES

Rushcutters
Bay

Wharf

PARK

YARRA-

NABBE

YARRANABBE

Thornton St

DARLI
POIN

New Beach Road

Bennett Ave

Hampden Ave

Beverley

Lin Rd

Yarranabbe

Wha

MC
Pe

POTTS
POINT

Manning St

Wayside
Chapel

Crick Ave

St Stephens

Hughes

Orwell

Victoria

St

Dowling

McElhone

Brougham

St

Roadway

Maclay

Greenknowe Ave

ELIZABETH
BAY

Gardens

FITZROY
GDNS

El Alamein
Foundation

Elizabeth Bay

Rd

Waratah

Goome

rah Cr

Darling

Point

Road

Etha

Mitchel

Rd

Yarranabbe Rd

Darling

Road

Eastbourn

Marathon R

1

Kings Cross
Railway
Station

Darlinghurst Rd

Kellett

Ward

St

St Lukes
Hospital

Roslyn

Clement St

Bayswater Rd

St

The Reg.
Bartley Oval

RUSHCUTTERS
BAY

RUSHCUTTERS
BAY PARK

New

Beach

Cruising
Yacht Club

Loftus Road

Mona

Road

Darling Point Rd

Annandale

Road

Greenoaks

St Marks

Ave

KINGS CROSS

Kings

Cross

Road

Cragend St

A

B

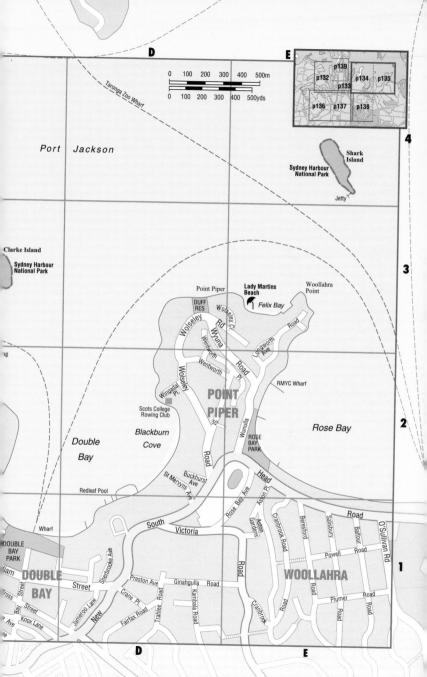

Taronga Zoo Wharf

Port Jackson

Shark Island

Sydney Harbour National Park

Jetty

Clarke Island
Sydney Harbour National Park

Point Piper

Lady Martins Beach

Woollahra Point

DUFF RES

Wolseley Rd

Wolseley Cr

Felix Bay

Road

Wolseley

Wyuna

Wentworth

Wentworth

Longworth Ave

Road

Pl

Wolseley

RMYC Wharf

Wingadal Pl

St

POINT PIPER

Scots College Rowing Club

Double Bay

Blackburn Cove

Wunulla

ROSE BAY PARK

Rose Bay

Buckhurst Ave

St Mervyns Ave

Road

Head

Redleaf Pool

Rose Bay Ave

Aston Pl

Road

Wharf

South

Victoria

Aston Gardens

Cranbrook Road

Beresford

Salisbury

Balfour

O'Sullivan Rd

DOUBLE BAY PARK

Road

Road

Road

Powell

Road

DOUBLE BAY

Street

Shernbrooke Ave

Preston Ave

Ginahgulla

Road

Road

WOOLLAHRA

Plumer

Road

Road

Crane Pl

Kambala Road

Cranbrook

Road

Jemeroo Lane

New

Fairfax Road

Trahlee Road

Knox Lane

p132   p139
p133   p134   p135
p136   p137   p138

0   100 200 300 400 500m
0   100 200 300 400 500yds

D   E

D   E

135

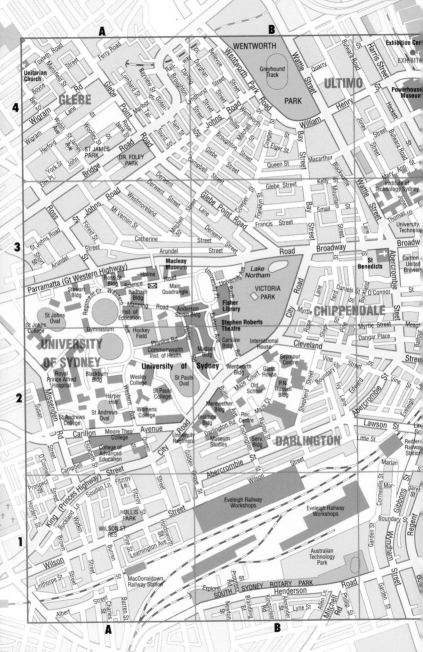

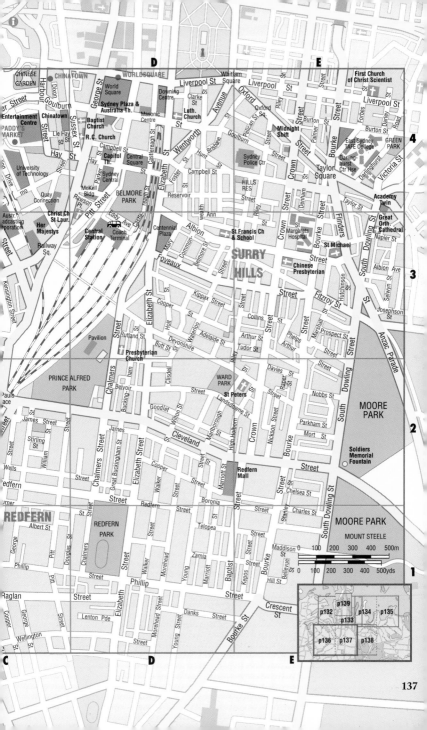

CHINESE GARDEN

CHINATOWN

WORLDSQUARE

Harbour Street

Goulburn Street

George St

Dixon St

World Square

Sussex St

Entertainment Centre

PADDY'S MARKET

Chinatown

Lie Hay St

Hay

Bagtist Church

R.C. Church

Campbell St

Capitol Th.

Central Square

University of Technology

Quay Connection

McKell Bldg

Rawson Pl

Pitt Street

Sydney Central

BELMORE PARK

Christ Ch St Laur.

Her Majestys

Railway Sq.

Kensington Street

Central Station

Coach Terminal

Eddy Ave

Austr. Broadcasting orporation

PRINCE ALFRED PARK

James Street

Chalmers

Stirling St

William

Wells

edfern

REDFERN

Albert St

James

Chalmers Street

Great Buckingham St

Elizabeth Street

George

Pitt

Douglas

Phillip

Raglan

George

Cooper

Wellington

Elizabeth

Lenton Pde

Phillip Street

REDFERN PARK

Chalmers Street

Walker

Morehead

Young Street

Street

Liverpool St

Downing Centre

Clarke St

Luth. Church

Masonic Centre

Castlereagh St

Elizabeth

Campbell St

Foster

Reservoir

Elizabeth

Wentworth Ave

Centennial Plaza

Mary

Foveaux

Albion

Commonwealth St

Belmore St

Cooper

Kippax Street

Holt

Rutland St

Devonshire

Butt St

Presbyterian Church

Clisdell

Buckland

Belvoir

Goodlet

Cleveland

Wilton St

Marlborough

High Holborn

Marriott St

Cooper

Walker

Boronia

Redfern

Telopea

Zamia

Marriott

Baptist

Kepos

Elizabeth Street

Whitlam Square

Oxford

Liverpool

Oxford Sq

Pelican St

Brisbane

Hunt

Goulburn

Campbell St

HILLS RES

Riley

Ann

Wexford

 St Francis Ch & School

SURRY HILLS

Chinese Presbyterian

Street

Collins

Adelaide St

Arthur St

Tudor St

Davies St

Raper St

WARD PARK

St Peters

Landsdowne St

Nickson St

Street

Cleveland

Street

Street

Crown

Liverpool

Riley

Oxford

Burton

Crown

Street

Midnight Shift

Bourke

Taylor Square

Denham

St Margarets Hospital

St Michael

Fitzroy St

Hutchinson

Marshall

Phelps

Arthur

Prospect St

Nobbs St

Bourke

South

Dowling

Parkham St

Mort St

Bourke

Street

Chelsea St

Street

Charles St

Stanley

Hill St

First Church of Christ Scientist

Liverpool St

Forbes

Burton St

Darley

Road

East Sydney TAFE College

GREEN PARK

Darlinghurst Ctr Hse

Palmer

Bourke

Academy Twin

Great Orth. Cathedral

Napier St

Albion Ave

South Dowling St

Belvin St

Josephson St

MOORE PARK

Soldiers Memorial Fountain

MOORE PARK

MOUNT STEELE

Maddison St   0   100   200   300   400   500m

0   100   200   300   400   500yds

Crescent St

Bourke St

REDFERN

Danks Street

p139
p132   p134   p135
p133
p136   p137   p138

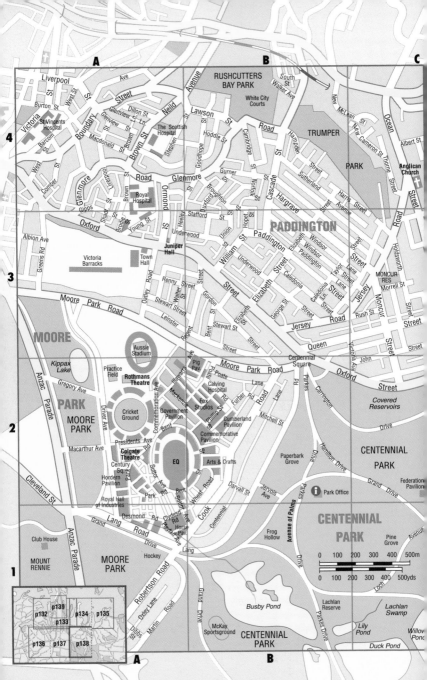

RUSHCUTTERS
BAY PARK

White City
Courts

TRUMPER

PARK

Anglican
Church

PADDINGTON

MOORE

PARK

MOORE
PARK

Aussie
Stadium

Kippax
Lake

Practice
Field

Rothmans
Theatre

Cricket
Ground

Pig
Pav.

Poate

Calving
Hospital

Fox
Studios

Cumberland
Pavilion

Commemorative
Pavilion

Government
Pavilion

Colgate
Theatre

Presidents

EQ

Arts & Crafts

Century
Sq.

Hordern
Pavilion

Royal Hall
of Industries

Horse
Pav.

CENTENNIAL

PARK

Covered
Reservoirs

Paperbark
Grove

Park Office

CENTENNIAL

PARK

Frog
Hollow

Pine
Grove

Federation
Pavilion

Club House

MOUNT
RENNIE

MOORE
PARK

Busby Pond

McKay
Sportsground

CENTENNIAL
PARK

Lachlan
Reserve

Lachlan
Swamp

Lily
Pond

Willow
Pond

Duck Pond

0   100 200 300 400 500m

0   100 200 300 400 500yds

p132   p139
p133   p134   p135
p136   p137   p138

138

Walsh Bay

DAWES PT

Sydney Theatre Company

Pier One

Sydney Harbour Bridge

Darling St Wharf

Hickson

DAWES PT PARK

Park Hyatt Hotel

Campbells Cove

The Earth Exchange

Campbells Storehouses

Sydney Harbour Tunnel

Sydney Opera House

4

Bradfield Highway

Lower Fort St

Pottinger St

George St Rd

Hickson Road

Towns Place

Sydney Theatre

Windmill St

Merchant's House

Sydney Visitors' Centre

THE ROCKS

Overseas Passenger Terminal

Sydney

Farm Cove Ct

Sydney Harbour Tunnel

Government House

3

Garrison Church

Argyle Pl.

Argyle

Argyle Stores

Cadman's Cottage

Cove

Kent Street

OBSERVATORY

Sydney Observatory

PARK

Cambridge St

Susannah Place

George St

Museum of Contemporary Art

Ferry Wharves

Circular Quay East

Macquarie St

Toll Gates

Ington St

FIRST FLEET PK

7 6 5 4 3 2 1

National Trust Centre

Cumberland

Harr.

Cahill Expressway

Alfred St

St Patricks Church & College

Grosvenor Place

Dalley St

Customs House

Lotus St

Street

Justice & Police Museum

Conservatorium of Music

2

Hickson Road

Grosvenor St

Bridge St

Department of Lands

Bent

Museum of Sydney

Rose Garden

Pioneer Garden

Maritime Centre

Kent St

St Philips Church

son St

Jami-York

Stock Exchange

BMA House

Street

Clarence

Westpac Plaza

Scots Church

Australia Square

O'Connell St

Bligh St

Phillip St

Shakespeare Place

Tropical Centre

Sussex

Citibank Centre

Hunter

Phillip

Herbarium Buildings

Sydney Distributor

Carrington St

Pitt Street

R. Johnson Square

Endeavour Fountain

St

State Library of NSW

Parliament House

THE DOMAIN

Western Distributor

Erskine St

Wynyard St

Kent St

George Street

Cenotaph

Martin

Fountain

Place

Castlereagh St

St Stephens Church

Phillip St

Macquarie St

Sydney Hospital

1

Darling Harbour Passenger Terminal

Barrack St

G.P.O.

MLC Centre

Elizabeth St

NSW Supreme Court

Theatre Royal

King St

Street

Glasshouse on the Mall

Strand Arcade

Mid City Centre

Sydney Aquarium

The Skygarden

Centrepoint

St

Old Supreme Court Bldg

St James Church

Queens Square

The Mint

St James Rd

Sydney (AMP) Tower

0 100 200 300m

0 100 200 300yds

C   **D**   **E**

139

E

p132 p139 p134 p135

p133

p136 p137 p138

Selective Index for Street Atlas

PLACES OF INTEREST

Andrew (Boy) Charlton Pool, The 133 E3/134 A3
Anzac War Memorial 133 D1
Archibald Memorial Fountain 133 D1
Argyle Stores 139 D3
Art Gallery of NSW 133 D2
Australia Square 139 D2
Australian Museum 133 D1
BMA House 139 E2
Cadman's Cottage 139 D3
Campells Storehouses 139 D4
Capitol Theatre 137 D4
Cenotaph 139 D1
Centrepoint 139 D1
Chinatown 137 C4
Cockle Bay Wharf 132 B1
Colgate Theatre 138 A2
Conservatorium of Music 139 E2
Convention Centre 132 B1
Cruising Yacht Club 134 B1
Customs House 132 C1
Domain, The 133 D2/139 E1
El Alamein Foundation 134 A1
Elizabeth Bay House 134 A2
Endeavour Fountain 139 E2
Entertainment Centre 137 C4
EQ 138 A2
Exhibition Centre 132 B1/136 C4
Fisher Library 136 B3
Fort Denison 133 E4/134 A4
Garrison Church 139 D3
Genesian Theatre 132 C1
Glasshouse on the Mall 139 D1
Government House 139 E3
Great Synagogue 133 C1
Harbourside Festival Market Place 132 B1
Her Majesty's Theatre 137 C3
Hyde Park Barracks 133 D2
Imax Theatre 132 B1
Juniper Hall 138 A3
Justice & Police Museum 139 E2
Macleay Museum 136 A3
Maritime Centre 139 C2
Merchant's House 139 D4
Mid City Centre 139 D1
Mint, The 139 E1
MLC Centre 139 D1
Mrs Macquarie's Chair 133 E3/134 A4
Museum of Contemporary Art 139 D3
Museum of Sydney 139 E2
National Maritime Museum 132 B2
National Trust Centre 139 D3
NSW Supreme Court 139 E1
Parliament House 139 E1
Pier One 139 D4
Powerhouse Museum 136 C4
Queen Victoria Bldg 133 C1

Regent Theatre 133 C1
Roma Theatre 133 C1
Rothmans Theatre 138 A2
St Andrews Cathedral 133 C1
St Georges Church 133 C1
St James Church 139 E1
St Marys Cathedral 133 D1
St Patricks Church & College 139 D2
St Philips Church 139 D2
St Stephens Church 139 E1
St Vincents Church & School 134 A2
Scots Church 139 D2
Skygarden, The 139 D1
Star City Casino 132 B2
State Library of NSW 139 E1
State Theatre 133 C1
Strand Arcade 139 D1
Stephen Roberts Theatre 136 B3
Susannah Place 139 D3
Sydney (AMP) Tower 139 D1
Sydney Aquarium 139 C1
Sydney Harbour Bridge 139 D4
Sydney Observatory 139 C3
Sydney Opera House 139 E4
Sydney Plaza & Australia Theatre 137 D4
Sydney Theatre 139 D4
Sydney Theatre Company 139 D4
Sydney Visitors Centre 139 D3
Theatre Royal 139 D1
Town Hall 132 C1
University of Sydney 136 A2-B3
Victoria Barracks 138 A3
Westpac Plaza 139 D2

PARKS

Belmore Park 137 D4
Beare Park 134 B2
Centennial Park 139 B1-C2
Chinese Garden 137 C4
Cook Park 133 D1
Dawes Point Park 139 D4
Double Bay Park 135 C1
First Fleet Park 139 D3
Fitzroy Gardens 133 E1/134 A1
Hyde Park 133 D1
Moores Park 137 E1-E2/138 A1-A3
Observatory Park 139 C3
Phillip Park 133 D1
Prince Alfred Park 137 C2-D2
Redfern Park 137 D4
Royal Botanic Gardens 133 D1
Rushcutters Bay Park 134 B1
South Sydney Rotary Park 136 B1
Sydney Harbour National Park 135 C3/E4
Trumper Park 138 B4-C4
Tumbalong Park 132 B1
Victoria Park 136 B3
Wentworth Park 136 B4
Yarra-Nabbe Park 134 B1-B2

STREETS

Abercrombie Street 136 B1-C2
Albion Street 137 D3-E3
Alfred Street 139 D3-E3
Anzac Parade 137 E2-E3/138 A1-A3
Argyle Street 139 C3-D3
Avenue of Palms 138 B1-B2
Barrack Street 139 D1
Bathurst Street 132 C1-133 C1
Bayswater Road 134 A1-B1
Billyard Avenue 134 A2
Boundary Street 138 A4
Bouke Street 133 D1-E2/137 D1-E4
Bradfield Highway 139 C4
Bridge Road 136 A3-A4
Bridge Street 139 D2-E2
Broadway 136 B3-137 C3
Brown Street 138 A4
Burton Street 137 E4/138 A4
Cahill Expressway 133 C3-D2
Chalmers Street 137 D1-D3
City Road 136 A1-B3
Circular Quay East 139 E3
Clarence Street 132 C1-C2/139 D1-D2
Cleveland Street 136 B2-E1/138 C2
College Street 133 D1
Cook Road 138 B1-B2
Cowper Wharf Roadway 133 E2/134 A2
Crown Street 137 E2-E4/133 D1
Cumberland Street 139 D2-D4
Darling Drive 132 B1/136 C4-137 C4
Darlinghurst Road 133 E1/134 A1/137 E4
Darling Point Road 134 B1-C2
Darling Street 132 A4
Druitt Street 132 C1
Elizabeth Bay Road 134 A1-B1
Elizabeth Street 133 C1-C2/137 D1-D4/139 D1
Erskine Street 139 C1-D1
Fitzroy Street 137 E3
Flinders Street 137 E3-E4
Foveaux Street 137 D3-E3
George Street 133 C1-C4/137 C2-D4
Glebe Point Road 136 A4-B3
Glenmore Road 133 A4-B4
Grosvenor Street 139 D2
Harbour Street 137 C4
Harrington Street 139 D2-D3
Harris Street 132 A2-B1/136 C4-137 C3
Henderson Road 136 A1-C1
Hickson Road 139 C2-D4
Hunter Street 139 D2-E1
Jersey Road 138 B3-C4
Kent Street 132 C1-C4/139 D1-C4
King (Princes Highway) Street 136 A1-A2
King Street 139 C1-E1
Lang Road 138 A1-B2

Liverpool Street 137 D4-E4/138 A4
Loftus Street 139 D2-E3
Macleay Street 133 E1-E2/134 A1-A2
Macquarie Street 139 E1-E3
Manning Street 134 A2
Market Street 132 C1-133 C1
Martin Place 139 D1-E1
Moore Park Road 138 A3-B2
Mrs Macquarie's Road 133 E2-E3/134 A3
New Beach Road 134 B1-B2
New South Head Road 135 D1-E1
Ocean Avenue 134 C1-135 C1
Ocean Street 138 C4
Onslow Avenue 134 A1-A2
Orwell Street 134 A1
O'Sullivan Road 135 E1
Oxford Square 137 E4
Oxford Street 137 E4/138 A4-C2
Paddington Lane 138 B3
Paddington Street 138 B3
Palmer Street 133 D1
Park Street 133 C1-D1
Parramatta (Gt Western Highway) Road 136 A3-B3
Phillip Street 139 E1-E3
Pier Street 137 C4
Pitt Street 133 C1-C3/137 D3-D4
Pyrmont Bridge 132 B1
Pyrmont Bridge Road 132 A1
Pyrmont Street 132 A2-B1/136 C4
Queens Square 139 E1
Queen Street 138 B3-C3
Regent Street 136 C1-137 C2
Riley Street 137 E3-E4
St James Road 139 E1
St Johns Road 136 A3-B4
St Pauls Place 137 C2
Shakespeare Place 139 E2
South Dowling Street 137 E1-E4
Sussex Street 132 C1-C3/137 D4/139 C1-C2
Sydney Harbour Tunnel 139 E3-E4
Taylor Square 137 E4
Thornton Street 134 C2
Victoria Road 135 D1-E1/137 E4/138 A4
Wattle Street 132 A1/136 B4-C3
Wentworth Avenue 137 D4
Wentworth Park Road 136 B4
Western Distributor 132 B1-C3
Whitlam Square 137 E4
Wigram Road 136 A4
Windsor Street 138 B3
William Henry Street 136 B4-C4
William Street 132 C1
Wilson Street 136 A1-B1
Wolseley Road 135 D2-D3
York Street 132 C1-C3/139 D1-D2

Index

A

Aboriginal culture **5, 28–9**
    art **28–9, 87, 115**
accommodation **70–77**
admission charges **50**
AMP Building **6**
AMP Tower **6, 7**
Andrew 'Boy' Charlton
    Swimming Pool **11,
    122, 128**
Anzac Memorial **7**
Argyle Stores **9**
Art Gallery of New South
    Wales **11, 50, 59, 85,
    128**
arts and culture **4**
Aurora Place **6**
Aussie Stadium **17**
Australian Centre for
    Photography **85**
Australian Chamber
    Orchestra **4**
Australian Museum **28–9,
    46, 84**
Avalon **25**

B

Bali bomb memorial **23**
Balmain **18**
Balmoral Beach **24, 38**
Bangarra Dance Theatre
    4
bars **30–37**
Basin, The **25**
beaches **4, 22–3, 38–41**
    Balmoral **24, 38**
    Bilgola **41**
    Bondi **4, 5, 22, 23, 28,
    38, 39, 46, 58, 130**
    Bronte **22–3, 38–9,
    58, 130**
    Clovelly **23, 39, 130**
    Cockle Bay **12**
    Coogee **23, 39, 122**
    Cronulla **39–40**
    Freshwater **40, 41**
    Lady Jane Beach **41**
    Manly **24, 25, 40, 58,
    130–31**
    Palm Beach **25, 41**
    Royal National Park
    beaches **41**

Tamarama **22, 40, 41,
    130**
Beare Park **15**
Bicentennial Park **95**
Bilgola **41**
Blackheath **27**
Blue Mountains **4, 26–7**
    accommodation **77**
    bars **37**
    cafés **45**
    restaurants **109**
Blues Point Reserve **94**
Bond Wharves **9**
Bondi **4, 5, 22, 23, 28,
    38, 39, 46, 58, 130**
Bondi Pavilion **22**
bookshops **78–9**
Botany Bay National Park
    96
Brett Whiteley Studio
    85–6
Bronte **22–3, 38–9, 58,
    130**
business hours **50**

C

Cadman's Cottage **8, 80**
cafés **42–5, 63**
Campbell's Cove **9**
Centennial Park **17, 21,
    49, 58–9, 94**
Central Business District
    6–7, 11
    accommodation
    70–71
    bars **30–32**
    cafés **42**
    restaurants **98–9**
children **46–7**
Chinatown **12–13, 59**
Chinese Garden of
    Friendship **12, 94–5**
Chinese Joss House **19**
cinemas **61**
    Chauvel Cinema **16,
    61**
    IMAX **12, 61**
    open-air **58, 61**
Circular Quay **6**
climate **27, 50–51**
Clontarf Point **130–31**
Clovelly **23, 39, 130**
Cockle Bay **12**
Coogee **23, 39, 122**
Cremorne Point **24**
crime and safety **51**
    drugs **14**

Cronulla **39–40**
Crown Street **17**
Customs House **10**
customs regulations
    51–2
Cut, The **9**

D

dance **88**
Darling Harbour and
    Chinatown **12–13, 58**
    accommodation **73–4**
    bars **33–4**
    restaurants **101–2**
Darlinghurst **15**
Darlinghurst Gaol **15**
David Jones **7, 57**
Dawes Point Park **9, 128**
Dendy Opera Quays **10**
disabled travellers **52**
Discovery Centre **80**
Domain, The **10–11**
Double Bay **20**

E

East Circular Quay **10**
East Sydney **15**
Eastern Beaches **22–3**
    accommodation **76**
    bars **36–7**
    cafés **45**
    restaurants **107–8**
Eastern Suburbs **20–21**
    accommodation **76**
    bars **36**
    cafés **44–5**
    restaurants **106–7**
El Alamein Fountain **14,
    15**
electricity **53**
Elizabeth Bay House **15,
    80–81**
Elizabeth Farm **81**
embassies and con-
    sulates **52**
emergency numbers **51**
environment **48–9, 126**
EQ **17, 46**
Experiment Farm Cottage
    81

F

fashion **4–5, 56–7**
Featherdale Wildlife Park
    47
festivals and events
    58–9, 66, 87   **141**

Biennale of Sydney **59**
Chinese New Year **59**
film festivals **59, 61**
Mardi Gras **67**
New Year **59**
Sydney–Hobart Yacht
    Race **20, 58, 121**
Sydney Marathon **122**
film industry **4, 15, 17,
    59, 60–61**
    film festivals **59, 61**
Finger Wharf **11**
Five Ways **16**
food and drink **62–5**
    beer **34, 64–5**
    coffee **43**
    wine **63–4**
foreshore **9, 10–11**
Fox Studios **17, 60**
Freshwater Beach **40, 41**

G

Gap at Watson's Bay **21**
Garigal National Park **96**
Garrison Church **9**
Gavala Art Gallery **13**
gay and lesbian Sydney
    16, 59, 66–7
General Post Office **7, 54**
George Street **7**
Giant Staircase **27**
Glebe **18–19**
Glebe markets **18**
Gordon Falls Reserve **27**
Gordon's Bay **23**
Government House **11,
    81**
Govett's Leap **27**

H

Haberfield **18**
Hambledon Cottage **81**
Hanging Rock **27**
Harbour Bridge Pylon
    Lookout and Museum
    81
Harbourside Shopping
    Centre **13**
health and medical
    matters **52–3**
    snake and spider bites
    48, 53
    swimming hazards **22,
    52–3**
heritage movement **8, 49**
historic houses *see*
    museums and galleries

Historic Houses Trust **50**
history **4, 5, 28, 68–9**
hotels *see*
    accommodation
Hyde Park **6, 7, 81–2, 94**
Hyde Park Barracks
    Museum **6, 80, 81**

I/J

IMAX cinema **12, 61**
Inner-West Suburbs
    18–19
    accommodation **76**
    bars **35–6**
    cafés **44**
    restaurants **105–6**
Italian Forum **19**
Juniper Hall **16**
Justice and Police
    Museum **82**

K

Katoomba **27**
Kelly's Bush **49**
King Street Wharf **12**
Kings Cross **14–15**
    accommodation **74–5**
    bars **34–5**
    cafés **43–4**
    restaurants **102–4**
Koala Park Sanctuary **47**
Ku-ring-gai Chase
    National Park **96**

L

Lady Jane Beach **41**
Lancer Museum **82**
Lane Cove National Park
    96–7
La Perouse Museum **82**
Leichhardt **19**
Leura **26, 27**
literature **78–9**
Lithgow **27**
Loop, The **15**
Luna Park **24, 25, 46–7,
    129**

M

Macquarie Lighthouse **21**
Macquarie Street **5, 6**
Manly **24, 25, 40, 58,
    130–31**
Manly Oceanworld **25,
    47, 131**
Manly Waterworks **25,
    47**

Market City **13**
Martin Place **7**
Metro Theatre building
    15
Military Road **24**
Millers Point **9**
Mint, The **6, 82**
money matters **53–4**
Moore Park **17**
Mosman Bay **24**
Mount Tomah Botanic
    Gardens **27**
Mount Wilson **27**
Mrs Macquarie's Chair
    11
Mundey, Jack **8, 49**
music **88–9**
    Australian Chamber
    Orchestra **4**
    Sydney
    Conservatorium of
    Music **11**
Museum of
    Contemporary Art
    8, 86, 128
Museum of Sydney
    80–81, 82–3
museums and galleries
    29, 80–89
    Art Gallery of New
    South Wales **11, 50,
    59, 85, 128**
    Australian Centre for
    Photography **85**
    Australian Museum
    28–9, 46, 84
    Brett Whiteley Studio
    85–6
    Cadman's Cottage **8,
    80**
    commercial galleries
    86–7
    Discovery Centre **80**
    Elizabeth Bay House
    15, 80–81
    Elizabeth Farm **81**
    Experiment Farm
    Cottage **81**
    Gavala Art Gallery **13**
    Government House
    11, 81
    Hambledon Cottage
    81
    Harbour Bridge Pylon
    Lookout and Museum
    81
    Hyde Park Barracks

Museum **6, 80, 81**
Justice and Police
    Museum **82**
Lancer Museum **82**
La Perouse Museum
    82
Mint, The **6, 82**
Museum of Contempo
    rary Art **8, 86, 128**
Museum of Sydney
    80–81, 82–3
National Maritime
    Museum **13, 83**
Norman Lindsay
    Gallery and Museum
    27, 86, 87
Old Government
    House **83**
Powerhouse Museum
    13, 46, 85
Rocks Visitors' Centre,
    The **8, 83**
S.H. Ervin Gallery **86**
Susannah Place
    Museum **83**
Sydney Jewish
    Museum **83–4**
Sydney Observatory
    84–5
Vaucluse House **21,
    84, 130**
Victoria Barracks **16,
    84**

N

National Maritime
    Museum **13, 83**
national parks and
    reserves **4, 48, 96–7**
Basin, The **25**
Blues Point Reserve
    94
Botany Bay National
    Park **96**
Garigal National Park
    96
Gordon Falls Reserve
    27
Koala Park Sanctuary
    47
Ku-ring-gai Chase
    National Park **96**
Lane Cove National
    Park **96–7**
Royal National Park
    41, 97
Sydney Harbour

National Park **97**
Newtown **19**
Nielsen Park **4, 20, 21,
    94–5, 129–30**
nightlife **5, 12–13, 14,
    66–7, 90–91**
comedy **90**
Norman Lindsay Gallery
    and Museum **27, 86,
    87**
North Shore **24–5**
accommodation **76–7**
bars **37**
beaches **40–41**
cafés **45**
restaurants **108–9**
North Sydney Olympic
    Pool **24, 122**

O

Opera House and The
    Domain **10–11**
accommodation **73**
bars **33**
cafés **42–3**
restaurants **100–101**
Old Government House
    83

P

Pacific coast **20**
Paddington and Surry
    Hills **16–17**
accommodation **75**
bars **35**
restaurants **104–5**
Paddington Markets **16,
    17, 46–7**
Paddington Town Hall **16**
Palm Beach **25, 41**
parks and gardens **94–7**
Beare Park **15**
Bicentennial Park **95**
Centennial Park **17,
    21, 49, 58–9, 94**
Chinese Garden of
    Friendship **12, 94–5**
Dawes Point Park **9,
    128**
Featherdale Wildlife
    Park
    47
Hyde Park **6, 7, 81–2,
    94**
Luna Park **24, 25,
    46–7, 129**
Moore Park **17**

Mount Tomah Botanic
    Gardens **27**
Nielsen Park **4, 20, 21,
    94–5, 129–30**
Parramatta Park **83,
    95**
Royal Botanic Gardens
    **4, 6, 11, 48, 49, 58,
    95–6, 128**
Tumbalong Park **12,
    46**
Parliament House **6**
Parramatta **81**
Parramatta Park **83, 95**
Pittwater **25**
plantlife **26**
Plaza Hotel **21**
population **4**
postal services **54**
Powerhouse Museum
    13, 46, 85
public holidays **53**
pubs **5, 9, 17**
Pulpit Rock **27**

Q/R

Quarantine Station **25**
Queen Vicoria Building **7,
    43, 112**
Redleaf Pool **20**
restaurants **4, 9, 98–109**
Rocks, The **5, 8–9, 33,
    49**
accommodation **71–3**
bars **32–3**
restaurants **99–100**
Rocks Market, The **8,
    117**
Rocks Visitors' Centre,
    The **8, 83**
Rose Bay **21, 129–30**
Royal Botanic Gardens
    **4, 6, 11, 48, 49, 58,
    95–6, 128**
Royal National Park **41,
    97**
Rushcutters Bay **20**

S

Scenic Railway **27**
S.H. Ervin Gallery **86**
shopping **7, 16, 20,
    56–7, 62, 65, 110–17**
tax refunds **113**
spas and beauty
    treatments **92–3**
Spit Bridge **130–31**

sport and activities
  118–23
  see also festivals and
    events
  adventure sports 26
  basketball 120
  cricket 17, 119–20
  cycling 122
  diving and snorkelling
    23
  football 119
  golf 122–3
  horse racing 120–21
  rugby 118–9
  sailing 20, 58, 121
  surfing 39–40, 121
  swimming 38–41,
    121–2
  tennis 123
  walking, jogging 25,
    26, 27, 122,
    128–31
  windsurfing 38
State Library 6
State Theatre 7, 125
Strand Arcade 7, 114
Surry Hills 16–17
Susannah Place Museum
  83
Sydney Aquarium 12,
  47
Sydney Conservatorium
  of Music 11
Sydney Cricket Ground
  17

Sydney Dance Company
  4
Sydney Fish Markets
  64–5
Sydney Harbour 20, 59,
  129
Sydney Harbour Bridge
  5, 9, 24, 123, 128–9
Sydney Harbour National
  Park 97
Sydney–Hobart Yacht
  Race 20, 58, 121
Sydney Hospital 6
Sydney Jewish Museum
  83–4
Sydney Marathon 122
Sydney Observatory
  84–5
Sydney Opera House
  5, 6, 10–11, 46,
  69, 88–9, 125, 128
Sydney Theatre 9
Sydney Theatre Company
  9
Sydney University 18, 19

T
Tamarama 22, 40, 41,
  130
Taronga Zoo 4, 5, 24,
  47
telephones 54
theatre 124–5
Three Sisters 27
time zone 54

tipping 54
toilets 54–5
tourist information 55
tours
  Aboriginal culture 29
  food and wine tours
    64
Town Hall 7
transport 126–7
Tumbalong Park 12, 46
Tusculum 15

V
Vaucluse House 21, 84,
  130
Victoria Barracks 16, 84
Victoria Street 15
visas 55

W
Watson's Bay 21
Waverley Cemetery 23
weights and measures
  55
wildlife 4, 11, 47, 48
  see also national parks
  sharks 4, 38
  spiders 48
wine 63–4
Woollahra 21
Woolloomooloo 11, 28,
  128

Z
Zig Zag Railway 27

Insight Smart Guide: Sydney
Text by: Ute Junker, Gabi Mocatta,
Kerry McCarthy
Edited by: Jason Mitchell and Jeffery Pike
Proofread and indexed by: Penny Phenix
Photography by Glyn Genin/Apa except:
Alamy 15T, 17, 40, 41T&B, 56/7T, 62/3T,
80B, 91B, 96; City of Sydney 58/9T, 59B;
Coo-ee Picture Library 68CB; Corbis 4T,
23, 25T, 69CT&CB, 63B, 90/1T; Jerry
Dennis/Apa 26; Ensemble Theatre 124/5;
Getty Images 60/1T, 66B, 66/7T, 69B,
118B, 118/19T, 120; Lansdowne Picture
Library 69T; Marathon Photos 123; Mary
Evans Picture Library 68CT; Gabi Mocatta
3B, 6, 16, 28B, 32, 46/7T, 42B, 42/3T,
43B, 44, 48B, 70/1T, 78/9T, 98/9T,
111B, 115TL, 116, 121BL; Robbi
Newman 68T; Palm Pictures 60B;
Tony Perrottet/Apa 9B, 39B, 54B, 94/5T;
Photolibrary 80/1T; Jeffery Pike 96; State
Library New South Wales 68B; Sydney

Hilton Hotel 70B; Tourism New South
Wales 12, 25B, 27T&B.

Picture Manager: Hilary Genin
Maps: Neal Jordan-Caws
Series Editor: Maria Lord

First Edition 2008
© 2008 Apa Publications GmbH & Co.
Verlag KG Singapore Branch, Singapore.
Printed in Canada
Worldwide distribution enquiries:
Apa Publications GmbH & Co. Verlag KG
(Singapore Branch) 38 Joo Koon Road,
Singapore 628990; tel: (65) 6865 1600;
fax: (65) 6861 6438

Distributed in the UK and Ireland by:
GeoCenter International Ltd
Meridian House, Churchill Way West,
Basingstoke, Hampshire RG21 6YR; tel:
(44 1256) 817 987; fax: (44 1256) 817 988
Distributed in the United States by:

Langenscheidt Publishers, Inc.
36–36 33rd Street 4th Floor, Long Island City,
New York 11106; tel: (1 718) 784 0055; fax:
(1 718) 784 0640l
Contacting the Editors
We would appreciate it if readers would
alert us to errors or outdated information
by writing to:
Apa Publications, PO Box 7910, London SE1
1WE, UK; fax: (44 20) 7403 0290;
e-mail: insight@apaguide.co.uk
No part of this book may be reproduced,
stored in a retrieval system or transmitted
in any form or by any means (electronic,
mechanical, photocopying, recording or otherwise), without prior written permission of Apa
Publications. Brief text quotations with use of
photographs are exempted for book review
purposes only. Information has been obtained
from sources believed to be reliable, but its
accuracy and completeness, and the opinions
based thereon, are not guaranteed.